THE HEALING OF THE MIND

The Technique of Psychoanalytic Psychotherapy

The Healing of the Mind

The Technique of Psychoanalytic Psychotherapy

by Reuben Fine, Ph.D.

DAVID McKAY COMPANY, INC.
New York

*For Charlotte
with love*

LIBRARY OF CONGRESS CATALOG CARD NUMBER: 70-134797
MANUFACTURED IN THE UNITED STATES OF AMERICA

Thou wilt leave everything that thou hast held
Most dear to thee, and that will be the bolt
The bow of exile arrows at thee first.
Thou wilt find out how much doth taste of salt
Another's bread, and how hard a road
Is going up and down another's stairs.

Dante: "Paradiso" XVII
Divina Commedia

Contents

Preface

In the course of teaching psychiatrists, psychologists, social workers, and other professionals the rudiments of psychotherapy over the past fifteen years, the need has often been expressed for a compact one-volume work that would serve as a guide through the bewildering world of mental healing. This book has been written to provide such a guide.

The beginner is all too often overwhelmed by the innumerable array of techniques put at his disposal by a variety of teachers. Analysis, analytic psychotherapy, rational therapy, schools with different theoretical bases, behavior therapy, and numerous others appear on the stage. One result has been that many practitioners operate in states of varying degrees of confusion about what they are doing, why they are doing it, and where they are going.

It is my conviction that there is one basic technique that underlies all attempts to help a suffering human being by psychological means. This technique, succinctly, is based on love and understanding. Yet, since the variety of problems faced in treatment is so great, while the underlying rationale remains the same, the actual measures adopted may range widely. My goal has been to make this underlying rationale explicit. In the last analysis, goals are more important than techniques, so that the student who acquires a thorough grasp of what he is trying to do will be able to adjust his activities to the problem at hand, rather than follow a prescribed procedure slavishly and, all too often, disastrously. Flexibility is the hallmark of the skilled practitioner, a flexibility that can only be learned on the basis of a thorough grounding in principles, rather than memorizing specific activities.

The basic systematic approach to psychotherapy derives more from Freud than from any other single individual. Yet it has also gone far beyond him in many respects, as the result of the contributions of many other analysts, including Alexander, Abraham, Federn, Jones,

Sullivan, Horney, Fromm, Erikson, Hartmann, Greenson, Glover, Menninger, Searles, and many others too numerous to mention. Modern psychotherapy should be learned as a synthesis of the best that is offered by many pioneers, whose early efforts have been sharpened and in many instances corrected by their numerous followers.

For the majority of patients encountered in ordinary clinical practice, the technique described in this book is the most suitable. It has been used over and over, for the past seventy years, on hundreds of thousands of patients, in many cultures, with patients with all kinds of clinical "diagnoses." It is certainly by far the best validated of all the techniques available.

Yet this is not to deny the usefulness of many of the experiments and innovations that have been introduced by a large number of clinicians. While most patients respond well to uncovering therapy, a number do not. For these some modifications are necessary, although the underlying principles do not remain essentially altered. As I have tried to show in various chapters, these are the patients who are unable to *relate,* and before anything else is done their relatability has to be tackled. To do this the therapist may be active, may intervene in the patient's life, may at times engage in social relations with the patient, or may do any one of a hundred other things that would ordinarily be contraindicated. What is vital is only that the technique should be adapted to the patient, not the patient to the technique.

It would have been confusing to discuss, together with the basic technique, the numerous deviations which varied circumstances could elicit. My experience has been that it is best for the beginner to master the essential technique before he experiments with the many novel approaches available. From the vantage point of the economy of learning, it is bewildering to try to master everything all at once.

No hard and fast line is drawn in this book between psychoanalysis and psychotherapy. Indeed, the research of the past twenty years has failed to produce even a definition of psychoanalysis that is fully acceptable to all who call themselves analysts. The field is still torn apart by vituperous theoretical dissensions, in which even persons of considerable stature have attempted to excommunicate others of stature who disagree on certain points of detail. The numerous splits in psychoanalytic groups are well documented, yet to the observer who approaches the situation dispassionately each group often seems to have something to offer. Thus at one time Fenichel tried to have Alexander read out of the Society. Fortunately, he failed. Both have made fundamental contributions that must be synthesized by the contemporary therapist.

Freud once defined analysis as any method that is based on the use of transference and resistances. This definition is sufficient for the purposes of this book, and allows one to incorporate the distilled experience of large numbers of competent therapists.

Perhaps the most original aspect of this work is its consistent emphasis on a philosophical basis. Psychoanalysis is seen as a philosophical approach to living, based on a scientific psychology. Ordinarily the psychology is overstressed at the expense of the philosophy.

It has seemed to me that the therapist from the very beginning should be fully consonant with the psychoanalytic image of health, which forms the basis of its philosophy. For this reason a special chapter is devoted to an exposition of the analytic ideal, contrasting it with the conventional image of "normality" embedded in the contemporary culture. At best, what passes for normality in our culture can be described as an adjustment neurosis; all too often it is a caricature of what man might really be.

Throughout the treatment of any patient, the therapist must have a clear image of how the patient might achieve happiness. Fundamentally, after all, people come to us because they are unhappy, and expect to leave when they have become happy. The potpourri of psychiatric diagnoses only serves to confuse everybody, psychiatrist and layman alike. Many have argued that the diagnostic approach to psychotherapy does more harm than good. In agreement with this point of view, I have consistently tried to help the budding therapist see the patient as a human being in a human situation, beset by difficulties in living from which everybody suffers. The therapist, if he is to do effective work, must have overcome to a greater or lesser degree these difficulties in his own life. Regardless of his professional background, his effectiveness as a therapist depends on the degree of happiness that he has achieved as a human being.

In consequence, the role that the personality of the therapist plays in the psychotherapeutic process has been discussed in many places. While there is disagreement on details, there is general agreement that the therapist must be a warm, empathic human being.

The point of view adopted here is that therapy is part of the growth process of the therapist. In order to begin doing therapy, the practitioner must have gone some way toward maturity, but he cannot be expected to have completed the process. When he turns to helping others, he is usually still in the middle of his own personal analysis. He is simultaneously patient and therapist, a regressed child in the morning, a mature adult in the afternoon. This unusual situation must be used constructively. Throughout I have tried to show how the therapist can use the problems encountered for the furtherance of his own growth and, further, that such an attitude makes for the most successful kind of therapy. The learning model should be seen as that of one human being, with some problems resolved but others remaining, helping another who has more problems. Nothing is more fatal to effective psychotherapy than the model of the "healthy" physician "curing" the "sick" patient. Such a model may turn the therapy into a cold scalpel that literally does more harm than good.

There is no doubt that psychotherapy is a learning procedure. Yet the nature of the learning process has never been clearly elucidated. Conventional learning theory, with its reliance on conditioning and other very simple forms of learning, has been at a loss to explain the results achieved in psychoanalytic therapy; as a natural reaction to this theoretical bafflement it has denied that there are any results.

Through the years psychoanalytic therapy has had to develop its own rationale for the kind of learning that goes on. I have tried to spell out this rationale in considerable detail in two chapters. Again, a careful study of how the patient learns to get better is essential to the whole process.

Inasmuch as the analytic ideal is at considerable variance from the social structure as it now exists, the growth of psychotherapy has been explosive, especially since World War II. It is still expanding at a phenomenal rate, in spite of the many critics who gloomily announce every year that psychotherapy is now a thing of the past. In New York City alone today there are probably more patients and more therapists than there were in the entire world twenty-five years ago. And it can only be anticipated that the growth will continue.

In the light of this growth, many critics have argued that the earlier techniques should be abandoned in favor of "innovative" approaches that will solve the problems more effectively. Unfortunately, time and again these "innovative" approaches have been discarded after a few years. It is certainly undesirable to look upon Freud as a God, yet it is still true that he made certain fundamental discoveries that are affirmed and reaffirmed every time a therapist sits down to help a new patient. Although psychotherapy has gone far beyond Freud, a firm grasp of his discoveries is still indispensable, even when the procedure adopted seems to be radically different from his original method.

Above all, my thanks are due to the many patients who have ventured to entrust their welfare to me, and to the many students whom I have had the good fortune to try to instruct over the years. In the numerous examples given for both therapists and patients, the facts have in many cases had to be altered somewhat to afford an adequate disguise. No intentional depreciatory remark has been made about any of the individuals cited. Many people have been kind enough to permit me to make use of their case histories for instructional purposes, and I wish to thank them especially for this kindness.

New York
November 10, 1969

CHAPTER 1

The Philosophical and Psychological Bases of Psychotherapy

Not contempt but grief
Does your sad state within me set so deep
That long it will be ere it wholly leaves me.

Dante: "Inferno" XV
Divina Commedia

In one form or another, psychotherapy has always existed. Man, frightened by pain, has sought ways to eliminate it, to deny it, to face it, or to relieve it. Originally, and for thousands of years, the distinction between physical and mental pain was virtually indistinguishable. The crystallization of the existence of *anxiety,* a psychic pain, entirely different from, though related to, physical pain, is one of man's great cultural achievements. It is an achievement that took thousands of years; for many today, even in the professions, it remains a mystery.

Historically, the development of psychotherapy as it is known today has gone through five major stages. In the first, *magic* played the dominant role. For most of human history, including today in many parts of the world, systems of magical beliefs have been dominant. In the second stage, magic gives way to *religion,* where the emphasis is on supernatural powers which must be placated to avoid inevitable suffering. Like magic, with which it is closely allied in many cultures, religion promises man surcease from pain if he will only obey its tenets.

Many men have valued the ethical precepts of religion, while disavowing the supernatural. This led to the third stage in the evolution of psychotherapy, *philosophy.* The word "philosophy" means literally love of wisdom. In Athenian Greece, where the word stems from, there was a group of philosophers called Sophists, who promised

1

happiness and well-being to any who followed their procedures. Since the Sophists, there have been many philosophical schools offering a solution to the problems of living. The one which has attracted the strongest following among contemporary thinkers is existentialism.

The fourth stage, based on the advance of science, is *medicine*. This rests upon the argument that for the alleviation of any condition a full scientific understanding is essential. Mental pain, while seemingly different from physical, must be derived from it in some way. Accordingly, if the correct diagnosis is made and suitable drugs or other physical approaches are devised, the anxieties should cease.

Medical beliefs, based on the extensive growth of science after the French Revolution, held sway until roughly the beginning of this century; in many quarters the conviction still holds that ultimately some simple physico-chemical explanation will be found for all the baffling phenomena that are called mind.

It remained for a man technically trained as a physician, Sigmund Freud (1856–1939), to shatter this complacent belief and introduce the fifth stage in the history of psychotherapy, *psychology*. The essential elements of Freud's system, the unconscious, psychosexual development, character structure, the division of the personality into id, ego, and superego, and a number of allied concepts, have become the heart of the contemporary psychological approach.

NORMALITY: THE ANALYTIC IDEAL AND THE SOCIAL REALITY

Psychoanalysis is both a philosophy of living and a system of philosophy. It differs from other philosophies in that it is based on a scientific approach to psychology; it differs from other psychologies in that it has a philosophical outlook attached to it.

The philosophy of living espoused by psychoanalysis begins with Freud's comment that the normal person is the one who can love and work. Further consideration leads to a description of the psychoanalytic philosophy along these lines: psychoanalysis maintains that man can attain happiness through a reasonable way of living, which involves the following: he must love rather than hate, seek pleasure, have sexual gratification, have a feeling for life yet one which is guided by reason, have an adequate role in the family, have a sense of identity, be constructive, work, be creative, have a role in the social order, be able to communicate, and be reasonably free of psychiatric symptoms.

Of the various components of the analytic ideal, the most central is the attainment of love. Love is the acme of gratification with another human being. Nothing is more important in the growth process and in the resolution of neurotic conflicts.

It is readily apparent that most of the disorders that people suffer from, if not all, involve some disappointments in love. These disappointments begin at an early stage, not infrequently within the first few months of life. The early frustrations lead to all kinds of distorted personality formations, which in turn affect the manner in which the individual reacts to later environmental stresses and stimulation.

A difficulty has arisen because psychoanalysts in their discussions of love generally deal with the clinical distortions of love rather than with what it might be ideally. In order to avoid confusion some clarification of the topic is necessary.

Most of what is described as love turns out to be a neurotic fixation when it is subjected to analytic scrutiny. Love may be a strong irrational transference, investing some shy, frightened, little girl with all the marvelous qualities the boy saw in his mother. Or love may represent a blind attachment, obviously self-destructive, yet one from which he cannot escape.

Love may be a reaction formation against hatred. It may be one form of masochism. Actually, a list of neurotic types of love relationships can be continued indefinitely. Suffice it to say that the characteristic element in a neurosis is the clinging to some earlier form of gratification, which does not suit the needs of the person or persons at the present age level.

For the mature individual five stages can be distinguished in the growth towards healthy love. These are: attachment, admiration, physical enjoyment, total enjoyment, devotion.

1. *Attachment* is an attachment to the mother originally. It leads, in Erikson's terms, to a feeling of basic trust in other people, since the infant has had the experience of being well taken care of when he is helpless.

2. *Admiration* refers to the father. He is the major source of strength in the family in relation to the outside world, and children of both sexes look up to him. This admiration leads to autonomy and initiative, since it is internalized as a feeling of self-confidence.

3. *Physical enjoyment* refers to sex and begins at puberty. Granted,

of course, that sexuality has a long history, the pubertal sex relations still remain markedly different from anything ever experienced before. In the early stages of puberty the desires are largely physical. It is no disparagement of love to think of it in this way; rather, the idea that love must be removed from the body is an expression of the split between tender and sexual feelings which has characterized Western civilization for many centuries.

4. *Total enjoyment* refers to both sexual and emotional intimacy with a person of the opposite sex. It comes in later adolescence and will normally lead to marriage.

5. *Devotion* is the basic parental feeling, maternal as well as paternal. The helplessness of the child calls for a long period of selfless devotion, even under the best of circumstances. At the same time the role of enjoyment in the parent's feelings about the child should not be forgotten. If it is forgotten, the result is a self-sacrificing kind of parent, who invariably creates deep guilts and neurotic conflicts in the children.

The psychotherapeutic process begins with an analysis of the neurotic love manifestations of the past and ends with the clarification of normal love. The discussion of love at the end of therapy should be specific and geared to the background of each individual.

In contrast to the analytic ideal, with its emphasis on love, pleasure, work, and so forth, what is found in our culture is hate, suffering, frigidity, lack of feeling, absence of family role, unwillingness to work, robotization, social disorganization, and isolation. The gap between the analytic ideal and the social reality is enormous. The immediate consequence is that virtually everybody in our society has a need for psychotherapeutic help.

The broader consequences of this gap are of inestimable significance for the practice and theory of psychotherapy. First of all, it will have been noticed that in the previous discussion of normality, nothing has been said about conventional psychiatric categories. This omission is deliberate. Traditional psychiatric classification, which, as Brill [1] has shown, has been altered almost every ten years since 1917, offers a picture of almost hopeless confusion. In practice, the therapist learns to pay less and less attention to the standard Kraepelinian categories, and to evaluate his patients along the lines indicated above.

Second, the widespread incidence of emotional disorder means that every case that comes to the attention of the practitioner is a character disorder rather than a symptom disorder. Every symptom is found within a character matrix, without which it cannot be understood. Reliance on traditional diagnostic categories represents a grave professional blunder. Every patient should be looked upon as a human being in a human situation, not a label to be compared to some textbook description.

Whenever possible, the therapist should set himself the task of altering the character structure to the extent that it can be altered. Where it cannot be changed to any appreciable extent, whatever aspects of normal functioning can be reached should become the goals of the therapeutic process.

Third, and in a sense the most important of all, the gap emphasizes the fact that the practitioner plays a special role in our social order. He cannot possibly set himself the task of merely adjusting people to a social order which is in the process of disorganization, or to a family system which is in a state of radical transition, or to a job the meaning of which will change from one decade to the next.

In reflecting on the issues involved in this scheme, the therapist becomes a philosopher as well as a healer. In fact, the psychotherapist should be looked upon as the real philosopher of our time. He is a philosopher who is willing to expose his views to everyday realities rather than to speculate on abstract theories that have little connection with man's real needs.

The training of psychoanalytic therapists has become fairly standard, whether it is conducted within a formally organized institute or outside. He goes through an intensive personal analysis, takes didactic courses in psychoanalytic theory, and does a number of analyses under supervision (controls). Most analysts have a preliminary degree in medicine, psychology, or social work, but there are some exceptions. Whatever the nature of the formal training, however, the decisive factor in therapeutic success is the warmth and maturity of the analyst's own personality.

SUGGESTIONS FOR FURTHER READING

The best systematic history of psychotherapy is W. Bromberg, *The Mind of Man* (New York: Harper and Bros., 1959). The most profound tracing of the interconnections between psychiatry and the social structure is G. Rosen, *Madness in Society* (New York: Harper and Row, 1968).

For the development of psychoanalysis, apart from Freud's works, the most authoritative single source is E. Jones, *The Life and Work of Sigmund Freud* (New York: Basic Books, 1953–1957). For a briefer summary of Freud's views and their present status, see R. Fine, *Freud: A Critical Reevaluation* (New York: David McKay, 1962).

The best extended discussion of the concept of normality is D. Offer and M. Sabshin, *Normality* (New York: Basic Books, 1966). The concept of the psychological reform of society is developed in a number of works. The best exposition of Freud's views in this area is P. Roazen, *Freud: Political and Social Thought* (New York: Knopf, 1968).

Numerous approaches to the analytic ideal can be found in the literature. Particularly useful: R. Fine, "The Goals of Psychoanalysis," in A. Mahrer, ed., *The Goals of Psychotherapy* (New York: Appleton-Century-Crofts, 1968). M. Brierley, "Psychoanalysis and Integrated Living," *Trends in Psychoanalysis* (London: The Hogarth Press, 1951). E. Fromm, *Man for Himself* (New York: Rinehart and Co., 1947). L. Feuer, *Psychoanalysis and Ethics* (Springfield, Ill.: C. C Thomas, 1956). H. Marcuse, *Eros and Civilization* (London: Routledge and Kegan Paul, 1955). H. Hartmann, *Psychoanalysis and Moral Values* (New York: Int. Universities Press, 1960).

CHAPTER 2

Overview of the Treatment Process

The relation of the child and the curriculum presents itself in this guise: of what use is it, educationally speaking, to be able to see the end in the beginning? . . . . Asking such a question suggests its own answer. To see the outcome is to know in what direction the present experience is moving, provided it moves normally and soundly. The far-away point, which is of no significance to us simply as far away, becomes of huge importance the moment we take it as defining a present direction of movement. Taken in this way, it is no remote and distant result to be achieved, but a guiding method in dealing with the present.

John Dewey: *The Child and the Curriculum*

While learning psychoanalytic technique, the emphasis throughout must be on goals rather than on specific procedures. Unless the therapist has the inner conviction and the theoretical background to back up his belief that the procedure he is using makes very good sense, it is more apt to fail than to succeed. A mechanical approach will never go far in therapy; the human situations involved are too varied, the emotions too powerful, the need for sincerity too great. The beginning therapist should be encouraged to question the value of every procedure until its underlying rationale really becomes second nature to him.

While the therapeutic process varies from person to person, a certain inherent structure exists in every course of therapy, and the structures are intrinsically similar. First, a relationship must be established between patient and therapist; without such a relationship nothing can be done. Then the patient is encouraged to talk as much as possible, with a view to clarifying the dynamics of his illness and of his psychic processes in general. Eventually, the therapist's summation of this dynamics is conveyed to the patient, who uses this knowledge to change either his feelings or his behavior or both. The

7

amount of change that can be effected varies considerably from one patient to another.

The rationale for this procedure is that the goal of the therapist is to bring the patient as close as possible to the analytic ideal; the goal of the patient is to get some immediate relief. The analytic therapist must perform an essentially educational process, to help the patient see what is really wrong with his life. This cannot be done by any superficial intellectual procedure, but must follow the deeper emotional experiences that the patient goes through in therapy.

In the course of working out the patient's problems, primary importance is attached to the *transference* and the *resistances*. These two phenomena are the cornerstones of all therapy. Why they become so central requires some explanation.

The patient enters therapy in a state of great emotional turmoil. To some extent, his defenses have been pierced, so that he is experiencing great anxiety. The childhood reaction to anxiety may be one of two kinds: phobic, to escape the feared situation, or clinging, to run to a protective parent-figure, ultimately the mother. Hence the patient in therapy is caught between fleeing the feared situation and clinging to his protective parent-substitute. The relative strength of these two factors determines the outcome of the early struggle.

In either case the analyst becomes a parent-figure to the patient. This leads to a heightened emphasis on the relationship between therapist and patient, a relationship that in its broadest aspects is called transference. Concomitantly, this relationship involves many of the emotional conflicts surrounding the original parents, which is the root of the variety of resistances manifested.

Transference is not sought out by the therapist; it is the product of the neurotic conflicts of the patient. In adult life the best way to handle anxiety is to sit back calmly and reflect on the best way to manage the threat. But the child does not have this rational control at his disposal; he must either flee or cling. If he flees the analyst, it is called negative transference; if he clings, positive.

Transference and its allied resistances form the heart of the personality structure. Their *working-through,* which involves consistently bringing them to consciousness, examining their roots, and looking at their numerous manifestations, is the basic method of psychotherapy. It is only by this consistent working-through, which always takes a lot of time, that deep-going changes can really be effected.

While the therapist has had a personal analysis, and is much more aware of his own motives, he is still caught up in certain emotional reactions to the patient. These are called *countertransferences.* Although in theory they should not exist, in practice they form a most significant part of the whole therapeutic problem. In general, it is assumed that when the therapist makes serious mistakes, especially those that mar the progress of therapy, it is because of unresolved countertransferences. An unremitting search for these unresolved countertransferences goes on in every well-trained therapist.

If the analytic ideal could be achieved once and for all, there would be no need to talk of countertransferences. The naive image of the well doctor treating the sick patient could be restored. But in actuality this is never the case, and never has been. The model taken should be rather that of one person (the therapist) who is closer to the analytic ideal, trying to teach another (the patient), who is further away. This model is basically more educational than medical, a vital point in understanding technique.

THERAPEUTIC ACCESSIBILITY: AN APPROACH TO DIAGNOSIS

Everyone knows that the conventional diagnostic system is of very little value. Anna Freud [2] says that ". . . the descriptive nature of many current diagnostic categories runs counter to the essence of psychoanalytic thinking," while Karl Menninger [3] states even more emphatically:

> Diagnosis in the sense in which we doctors have used it for many years is not only relatively useless in many cases; it is an inaccurate, misleading, philosophically false predication.

It is useful to inquire why traditional diagnosis has been found to be so unsatisfactory. One reason is that it ignores four vital aspects of the individual's functioning: intelligence, socio-economic status, age, and sex. These are all incidental in any standard medical diagnosis and consequently it was assumed that they were also incidental in mental disorders. Nothing could be further from the truth.

In the exploration of intelligence a great deal of progress has been made, primarily because as a working tool the researcher has been guided by the idea that it is basically a measure of learning ability. If such a guideline could be found for personality, the question of diagnosis could be resolved more readily.

Menninger [4] has shown that the conventional psychiatric nomenclature has changed but little over the centuries. Alexander [5] has also shown how ideas once forgotten are revived to crop up over and over again. Jung [6] in his delineation of introversion and extraversion has a lengthy historical section in which he demonstrates how in one form or another the polarity of extravert-introvert has been found throughout the history of Western thought.

Since psychotherapy scarcely existed before Freud, the traditional systems took as their base line the functioning of the individual in society. If he could function, he was "sane"; if he could not, he was "insane." All the research of the last fifty years has dealt a telling blow to this idea. We know now that people can get along in certain cultures with all kinds of psychopathology, including the most severe forms of mental illness, while others who are psychologically healthy are at odds with the culture in which they live. Normality and social functioning cannot be equated outside an ideal society, and no such society has ever been found.

Faced by a dilemma of this kind, it is best to replace the strife of words by rational inquiry. What we want to know when we see a patient is: Does he have the capacity to change in the desired direction or directions? How much change can be expected? How durable will it be? In other words, the clinical approach is based on *therapeutic accessibility*. It is wise to make this as well the basis of the theoretical system of classification.

Knowledge of therapeutic accessibility is still largely clinical, though supplemented by many empirical studies. This experience leads to a number of significant findings that may be summarized here:

1. No essential difference is found between those who come to therapy and those who do not. Hendin, Gaylin, and Carr,[7] attempting to apply a research method based on psychoanalytic theory, used nurses as subjects. They called them non-patients (some had been in therapy and stopped, but they were chosen essentially at random from the nursing staff of a large hospital). Even on this superficial basis, they displayed many problems that called for therapy.

Therapy is a form of self-study applicable to everybody. It is not a cure of the sick in the statistical sense, but only in the ideal. It thus resembles religion, which calls upon mankind to seek salvation; or education, which offers to teach anyone who can benefit from the teaching, much more than conventional medicine, with its emphasis on illness and treatment. (It should be noted, however, that it does not differ so radically from medicine in the broader humanistic sense which seeks to prevent illness as well as to cure it when it arises.)

The implications of this finding can scarcely be overestimated. Above all, it means that therapy should be looked upon as a positive action designed to reach happiness rather than a negative one meant to alleviate illness.

In a great many cases, a subtle change takes place in the attitude of the analytic patient toward his illness. At first he comes to treatment in a state of despair (as most people still do on the contemporary scene), convinced that he is far sicker than those around him. Gradually, as he discusses his family, his friends, his acquaintances, colleagues, superiors, and inferiors, this attitude changes. It undergoes a radical reversal. Instead of feeling sicker than others, he becomes acutely aware of the illness which is hidden behind their façades, and gets to feel that at least he has done something about his illness and is doing more. The "sick" are healthy because they are doing something about their illness, while the "healthy" are sick because they stagnate in their defensive rituals. Saul and Wenar [8] put this very well:

> The inevitable and simple conclusion is that if all children were properly reared we would have a world of emotionally mature men and women. What we see instead is not human nature, but a variety of characterological disorders which are so nearly universal that we mistake them for human nature.

2. Most people who engage in therapy seriously derive benefit in terms of improved self-understanding, functioning, and well-being. Some benefit more than others. Some feel their lives totally transformed; others experience lesser changes. But the great majority are helped in ways that are made intelligible by the analytic ideal.

3. For successful therapy a certain openness to the inner life is a highly desirable prerequisite. Those who do not have this openness are: a) people with a low I.Q.; b) many with low socio-economic status; c) those with excessive hostility; d) the excessively suspicious ("paranoid"); e) the excessively rigid; f) those with too little real-life hope (e.g., the terminally ill).

4. For many who are not amenable to the basic procedure certain modifications have proved therapeutically beneficial.

5. The goal is not cure but improvement. Therapy is in every respect a learning procedure.

In the light of the above, therapy can be reevaluated as a method of helping people come as close as they can to the analytic ideal. This ideal has been defined above (see Chapter 1) as consisting of love, pleasure, sex, feeling, reason, family role, sense of identity, work, role in the social order, creativity, communication, absence of psychiatric symptomatology. On the basis of this schema the clinician is able to place the patient on a scale of mental health. Such an evaluation should consistently replace the conventional diagnostic approaches.

TREATABILITY AND ANALYZABILITY

As long as the medical model holds in psychiatric investigation there will be constant discussion of treatability and what is meant by a cure. This discussion has gone on over the decades without reaching any concrete conclusion. In general, as Freud had already pointed out in his 1905 paper on psychotherapy (his first published paper on the theme), the analytic procedure is especially suitable for persons who are fairly intelligent, somewhere between 20 and 50, and do not have too many disabling symptoms. In broad outline these criteria still hold.

But by now it is possible to say much more. Apart from the general criteria of age, intelligence, and real life obstacles or advantages, two factors stand out prominently if the patient population in psychotherapy is surveyed. These two are *guilt and accessible fantasy*.

1. Guilt

The person who has a fair amount of free-floating or bound guilt is sufficiently motivated to seek the cause of his misfortunes in himself, an indispensable first step in the therapeutic encounter. With the guilt he says: I have done something wrong, and unconsciously (sometimes quite consciously) adds: Punish me. In effect the analyst replies: In some way you have been hurting yourself. Let us explore your life together, find out what you have been doing, and correct it.

By contrast, the person who feels no guilt seeks the cause of his misfortunes in outside circumstances or in other people. Accordingly, he comes to the therapist, when he does come, with the request: Help me change other people. In effect the therapist replies: I cannot help you change other people. I can only help you to make yourself stronger so that you can handle them better. If the patient makes excessive use of denial or paranoid mechanisms, the therapeutic encounter is destroyed by his obdurate refusal to look into himself.

2. Accessible Fantasy

The primary material of psychotherapy is the fantasy life of the individual; hence, the more fantasy there is the more accessible the patient is to treatment. By "accessible fantasy" is meant simply fantasy that can be brought out in the treatment, such as dreams, daydreams, memories, associations, and so on. In effect, the analyst says to the patient: Let us explore your fantasies together to find out why and in what ways you are doing things to hurt yourself. Further in the background the therapist has the goal of the analytic ideal, to which he will try to direct the patient when the time is ripe.

A word should be said here about the various misconceptions of the schizophrenic that are current. The schizophrenic is characterized by an inability to distinguish fantasy from reality, not by his wealth of fantasy. His loss of fantasy is due to a sense of despair about ever finding any real satisfactions in his human relationships.

Both guilt and fantasy must operate within tolerable limits. If the guilt at the beginning is excessive, it creates a special problem which must be handled first.

> Daisy, a 19-year-old girl, spoke in such a low voice that the therapist could scarcely hear her. When she was asked what she had said, she took this as an indication that what she had said was wrong, and then reformulated her statement. In the beginning it was necessary to impress upon her that all that was needed was for her to repeat what she had said in a louder tone of voice.

Likewise the fantasies must be within certain bounds. If the fantasy life is excessive, the therapist will be barraged by a flow of material too complex to handle; Reich called this a "chaotic situation." In such cases it is sometimes advisable to ask the patient to concentrate on real-life material, and to limit the production of fantasy for a while.

Patients who have a fair amount of guilt and adequate fantasy establish a relationship most readily, provided the therapist does not make any serious mistakes.

With other patients, the preliminary period of therapy is one in which they are led into this framework. Whatever they come with, the therapist tries to establish a relationship in which there is enough guilt to motivate the patient to look into himself, and enough production of fantasy material to allow for a meaningful therapeutic encounter. This is the task of the initial period of therapy, when a relationship is being established. The first strong resistance, or treatment crisis, comes about because the wealth of fantasy material arouses so much guilt that the previous defenses are not strong enough to handle it.

Looked at in this light, suitability for therapy depends on the presence of an optimal combination of guilt and fantasy; conventional diagnosis is almost entirely irrelevant, with the exception of a differentiation between patients who should be hospitalized and those who should not.

If the guilt-fantasy combination is inadequate for the basic model technique, then other procedures have to be adopted to get the patient to that point. Here much confusion has arisen because of the failure to differentiate between *techniques* and *goals*. In terms of goals, outlined above in the analytic ideal, everybody is suitable for therapy, since virtually no one in our society succeeds in reaching the analytic ideal unaided. But in terms of techniques, the basic model is applicable to a much smaller number of individuals, although the number is much greater than many critics of psychoanalysis would have the world believe.

In the course of time various techniques have been devised to make therapy available to virtually all kinds of patients. Freud's contemporaries (Déjerine, Dubois), and predecessors knew only rational therapy, hypnosis (with either catharsis or suggestion), and the meaningless electro-therapy (faradic shocks). It was Freud who introduced the systematic exploration of the fantasy life which has become the heart of the basic model technique. But Freud also introduced the concept of goals of analysis that go well beyond what is accepted as normal in our society or any other; i.e., an image of happy living which goes far beyond the confines of the immediate environment.

Since Freud, modifications of technique have served to bring virtually the entire gamut of psychopathology within the range of the analytically trained therapist. Melanie Klein [9] and Anna Freud [10] widened the process to include children. Sullivan [11] was the first to treat schizophrenics successfully on any extended basis. Later Rosen [12] showed that severely regressed (back wards) schizophrenics are also amenable to treatment. Aichhorn [13] initiated the treatment of adolescent delinquents. This has since been extended to include adult criminals; Maxwell Jones [14] has even succeeded in helping the most intractable criminals by gathering them together in a therapeutic community. Alexander [15] devised a simplified approach for patients with severe psychosomatic problems, most of whom reject the standard technique.

The mentally retarded have been brought within the purview of the analytically trained therapist, although their therapy consists largely of affective release.[16] The terminally ill have been helped by Eissler [17] and others who seek either to prolong life somewhat or to make the end somewhat more comfortable.

In short, from the point of view of goals there is not a single kind of patient who has not at one time or another been helped by one therapist or another. This help ranges from the supportive handling of the terminally ill to the full analytic reconstruction of the normal-neurotic.

If the question is now put: Who needs treatment? the answer must be: Everybody who has not yet reached the analytic ideal. As pointed out above, this includes virtually the entire population. The difference is only that with presently available techniques some can be helped a little, while others can be changed a great deal. Thus the question:—Who needs treatment?—is a futile one; what is operationally more significant is this question: How much benefit can this patient expect to get from such-and-such form of treatment?

When clinical experience is reformulated in this light, many of the practices common on the current scene are seen to be senseless or directly harmful. It is not up to the internist or any other medical specialist to decide who needs treatment, since there is too little in his training or experience that permits him to answer the question in a rational way. The same holds true for guidance counselors, teachers, lawyers, and so on. The delineation of how much help any given individual can expect from psychotherapy should be left to the experts in the field.

With *analyzability* the problem is somewhat similar to treatability. Again, here the trouble arises because an insufficient distinction has been drawn between technique and goals. Thus, when it was first shown by Federn,[18] Sullivan,[19] and others that schizophrenics could be helped by psychotherapy, a proposition Freud had questioned, it was argued that what these patients received was not psychoanalysis but "dynamically oriented psychotherapy." Certainly in terms of technique the schizophrenic is not put on a couch and asked to free-associate. But in terms of goals the ultimate direction is the same. If the patient is too sick to get as far as some other patients, that does not alter the fact that the process is essentially psychoanalytic.

ESTABLISHING THE RELATIONSHIP

The first stage in therapy is the establishment of a relationship; in the beginning everything else is of secondary importance. The focus must be on what facilitates and what impedes this relationship.

The most effective way of establishing a relationship with the average ambulatory patient is to *listen*. As a rule, from the mere unburdening of hitherto secret thoughts and feelings, the patient experiences some relief and comes to value the relationship. Frequently he is not in a position to put his finger on what is helping him, but he goes around with the feeling: I'm not sure of what's going on here, but it's making me feel better.

In this ideal situation, where the therapist need do little more than listen, the patient concentrates on the *production of material*. If the patient falters, a helpful formulation is: Tell me more about yourself; the more I know about you, the more I'll be able to help you. The patient talks about his childhood, his mother, father, friends, dreams, hopes, fantasies, life history, symptoms, fears; everything is grist for the analytic mill.

What the therapist does in the beginning should be thought of as *dynamic inactivity,* rather than as passivity. He should recognize that the beginning of analysis sets off a dynamic process in the patient over which the therapist has only a limited amount of control. His efforts should be geared toward understanding this process, which differs from patient to patient.

Usually it is difficult for the beginning therapist to sit back and listen calmly. He is anxious about the start of a practice; he is surprised and bewildered by the kind of material that is offered to him; he is annoyed at the resistances, some of them glaringly transparent, that he has to handle. To overcome this anxiety, he feels that he has to offer the patient something. And so he begins to interpret, prematurely. *The besetting sin of the beginning therapist, common to almost all, is excessive interpretation.* Related to this is excessive activity of other kinds, such as needless advice, or intervention in the patient's life.

All of this hampers the development of a relationship. More often than not, technical mistakes by the therapist in the beginning, involving overactivity of all kinds, chase the patient away.

To give the beginner some overview of what a successful therapeutic experience can look like, the following case history is reproduced *in extenso.*[20]

Illustrative Case *

Even before the first interview, Jim manifested considerable anxiety. He had had no direct referral to the analyst, but had merely heard a general comment about him from one of his school instructors. His first call had come while the analyst was on vacation, and he was so informed by the answering service. In spite of this, he called several more times, and was obviously impatient for contact when the analyst was finally reached.

After listening to more details of the history, including a psychological examination done some three years previously, the analyst suggested to him that his problem was not vocational but emotional and that he should try analysis. At this he balked rather strongly, objecting pointedly that he did not feel his problem to be so deep-seated. Although he was then 37 years old, without a job and without a girl, he felt no problems. He wanted the analyst to tell him what could be gained by such a procedure. To this the analyst replied that an intellectual discussion would be of little avail, but that in such cases it was customary to have a trial period of two months, at the end of which time he would have a better idea of what the analytic experience was. This he accepted. He could not come more than twice a week, ostensibly for financial reasons.

A summary review of his life history revealed that it had been pervaded by a sense of aimlessness for a period of many years. He was the second of three children; both the others were girls. Soon after reaching adolescence a severe withdrawal pattern made itself apparent. He went to college in another city, but dropped out before getting his degree. There was no purpose in college for him. During this period, there was still some contact with his family. Then he left his home entirely, moving to the Pacific coast, where he went to a theological school for a while, supporting himself by odd jobs as cook, dishwasher, etc. Before leaving home he had almost no dates with girls, and no sexual experience of any kind. In the Pacific city he went steady with

---

* Throughout the remainder of the book this case will be referred to as "the illustrative case" or "Jim."

a girl for some time, but was too frightened to have any physical contact. In this period he had one brief homosexual experience, when he was masturbated by an older man.

The theological studies were abandoned, and soon thereafter he was inducted into the Army. Almost from the first day he showed tremendous resentment. He would not march, he would not drill, he would not obey. Because of a hearing deficiency he was assigned to limited service; here, too, he rebelled at the work assigned to him. Demerits piled up; he was threatened with court-martial. Nothing moved him. His resentment mounted, and he finally had a severe anxiety reaction for which he was hospitalized. For months he remained in the military hospital, crying all the time. There was no psychotic ideation; it was a breakthrough of so much of the affect stored up over a lifetime. No treatment was given during his hospital stay. After several months he was discharged from the service, with no disability pension, because it was decided that his hearing deficiency antedated the Army. Typically, he was indifferent to the decision and made no attempt to appeal it.

After discharge, he did not return home, but remained in the city in Texas where he had been stationed. The Army doctors had advised him to seek out psychiatric treatment; he could see no necessity for it. He spent his time drinking and gambling, with some sporadic contacts with women. One W.A.C. he remembered from this period was very sweet to him, but as usual he was indifferent. At this time he had his first heterosexual experiences with prostitutes and, curiously, reported no difficulties. When his money ran out, he left Texas and returned home. Significantly, although he was now living in the same city, he shunned his family, particularly his mother.

Vocationally his situation improved. He took some business training and succeeded in clerical-administrative work. But it did not take long to make him feel dissatisfied, and he drifted through several jobs. He finished college, though still with no idea of what he wanted to do.

Emotionally, the outstanding change in the post-war period was an active homosexual life. He went to live with a gifted artist whom he admired very much, who he said opened a whole new world for him. The sexual contact was confined largely to mutual masturbation. After breaking up with this friend, he repeated a similar relationship with another strong personality, also a creative individual. This too ended in an unsatisfactory way. During all this time he avoided any close contact with girls.

With such a history the first point that had to be understood was the resistance to therapy. He was after all a highly intelligent person with some knowledge of modern psychology. He had had a nervous breakdown in the Army, for which treatment had been recommended and refused. His lifelong experiences had been ones of inadequacy, blocking, and frustration in all the major areas of living. Most of his life he had felt subjectively quite miserable. Objectively he knew that many people with such conflicts were helped by psychotherapy; in fact, at one time he had even thought of becoming a social worker. Why then had he fought therapy so strongly? Even in this analytic situation he had begun, so to speak, on the sidelines. He had come for "vocational guidance." Initially he had not known that the writer was an analyst, knowing of him only as a clinical psychologist. In fact, had he known it, he might not have come. He did not see the need for more intensive treatment or more frequent visits. Actually, he said, he was just coming to see what this was all about, and did not know how long he would stay.

As the analyst repeatedly called attention to the discrepancy between the severity of his problems and the reluctance to do anything about them, it gradually dawned on the patient that his life up to that time had been pretty aimless, and that he really had no idea of how he could go about changing this sense of aimlessness on his own. It also became clear to him that this aimlessness had been with him for a long time. The unnecessarily long trip to go to college he could now see as a needless detour. When he left college without a degree it was because there was no purpose in anything. Various enthusiasms had temporarily covered up the feeling of aimlessness. For a while it was a famous professor in college. Later it was Zionism. In the Army he had really let himself go emotionally—particularly in drinking and gambling. After the Army it was homosexuality. That too passed. At the time the analysis began it was masturbation and movies. Outside of these two pastimes, everything was frustrating and disappointing, and all the passions of the past had been forgotten.

To trace the meaning of this aimlessness then became the central topic for him in therapy. It did not take long for him to see that his conflicts derived from the lifelong battle with his mother. Jim, who at the time of beginning treatment was 37 years old, had very vivid memories of his mother and her domineering ways. For quite a while the complaints poured out in an almost never-ending stream; in milder form they continued until the end of therapy. For the first six years of Jim's life the family had lived on a farm in Pennsylvania, but the father had no talent for farming, and they had to return to New York. The father then went to work for the mother's brother who, according to Jim, was a modern Simon Legree. After many years of this drudgery the parents bought a small candy store, which they still had at the time he came to see the writer. This prospered because, it was said, the mother took over. She had sole charge of the cash register. Once the father had gone to the register to pay some bill, which turned out to be not due. Ever since, the mother had redoubled her vigilance, because if left in the father's hands the business would go to rack and ruin. The father was deprived of the right to handle money.

In the household the mother also bossed the father completely. She even prepared his food down to the last slice of bread and butter, and he was obligated to eat it. Several times—once even during therapy—the father had simply thrown his plate out *in toto,* in protest against being spoon-fed. The protest did not last.

Extreme vigilance was practiced by the mother to see to it that the daughters did not stray from the righteous path. Her suspiciousness was so great that when they went swimming the father was ordered to go along secretly and make sure that no wrong was done. It was no wonder that the older sister was reported to be dull or feeble-minded, and had dropped out of school at an early age. The younger sister seemed to have escaped relatively unscathed.

Jim felt very bitter towards his mother. When he was a child she used to beat him severely; against this he built a hard-shell defense. His greatest victory came when his mother beat him with a strap and he could hold back his crying. He was force-fed. No interest was shown in his schooling; his mother could see no point in buying a book for him. He had no close friends because he could not bring them home. The household, as he remembered, was one with no cohesiveness; everybody lived in an isolated world. His mother, he felt, had great contempt for him; she compared him unfavorably with his cousins, many of whom became successful professional men, and predicted that he would come to no good end. The mother permitted herself no enjoyment of any kind. She lived near the store and never left the neighborhood. By the time he was grown up, the parents had amassed a considerable amount of money, which Jim contemptuously referred to as "mattress money"; it was merely saved, never spent.

While these initial insights allowed him to make more sense of his life than ever before, they were still highly intellectual and in theory would produce no deep or lasting effect.

During the two-month exploratory period, which ended quite successfully in that he could see his need for analysis and determined to finish it, a number of transference-resistances came out and were analyzed. First of all, he experienced deep resentment toward the analyst, especially when any interpretation was given not to his liking. At other times, he recognized, such resentment would have led him to break off the relationship. Here he could see that the resentment toward his mother was being carried over inappropriately, and he changed his reaction accordingly. Bringing this resentment to consciousness helped him for the first time in his life to see the dynamics of his repetitious withdrawal; oral frustration → oral aggression → withdrawal, since the oral aggression toward his mother always had to be inhibited.

At the same time, he showed great ambivalence about the manner in which he paid the fee. Sometimes it was by the session, sometimes by the week, sometimes every two weeks, but almost every week it was different. Analysis of this ceaseless variation brought out several significant points. He was not short of money. In fact, he had a sizable amount saved up, again something he did not want people to know; it was his own "mattress money." Yet he never kept much with him. He liked to go to the bank and make withdrawals of small sums. For a period he did this several times a day until things came to such a pass that the bank asked him to transfer his account. This made him very angry with the bank; they made enough money on him, paid him only 2½ per cent, and ought to serve him. It thus became apparent that the bank was like a mother who should always have the food ready for him whenever he came to eat, and should make no demands on him. Underneath the hatred of the bad mother lay revealed the yearning for the good mother, and it was only when this hidden yearning was brought to light in the transference situation that any real change in ego structure could be effected. By switching the manner of payment of the fee all the time, he was testing the analyst out to see what kind of a mother he would be.

After the withdrawal, resentment, and testing, the next transference manifestation that came to light was the transfer of omnipotence. The analyst became a magical figure who could by a wave of his finger solve all the patient's problems. This first came to light in a dream around the 20th hour: "I go to a dentist, a woman, she drills my tooth." In associations to this dream, the dentist was described as a woman of about 30. To the drilling he associated the analyst. The dentist is made into a woman to facilitate sexual contact. Often we find that the first dream in analysis combines the core of the neurotic problem with its attempted solution. Here, too, this is the case. He wants to be drilled by a woman; the sore tooth is symbolic of his inadequate self and body-image; the drilling makes him a passive recipient of sex. Dentist-analyst-lover are all one, making no demands on him.

The self-depreciation (severe superego derived particularly from the mother's continual depreciation of him) was seen to be another important source of his withdrawal. He felt sure he would be defeated, and therefore developed the formula: "If I don't play, I can't lose."

Although compulsive masturbation was one of the main complaints in the early part of analysis, he completely denied any connection between masturbation and sexual frustration. The masturbation was free of fantasy; it was a purely mechanical stimulation. The absolute denial of any sexual desire naturally required analysis. No insight dawned upon him, however, until he had relived an experience from earlier days. Several years before, he had been friendly with a group of people in analysis, for whose attachment to their analysts he had nothing but contempt. One of these people was a girl who had a great need to "make" every man she came across. Inevitably the patient, who acted indifferent to her, became a great object of desire. She did everything she could to get him to have sex, even appearing before him in the nude, and going to bed in the next room with another man while he was present and could surmise what was going on. Consciously, Jim felt great contempt for this girl, yet he continued to visit her regularly. He could now see what he was doing. On the one hand he derived gratification from being a voyeur and rejecting the eager woman (revenge on mother). On the other hand, he could now admit that he had some sexual desire for her, and that this desire could come out only when he was physically thousands of miles away from his mother. Consequently, he could see that his vehement denial of sexual desire to the analyst was again a transference of feelings called out by mother.

With this memory and transference insight, the sexual feelings began to break through. Sexual and aggressive dreams served to mitigate the severity of the superego sufficiently to seek out contacts with women. Characteristically, he sought out Sally, who had been a great admirer of his for many years. He had to be certain that there would be no rejection before he could allow himself to feel more deeply.

Not long after, when the analysis was in its 14th month, he had his first heterosexual experience with Sally. A general loosening of the personality set in. He became much more relaxed. His job, which had hitherto been an impossible chore, became much more acceptable. The deep dissatisfaction with everything in his life disappeared. He would come in beaming, and often remark on what a wonderful place the world was. His hostility toward his family became manageable. The central problem now became the working out of his relationship with Sally. Certain resentments cropped up, especially once when she was sick. But everything could be handled. After some 20 months of analysis he felt that he had come far enough to marry, and broached the subject of termination. Although there certainly was a strong element of dependency in his feelings about Sally, it seemed to be normal in the circumstances. In the year or so in which he could be observed with her, it seemed to be in every respect an ideal relationship for him. Sally was past the child-bearing age, but she had a 9-year-old son to whom he became very devoted.

Toward the end, the psychological tests were repeated. The two Rorschachs, given by the same examiner at an interval of about five years, confirmed that many far-reaching changes in positive directions had occurred.

With his marriage the analysis was terminated. It had lasted some 175 hours over a two-year period. The termination left the road open for further treatment if the need should arise. But in the twenty years that have passed since, no such need has arisen.

SUGGESTIONS FOR FURTHER READING

On the general problem of diagnosis see: T. Szasz, *The Myth of Mental Illness* (New York: Hoeber-Harper, 1961) and L. Eron, *The Classification of Behavior Disorders* (Chicago: Aldine, 1966). Suggestions for revision along more dynamic lines are found in A. Mahrer, ed., *New Approaches to Diagnosis* (New York: Columbia U. Press, 1970).

The topic of treatability generally centers around the therapy of schizophrenia. For the most systematic discussion, see G. Bychowski, *The Psychotherapy of Psychosis* (New York: Grune and Stratton, 1952). Sullivan, a pioneer in the field, never presented a clear exposition of his technique, but see his *Schizophrenia as a Human Process* (New York: W. W. Norton and Co., 1962). The most recent summary is in L. Bellak and L. Loeb, *The Schizophrenic Syndrome* (New York: Grune and Stratton, 1969). Inspiring is the heroic work of H. Searles, documented in *Collected Papers on Schizophrenia and Related Subjects* (New York: Int. Universities Press, 1965).

On the opening phase an especially good discussion is to be found in E. Glover, *The Technique of Psychoanalysis* (New York: Int. Universities Press, 1955).

CHAPTER 3

Transference: General Considerations

Transference is a universal phenomenon of the human mind, it decides the success of all medical influence, and in fact dominates the whole of each person's relations to his human environment.

Freud: *An Autobiographical Study* (1925)

In the area of technique Freud's most fundamental discovery lay in his elucidation of the importance of transference and its concomitant resistances. With these concepts a variety of different types of therapeutic experience can be readily understood.

However, Freud tended to use the word "transference" in two different senses, which has created a certain amount of confusion. He used it first to describe the general emotional relationship between patient and therapist, and second in the more narrow sense of the intense feelings toward the therapist that are aroused in the patient. These two senses, the broad and the narrow, are not entirely different; the second is a special case of the first. We prefer to use the term transference in the broad sense, and transference neurosis for the narrower meaning.

In the broad sense, every patient has some kind of transference; i.e., he has some kind of reaction to the therapist, if indifference or a lack of reaction is included. In the specific sense of a transference neurosis, the issue is the intensity of the feelings developed by the patient toward the analyst; these vary considerably.

Transference is explained by childhood experience, but is not identical with it. This has led to a further confusion between the present-day reactions and their origins in the past; at times transference is used to describe both. A clear distinction must be drawn between the phenomenological observation of present-day transference manifestations, and their referents in childhood. In therapy it is necessary to deal with both the present and the past.

No sooner does the patient come to treatment—many times no sooner does he think of treatment—than he becomes involved in an emotional relationship with the therapist that takes precedence over everything else. Transference is forced upon the therapist by the reactions of the patient. Because of the transference therapy can never become an intellectual exercise.

Psychoanalytic therapy is set up in such a way that the patient is given optimal opportunity to produce transference manifestations. Transference exists everywhere but it is hard to prove. The therapist creates a special relationship to the patient, he sees him at certain times, for an agreed-upon fee, he eschews social contacts with him, his family, or his friends. All of this is done in order to give the patient a chance to see what his real transference reactions are. Any violation of these rules, such as encouraging social contacts, interferes with the transference to such an extent that the whole therapeutic process is vitiated. The generally passive position of the therapist in the beginning likewise is adopted in order to give the transference reactions a chance to appear; if the therapist is too active, the patient will rightly say that he is reacting to his activity, so that he will be unable to see his own contribution to the problems.

CLINICAL MANIFESTATIONS OF THE TRANSFERENCE

Transference is inferred from the totality of all the responses made by the patient. It builds up, like any other emotional reaction, and expresses itself in a variety of ways. The therapist, aware that this is the central experience in therapy, is content to wait for its manifestations to reach a point where they can be called to the attention of the patient, and correlated with other phenomena in his life. On the other hand, the patient, totally oblivious even to the concept of the transference, has other concerns. He must gradually be taught how significant his reactions to the therapist are, how they are related to his general life difficulties, and how once they are put in proper perspective his life begins to look different. This is an enormously complex process, the working through of the transference; it occupies the major portion of therapy.

In accordance with the general principle that the major demand on the patient, especially in the beginning, is to produce material, the therapist defers any interpretations or conflict-laden comment until he has sufficient material at his disposal, and until the patient is emotionally able to handle it. How he handles this material is a complex question; actually, this entire book is devoted to it.

At the beginning of therapy three demands are made on the patient: to come at a certain time, to talk, and to pay a fee. It is amazing how many variations there are in the ways in which different patients handle these three simple demands. Some come early, some late, some pay on time, some are behind in their payments, and so on. From the way in which the patient handles these three simple requests come the first clues to the nature of his transference reactions.

Since the patient guards against revealing his feelings too openly, the therapist must use his skill to get him to bring these feelings out in words, when they can be discussed. Often the way in which the patient handles the three basic demands provides a convenient avenue to the transference reactions. The first step, as in all interpretation, is *confrontation*.

Behavior by itself can be interpreted in many different ways; what sheds light is the fantasy connected with behavior. Consider, e.g., the question of time. Some patients are consistently early. At times it is because they feel hopeful of a solution to their difficulties. In other cases, however, it may be the expression of a deep-seated dependency: by submitting to the analyst, some magical benefits will accrue. Many times it is only the pursuit of some repetitive pattern, together with some seemingly insignificant detail, that manages to bring out the real feelings.

To the therapist the most conclusive evidence of transference is the variety of different reactions he gets to the same objective event. In a series of patients there will sometimes be as many reactions as there are people. The only explanation of the multiplicity of responses lies in the personality of the patients; i.e., the transference in the broad sense.

While transference is related to childhood experience, the family environment differs from child to child. It is instructive to examine the transference reactions of two members of the same family to the same therapist.

Bryan was the first to enter treatment. He was the youngest of three children. Mother had been a serious depressive, who spent much of her time crying that she was dying. She died relatively young of cancer. Father then remarried, but died two years later. Bryan was then 18.

The oldest child, a boy, had been hospitalized twice for schizophrenia. Now he was out of the hospital living with his stepmother, but otherwise completely isolated from human contacts.

Since his father's death Bryan had been suffering from severe anxiety attacks. These led him to retreat from relationships with women, because he had once made a pact with God that if God would get him over one of his attacks he would never have sex before he was married. The attack did end, which he attributed to God's intervention, and he refrained from sexual intercourse.

The transference was almost bitterly negative from the very beginning. The therapist represented the distant intellectual brother (they were about the same age and according to Bryan even looked alike) who was always critical of anything that he did. Bryan doubted all the major tenets of psychoanalysis, and was convinced that some day a drug would be discovered which would put all psychotherapists out of business. It was only after many years that he was able to change his hostile attitude.

Although Bryan's analysis was of many years' duration, his sister Judy came for only six months. She too had many anxiety problems, particularly a severe agoraphobia which in the beginning prevented her from coming to treatment alone. She was married, with one child. Her transference, in contrast to her brother's, was intensely positive. A hysterectomy at 30, together with a husband who was almost impotent, combined to give her almost no sexual satisfaction in real life. She fell in love with the analyst, had constant thoughts of sex with him, would think about him all week, at times concentrating particularly on his lips, which reminded her of her father who had also had such thick, kissable lips.

During the therapy, which for financial reasons was limited to a once-a-week basis, she grew more and more anxious about her sexual feelings. Finally she terminated. After termination her symptoms began to subside, and she made some rather remarkable progress.

In this brother-sister combination, who were treated by the same analyst, the variability and unpredictability of the transference are seen. Bryan concentrated on the negative feelings about the hated older brother, using the sessions to release his hostilities. Bryan had had positive feelings about his father as well, yet these rarely came out. Judy made a transference to the therapist as a father figure, for whom she still retained warm feelings. Just why she reacted to the therapist as if he were her father, while her brother made a brother-figure out of him, is hard to explain.

In the present stage of knowledge the kind of transference any patient will make can be predicted only in a fairly general way. There are still too many unknowns. This is another reason why the therapist should adopt a fairly passive role in the beginning, allowing the transference manifestations to accumulate until the pattern has become established. Except for strong negative reactions, the analysis of the transference only comes about much later.

The problem in the beginning is to get the patient to verbalize his feelings about the therapist. Sometimes he has direct fantasies or dreams; these are very useful. But more often whatever he feels crystallizes slowly to the point where it can be verbalized. With patients who say little about the transference it is useful to ask them once in a while whether there are any feelings about the therapist that they have been unable to mention for one reason or another. If there are any, this provides helpful material. If there are none, the patient can be asked to bring up anything that might come to mind as the therapy proceeds. In most cases this will provide sufficient impetus for therapeutically helpful verbalization.

VARIETIES OF TRANSFERENCE

Three major kinds of transference reactions can be distinguished: positive, negative, and indifferent. Since human relationships have such a marked degree of ambivalence these three alternate at various times in the therapy. Positive turns to negative, and vice versa. But the predominant tone of the transference maintains a certain constancy that eventually becomes the major object of scrutiny.

DIMENSIONS OF THE TRANSFERENCE

Three aspects of the transference are particularly important: intensity, variability, and accessibility to consciousness.

1. *Intensity*: The transference may be extraordinarily intense, or so weak as to be scarcely noticeable.

2. *Variability*: The patient's feelings may persist in the same form, or may change markedly, sometimes even within one session. In many cases, the transference may remain positive for some months, then turn negative.

3. *Accessibility to Consciousness*: The patient may be fully aware of his feelings, or they may come out in dreams, acting-out, or other disguised forms. Those who are aware of their transferences are easier to handle.

TRANSFERENCE AND REALITY

Inasmuch as it involves a distorted perception of the therapeutic relationship, transference per se has little to do with reality. It can seize upon any triviality in the office environment, blowing it up all out of proportion. No matter what evidence to the contrary is presented, the patient in strong transference may insist on his version of the matter.

In recent years it has been argued that the transference is closer to reality than had been supposed. After all, the therapist is a real person, with real strengths and weaknesses. Some of these weaknesses inevitably impinge upon the patient, who then becomes aware of them and discusses them accordingly. Szasz [21] has even argued that poorly trained therapists may use the transference as a screen behind which they can hide their own problems. No doubt this is true, but it should be used as an argument for better training rather than a polemic against the idea of the transference.

While the emphasis on reality contains a kernel of truth, it still misconstrues the relationship of therapy to reality. In theory, when the analytic approach is adopted, the therapist does not thereby ignore reality. What he is doing is assessing the situation as one in which the patient can handle reality, to build up the patient's strength accordingly. If the patient is too regressed to handle reality situations without help, as happens in many schizophrenics or borderline cases, the therapist should at times intervene in reality matters.

If the patient is in sufficient contact, or has a strong enough ego, he can release his fantasies about the therapist, look at them, and benefit from their systematic interpretation. Most of the time what the patient fantasizes is untrue. But even when it is true, or a correct observation, it may still be so tied up with his entire relationship with the therapist that it can be used to therapeutic advantage.

Jerry, in a state of great anxiety, was given permission to call the analyst at any time of day or night. One night he called at about 4 A.M., waking the analyst out of a sound sleep. The patient's first remark was, "You sound sleepy." This was an entirely correct observation, but completely missed the dynamics of what was going on.

What should be kept in the foreground in all these discussions is the goal rather than the technique; technique follows goal, not vice versa. The goal is to help the patient become aware of the distortions in his fantasies, a goal for which the analysis of the transference is eminently suitable. The technique will vary from one patient to another. When the patient's ego is sufficiently strong, he can grasp the transference fantasies and remodel his life accordingly. When his ego is too weak, he needs much more support while the transference is being analyzed, or before it can even come to that. In other words, the role that the therapist plays will vary with the ego strength of the patient, but the basic technical ideas remain the same in every case.

It is important for the therapist to be as real a figure as is consistent with the needs of the patient. In some cases therapists do take advantage of the theory of transference to throw everything back at the patient, instead of being honest about what is going on.

> Katherine, a young girl of 25, started therapy with a woman therapist, who took notes all the time. This note-taking irritated the patient. When she protested, instead of asking for fantasies, the therapist replied, "I have finished my analysis, you must face *your* problems here." Actually the therapist was taking notes because she was still in supervision (which the patient suspected) and it would have been much better to say that. At one point some factual disagreement came up between patient and analyst, who tried to settle it by referring to her notes. The patient, enraged that the analyst remembered so little about her, left treatment.

> In a second treatment situation, Katherine put up a furious resistance to the idea of transference, falling back on her experience with the previous therapist. This was part of her lifelong feeling of being blamed for everything. Partly because of the previous fiasco, it was quite difficult to overcome this resistance.

Psychotherapy is by no means as routinized a procedure as, say, surgery, or even ordinary classroom teaching. Only the outline can be given to the student; the details have to be filled in through extensive experience.

Accordingly, it is not surprising to find that therapists make all kinds of mistakes. Whenever possible, if the patient picks up a mistake by the therapist, it is best to admit to it frankly; full explanation may, however, be out of the question. What counts is that the therapist should come across as a truly sincere individual, dedicated to the patient's welfare, even if he occasionally falters in his task.

An experienced analyst once fell asleep during a session with a homosexual male patient. The patient interpreted this as a sign that the therapist trusted him, for if he did not trust him he would never have fallen asleep and exposed himself to a homosexual attack. The therapist admitted that he had fallen asleep because he was tired, but refrained from further details. Actually, he had stayed up late the night before in a quarrel with his wife. It was much more important to analyze the patient's feeling of trust, and the concealed homosexual wish on his part, than to go into any details of the therapist's life situation.

THE CHILDHOOD ROOTS OF TRANSFERENCE

While transference is always traceable to childhood, no simple one-to-one correspondence between past and present can be delineated. Sometimes there is a direct repetition, sometimes there is a compensatory fantasy to make up for what was lacking in childhood. It is the business of the therapist to help the patient trace the complex path from earliest experiences to the present.

In the illustrative case (see pp. 17–23) the transference, at first rather negative, soon became moderately positive. For a while it was quite intense. One may well inquire in this positive transference what kind of childhood figure the therapist represented. He was not similar to anybody in the patient's early environment. Rather, he was the ego-ideal of the patient, who after many disappointments with his own parents built his hopes on the learned professors that he found in school and college. Thus the transference represented a compensatory fantasy.

There are cases where a repetition of a childhood experience is quite direct. Yet here, too, as the following case vignette shows, the total emotional climate is more important.

Mary, a 22-year-old girl, had a dream that as she was coming out of the therapist's office she was greeted by ten high school girls. In association to this dream she stated that when she was about six months old her mother became ill and Mary was sent off to another woman for a while. The other woman had ten children.

Yet this repetition was less significant than the total transference Gestalt. Mary had a most pathological background, sleeping with her father until the age of 13 while her sister slept with the mother. The father was about 20 years older than the mother. When Mary reached puberty she was convinced that her father would rape her, and moved her bed elsewhere without telling anyone why.

The transference became an intensely positive one, with the therapist the good father-figure. Later she went to live with a man who was old enough to be her father; this too, failed. Her life was a series of disappointments with father-figures; for a short while it would go well, then came the disillusionment.

Many patients will balk at the assumption that their present-day character structure stems from their relations with the parents. Although as obvious as ABC to the therapist, the relatively naive patient will frequently go through the gamut before he can accept this basic psychological proposition. Ontogeny recapitulates phylogeny; parallel to the historical development of psychotherapy is the sequence of resistances that the patient puts up. He resorts to magic, religion, philosophy, medicine, before he will get to the illuminating insights of psychology. Some fight the genetic point of view so hard that they run from treatment, sometimes to therapists whose theoretical persuasion is that the past does not count. Most, however, will stay to undo gradually the rupture of the present from the past which has cost them so much in terms of human happiness.

TRANSFERENCE IMPROVEMENT AND TRANSFERENCE CURE

The therapeutic relationship is such a powerful curative force that in many cases a considerable improvement results, even when the therapist does virtually nothing. This is the analytic honeymoon, sometimes the flight into health, described in later chapters (see pp. 38–49).

If nothing further is done, or if the patient leaves treatment at this point, his condition is apt to deteriorate. Improvement has been based on the fact that he could release his deepest feelings to an understanding person; when this outlet is gone, he feels bad again. Customarily, in any extended analysis after the initial improvement there is a relapse, then a turn for the better again, followed by a long series of ups and downs. It is only after these ups and downs have been sufficiently elucidated that the patient reaches a greater degree of equilibrium.

The transference cure is one in which the symptom disappears because of the therapeutic relationship. In some cases of this kind, the patient sees no reason for going on with the therapy; in others, enough has been learned about the character structure to maintain a desire for further change.

Since the ultimate goal of analytic therapy is to move the patient as close as possible to the analytic ideal, quick changes for the better or for the worse must be evaluated by this standard. Symptoms often yield to some quick form of treatment, character structure never. The well-trained therapist will be able to distinguish between a superficial removal of a symptom and a deep-seated alteration in the character.

THE TRANSFERENCE NEUROSIS

The *transference neurosis* represents an intensification of the transference to a point where it becomes the center of the patient's life for as long as it lasts, which may be anywhere from a few months to a few years. Usually it takes some time for the transference neurosis to come out in full force. If it should come out too soon, its very intensity, as in the violent erotic transferences, may be so great that it becomes unmanageable.

There are basically two kinds of transference neuroses: positive and negative, love and hate. Because of the overwhelming significance of these emotions the transference neurosis resembles a torrid love affair more than anything else, except that the protestations of love and the rage reactions when the other person does not respond are limited to one side. And indeed, through the knowledge of the love affair the psychology of the transference neurosis can become most readily intelligible.

Notoriously, love affairs are short-lived, stormy, defiant of sober "common sense," full of wild sweeps of the imagination, riddled with contradictions. On the one hand the deep passion is admired, as in the phrase, All the world loves a lover. Yet on the other hand its irrational nature is recognized in other phrases such as, Love is blind.

The analogy with love is particularly useful because one major goal of analysis is to teach the person how to love in a mature way. This can only be done by careful investigation of the immature ways in which the person experiences love. Through the exploration of the transference neurosis these immature ways of loving are brought out more clearly than in any other manner.

Not everybody goes through a transference neurosis, nor is the intensity of the neurosis as great with some as it is with others. Those who do are by and large better off, as the analogous saying goes about love: Better to have loved and lost than never to have loved at all. Love is an attempt to bridge the gap between people, and penetrate to the deepest reaches of interpersonal relatedness. Similarly, in the transference neurosis the patient wishes to come closer, to break down the barriers that seem to separate him from the therapist like high shutters.

Sharp swings from love to hate and back again are to be expected. The danger to be warded off is that in the course of those swings the patient may be so overcome by his longings that he will engage in some self-damaging actions.

> After the initial analytic honeymoon, Dan (cf. pp. 44 and 129) was in a strong transference neurosis. He could think of nothing but the analyst, fantasized extra sessions and conversations, thought of how it would be to live with him, etc. Sometimes he would call him up just to say I love you.
>
> This was followed by a period of acute depression. Dan had not yet been able to engage in relationships with girls, which bothered him immensely. Any rejection would set him off.
>
> Then came a period of tears. Dan could not seem to hold back his crying, in spite of the shame attached to it. He could control it in public, but in private he cried and cried. Once he isolated himself from his friends and cried for a whole day, bewailing his "miserable fate."
>
> Along with the crying came a period of reckless driving, which led to several near-accidents. At times it seemed as if the motion of the car was all that could hold back the deep depression.
>
> Fortunately, in a longish period of working-through these various transference feelings could be successfully analyzed.

The demands made on the analyst during this period may become overwhelming. Suicidal threats, even attempts, may occur. This is particularly dangerous; sometimes the patient may have to be hospitalized temporarily. But usually the feelings of rejection can be worked out. It may be noted incidentally that in love affairs suicide is not too uncommon when there is a rejection by the beloved.

The patient gives up outside figures, concentrating his libido entirely on the analyst, or at most substitutes for him. He wishes to see the analyst all the time. Yet no matter how many sessions are scheduled per week it is not enough. There is a desire for an almost literal symbiosis with the therapist. Since this can never be gratified, sharp flashes of rage are always to be anticipated in such a period.

Caught up in a web of powerful emotions, the patient can only talk about present-day conflicts and satisfactions. The past is forgotten; when the therapist tries to tie up the present with the past his efforts are resented. What does my childhood have to do with it? the patient keeps on saying, I want love now.

The demand that the therapist should reciprocate the patient's feelings is a natural one, yet of course it has to be denied. It is true that many times the therapist may have strong feelings about the patient, but it is best to conceal them, or at least present them in diluted form, because they are never as strong as the patient's, and would therefore be misleading to her. Besides, the therapist should have enough gratifications in his own love life, so that his feelings for the patient who is starved for love are not apt to be nearly as strong as her feelings for him.

While the transference neurosis presents itself as a state of great excitement and elation, deep undercurrents of depression are present. Essentially, the patient is going through an experience of unrequited love, yet one that neither she nor the therapist can avoid. As mentioned before, suicide is a threat, especially in patients who have a history of suicidal attempts. But even when there is no suicidal threat, the depression can be quite profound. There may be a breakthrough of feeling that leads the patient to cry much of the time.

A deep transformation of all values takes place. The old superego is given up gradually, and a new superego figure is developed, based on the person of the therapist. Eventually, as a result of the analytic work this new superego figure is also dissolved into a realistic resolution of life's difficulties, but for the time being the analyst becomes the standard for all things.

In the case of Jim, cited *in extenso* above (see pp. 17–23), the acute transference neurosis came on after about three or four months of therapy, and lasted about a year. There had never been anything like that in childhood; it was a compensatory fantasy. It was only when a woman came along who offered more reality satisfactions than the analyst that he was able to give up the transference. Actually, from a dynamic point of view his relationship to her was a transference neurosis of another kind, but since its reality consequences were on the whole very favorable, the neurotic elements in it could be ignored.

It is surprising to find that when the transference neurosis is negative, consisting mainly in the release of hateful feelings, it too can go on for a long time. One often wonders what drives the patient to continue in this therapy where the other person is seen as dull, incompetent, unimaginative, even a charlatan. Yet the patient comes back the next time, ready to let loose his quiver of arrows all over again. These are generally people who have so much hostility, which is qualitatively and quantitatively so burdensome, that other people will not stand for it.

> Carole was full of violent thoughts about the analyst. He was insensitive, did not treat his children right, gave wrong interpretations, abandoned her on long vacations, was so bad in fact that nobody in his right mind would go to him. In high dudgeon she finally left treatment. Three days later she called to ask if she could come back. When she did return she explained that on reflection she had decided that this was the one place in the world where she could say everything that was on her mind, and that this alone was worth more than anything else.

Nowadays, when some knowledge of psychoanalysis and psychological theory is possessed by many in the better educated classes, patients often come to therapy with some preconceived notion of what the transference neurosis should be. They know that they are "supposed" to fall in love with the analyst, or that they are supposed to "let him have it" if they feel like it. Sometimes they come with the idea that if they establish a "transference" they will not need any other person in the world. Needless to say, these preconceptions add a complication to the therapeutic procedure, but it suffices to bring them out into the open. Even with all this foreknowledge the course of therapy is not materially altered.

SUGGESTIONS FOR FURTHER READING

An excellent summary of the literature on transference to 1953 is D. W. Orr, "Transference and Countertransference: A Historical Survey," *J. Am. Psychoanalytic Assoc.* 2, 1954, 621–670.

Significant books or papers which have appeared since on the general topic are: E. Racker, "Notes on the Theory of Transference," *Psychoanalytic Quarterly* 23, 1954, 78–86. E. Racker, "A Study of Some Early Conflicts Through Their Return in the Patient's Relation with the Interpretation," *Int. J. Psychoanalysis* 41, 1960, 47–58. H. Searles, "Transference Psychosis in the Psychotherapy of Schizophrenia," *Collected Papers* (New York: Int. Universities Press, 1965) and Chapter 12 in the same book, "The Evolution of the Mother Transference in Psychotherapy with the Schizophrenic Patient." E. Zetzel, "Current Concepts of Transference," *Int. J. Psychoanalysis* 37, 1956, 369–376. T. S. Szasz, "The Concept of Transference," *Int. J. Psychoanalysis* 44, 1963, 432–443. L. Stone, "The Psychoanalytic Situation and Transference," *J. Am. Psychoanalytic Assoc.* 15, 1967, 3–58. E. Racker, *Transference and Countertransference* (New York: Int. Universities Press, 1968).

On the issue of transference and reality, see especially R. Greenson and M. Wexler, "The Non-Transference Relationship in the Psychoanalytic Situation," *Int. J. Psychoanalysis* 50, 1969, 27–39. M. Kanzer, "Past and Present in the Transference," *J. Am. Psychoanalytic Assoc.* 1, 1953, 144–154. E. Weigert, "The Importance of Flexibility in Psychoanalytic Technique," *J. Am. Psychoanalytic Assoc.* 2, 1954, 702–710. A. Roland, "The Reality of the Psychoanalytic Relationship and Situation in Handling of Transference Resistance," *Int. J. Psychoanalysis* 48, 1967, 504–510.

On the transference neurosis, the discussion in Glover, *op. cit.,* is particularly instructive.

CHAPTER 4

Positive Transference:
The Analytic Honeymoon

> . . . a healthy child and a healthy mother are so well adapted to each
> other that the same action inevitably brings gratification to both . . . the
> theory of primary love presupposes the experiencing of an external world,
> but it assures that there exists a harmony between the individual and
> his world; that is, there is not—and cannot be—any clash of interest
> between the two.
>
> M. Balint: *Thrills and Regressions*

The most striking form of positive transference in the early stages
is the *analytic honeymoon.*

As the name suggests, this is a period of blissful expansion for the
patient. Everything seems to be going well. He has one new insight
after another, feels better on his job, functions better in his family.
The whole experience is entirely new to him. If the therapist maintains a proper degree of interest coupled with attentive silent listening, it occurs in a goodly number of patients. For the therapist it is
particularly gratifying; he feels like a fond parent watching a child
grow up; little need be done other than to provide the setting in which
the growth can take place.

Although almost invariably followed by a *first treatment crisis* (see
Chapter 7) the analytic honeymoon may last anywhere from several
months to several years. The only thing that stops it from being completely delightful is that certain nagging problems persist, in spite of
the general feeling of euphoria.

To bring about the analytic honeymoon, the therapist must feel
warm and sympathetic, yet dynamically inactive. The more he does,
the more likely he is to interfere with the patient's growth.

The patient talks freely, begins to put his life in order, and is able
to face a variety of exciting new experiences which had been denied

to him before. The therapist listens, limiting himself to comments which help the material to flow more freely. If minor resistances crop up they should be handled, but, on the whole, during the analytic honeymoon resistances are at a minimum.

There are a number of dynamic factors that explain the appearance of the analytic honeymoon.

1. *Catharsis:* The patient has a chance to unburden himself. He can talk and talk and talk to his heart's content. He reveals himself as never before to any other human being. The illustrative case is one example.

> Stuart, a 37-year-old man in deep marital trouble, came for help ostensibly because of his vocational problems. When the vocational adviser suggested therapy he was quite pleased. He called on a Thursday and was given an appointment for Friday. When he came he said that a great load had fallen off his shoulders as soon as the appointment was made. The analytic honeymoon lasted more than six months with him.

2. *Lack of Superego Criticism:* Most patients come into treatment with some secrets which weigh them down with guilt. The secrets are revealed to the analyst, who passes no judgment on them, merely analyzes, or often enough just listens. The patient experiences a tremendous sense of relief when the anticipated punishment is not forthcoming. Here again silence is usually the most effective weapon in the analyst's arsenal.

> Sol was a man in his 40s, well up in his profession and ostensibly happily married. But he had a compulsion to visit other women, especially prostitutes, which made him terribly ashamed. Once on a business trip out of town he picked up a prostitute who suggested to him that he hire another girl and see the two perform a Lesbian act. He consented. The guilt following this pick-up was enormous. Eventually it was the conscious reason that drove him to analysis.
>
> When he revealed what he had done the analyst said nothing. Sol could then calm down sufficiently to look more dispassionately at the dynamics of his action, why he went with prostitutes, why he had to choose two women, what the meaning of homosexuality was to him, etc.

3. *Production of New or Hitherto Unnoticed Material:* In the early stages, when the patient is permitted to unburden himself freely,

either new or hitherto unnoticed material comes out. In some patients new memories come to light. Others will begin to pay more attention to facts of their lives which had previously been glossed over. In either case, what is therapeutic is the consistent concentration on a different attitude towards the person's life—the fundamental shift to inner exploration. The therapist neither praises nor judges; he tries to help the patient to understand.

4. *Establishing a New Kind of Relationship:* The therapist, if he performs his functions properly, is different from any other kind of person in our society. There is no other interpersonal situation in which exactly these roles are carried out. If a patient reacts positively, he experiences this as the bridge to a new world. No condemnation, no orders, no bribery, no quarreling—just acceptance, and listening.

5. *Absence of a Time Limit:* The fact that therapy is of indefinite duration is one of its greatest advantages. No one can predict with certainty how long any therapeutic experience will last. The patient who at this stage welcomes especially the warm feeling of acceptance by the therapist is particularly pleased that it is not due to come to an end at some predetermined time, as would be the case with a kindly professor at school. As Shakespeare put it, love is not love which alters when it alteration finds. The patient could paraphrase this for the therapeutic situation: Acceptance is not acceptance which changes when it changes finds. The patient has the conviction that no matter what he does he will be accepted by his therapist. And this conviction, reinforced by everything else that is going on, heightens his sense of well-being.

6. *Reestablishment of Hope:* As a rule, when the patient enters therapy he is in a state of bewildered despair. All he knows is that he is faced by terrible problems with which he is unable to cope. He has no idea what these problems are connected with, nor how they can be solved. For most patients it is a mystery how talking can make them feel less depressed or overcome a persistent pattern of overdrinking.

Through the persistent exploration of the therapeutic material the patient gradually gets the idea that he is neither a devil who is to be held morally responsible for his sins nor a God who is expected to dispel all his troubles by one sweep of the hand. He is a human being, molded, like all other human beings, by the accidental circumstances of birth and environment. What has been done by fumbling parents can still be undone. Hope reenters the picture.

This hope is part of the fundamental shift to a psychological way of thinking. Without being able to formulate it in that way, the patient becomes a psychologist, examining his and other people's motives, exploring the family backgrounds of himself and his friends, seeing the interrelationships of fears and wishes.

Though simple, the insights which this new way of thinking affords produce a sense of great optimism. A 28-year-old man, verging on the brink of homosexuality, was convinced that he was by nature incapable of being a normal male. Accidentally, he ran across Bergler's book on homosexuality; the mere statement that homosexuality is due to infantile frustration aroused so much hope in him that he sought out therapy. It was not surprising that he began with an analytic honeymoon.

While the analytic honeymoon is normally followed by resistances of varying degrees of severity, there are cases where the entire therapy proceeds in a positive state. They are rare, yet instructive when they occur. The following is an unusual case of this kind.

Caroline was a 24-year-old divorcee who came to treatment because of depressions, fears, and general unhappiness with life.

She was the younger of two sisters. Father was a taxi-driver, mother a housewife. Mother showed much depression; she would sit around the house for hours in the dark, doing nothing but staring into space. The sister had refused to go to school for a period during childhood, when she was placed in therapy with symptomatically satisfying results. An aunt had also had some psychiatric treatment.

Throughout her life Caroline had suffered from many phobias. Up to 22 she had been afraid of the subways, and had never been on one alone. Somehow she got over this subway fear. In early childhood she had had a deathly fear of witches, with many nightmares about them, some of almost hallucinatory intensity.

She became a lively, outgoing girl, interested mainly in a variety of artistic pursuits. Performance in school was mediocre, and she left after graduation from a commercial high school. She worked as a typist. She liked to dance, paint, and sing; at one time she even thought that she might become a singer for a band, but her voice was not good enough.

At 18 she married Jim, had one child, a girl. Sex with him was not too good. He was a brutal man, who hit her a number of times. After several years of marriage Jim cracked up, and was hospitalized. There was chiefly a withdrawal from life, with loss of interest in the child, in sex, and in work. He blamed all his troubles on her. After a great struggle she succeeded in leaving him. She lived near her in-laws, who gave her help in bringing up her daughter; there was one first cousin who was almost the same age as her child.

After her divorce she began to run around with a lot of different men. One girl friend, Charlotte, was acting out in many different ways. One was constant pot parties; these intrigued Caroline but also frightened her. Sometimes they would go out and pick up men together. Charlotte also seemed on the verge of Lesbianism.

At a party one time she met a fellow who introduced her to analytic ideas. Despite her lack of education she showed a fantastic aptitude for grasping psychological insights. She began to study her own life, with his help, and filled several notebooks with the story of her life, and her analyses of her actions. This self-analysis was quite a remarkable achievement. Partly because of it she was accepted for treatment at a reduced rate, though even then she could only come once a week.

The transference was positive from the very beginning; in fact, as mentioned, the whole therapy was an analytic honeymoon from start to finish. The need to submit to men, recapturing the good daddy of her childhood, came out very quickly as one prime motive for her sexual activities. However, when men mistreated her as they often did, she was able to overcome the transference needs and give them up. One boy friend took her to a motel one night, then left at 2 A.M., saying that he had an appointment elsewhere. This was too much for her, and she began to look more searchingly at the men in her life.

There was a strong temptation to act out with Charlotte in pot parties, drinking, and Lesbianism. But this too she could analyze as a reaction to the depressed mother, and the nightmares of witches in childhood.

The only complication presented by the transference was that at times it became somewhat insistently sexual. She would say that she had heard that sooner or later all analysts ball their patients, especially the pretty ones. At this point she resumed an old affair with a physician, who was of about the same age as the analyst. It was not hard for her to see the transferential character of this affair, and she soon dropped it.

An old suitor now came along, whom she had previously rejected because he was too "square." With her new insights she took a second look at him. In many ways he was like the good father of childhood; there was even a physical resemblance. She began to see more of him, and he proposed marriage. She accepted, became pregnant, and terminated the analysis with the consent of the therapist.

About six months after termination the therapist received this letter from her:

Dear Dr.,

I am feeling so happy that I had to drop you a line to let you know. You have succeeded in helping me make a happier life for myself. My new baby will be coming in November and I find myself thrilled over the new addition. Most of my fears over the baby have gone, and I can easily enjoy looking forward to the baby.

I have not had to go for help out here and been able to handle things pretty nicely. I have really surprised myself. If ever I get confused or upset I just think of you and I know in some way I don't know how you do it, you would make me feel like, whatever it is that I feel, is not so drastic or terrible and is not the worst thing. It will pass, and then I'll think of it later on and say "How silly. What a ridiculous thing to get upset over. It doesn't even matter." So all I do is think of you and then I really can't fool myself into getting that upset anymore, for with your help I have learned a much better way.

I still don't know how or what to feel towards you and it strikes me funny, for the main thing is that you succeeded in helping me. The word friend comes to my mind, but somehow it doesn't fit. It's like somebody way out there, that knows all about me but that I know nothing about.

Since I have never experienced this type of relationship with anyone I'll have to refer to you as my odd friend.

Sincerely,

THE LIBERATION ANALYSIS

When the analytic honeymoon is handled properly, it frequently becomes part of a *liberation analysis,* in which the patient goes from one gratifying positive new experience to another, both within and outside the therapeutic situation. For the analytic therapist, this is one of the most pleasing of all situations to encounter. Its frequency, however, depends on the kind of clientele at his disposal.

What the patient does in his liberation experience depends a good deal on the potential that he brings into therapy. Not everyone is capable of everything. And yet there are a good many people, bright, gifted in many ways, who are prevented from realizing their potential by some neurotic blocks. These people, underachievers in life's struggle because so much energy has been diverted to the neurotic battle, find a sympathetic and understanding ear in the therapist. Encouraged by him, their lives move back into more constructive paths. Before drawing any general conclusions about these patients, we would like to cite a few more cases.

Dan, a 28-year-old scientist, entered treatment to work out a bad marriage relationship. Soon he got away from the concentration on the marriage, and began to explore his own life directly.

He was the younger of two children. Father had deserted the family when he was 2, leaving the mother to fend for herself. This left a bitter taste in her mouth, which she never concealed from anybody, least of all the children. Men were no good, she screamed, and women were no better. In fact, in her opinion she was the only decent person in the world. Dan became the apple of her eye. He was groomed to get out of school young, get a good job, and support her for the rest of her life. It was predictable that a highly ambivalent relationship between mother and son resulted, especially when mother ostentatiously refused to even consider remarriage because of the effect it would have on her son.

In his early life Dan was highly successful, running away with many honors in school, and graduating at an extremely early age. But then came the rebellion. Unconsciously he was most reluctant to devote his life to his mother, as she allegedly had done for him. He ran away, to make his fortune in another part of the country. There he met a young girl, physically very much like his mother, whom he married. It was this early marriage, now on the rocks, which brought him to a psychoanalyst.

In the therapy Dan made rapid strides for a long time. The relationship with the therapist was marvelously positive. He saw the pattern of his life very quickly. Then he began to undo some of his inhibitions. Difficulties with women, and certain sexual problems, were ironed out. He resumed progress in his branch of science, progress which had previously been interrupted after a brilliant start. He began to grow in other ways, particularly in artistic directions, which before had been foreign to him. He wrote poetry, songs (he had done a little of this as a child), danced, painted, became a social butterfly, and expanded along many different lines. Life had never been so rich or rewarding.

The price that Dan paid for this liberation was an excessively positive transference. After a while his needs for the therapist became so overpowering that sometimes he could think of nothing else. It was then that the first negative manifestations, the first treatment crisis, occurred. But the long positive period of liberation stood **him** in good stead, and the difficulties were eventually ironed out.

Frank, a 35-year-old businessman, had been suffering from anxiety spells for many years. Neurologists, whom he consulted regularly, found nothing wrong and prescribed some innocuous medication; none ever suggested psychotherapy. Finally he decided on his own that since his problems had repeatedly been found to be psychological, he should look into a psychotherapeutic approach.

In therapy he made exceedingly rapid progress. For several years, in fact, he announced at every session that he felt better than the previous time. His anxieties diminished. He functioned better at work. He was able to face most situations that had frightened him before. In his private life he began to enjoy his wife and children. Hobbies, which he had always had in abundance, now became more pleasurable for him. For the first time he was able to take up a sport, at which he became quite proficient. The most notable new experience, apart from this, was painting, at which he became quite adept. When he won a prize for one of his paintings in an amateur show, he was quite thrilled.

Frank was an only child. Besides his parents, there were an aunt and uncle living with them, so that he was the spoiled darling of four adults. In childhood, which he remembered as extremely unhappy, he was a rebel all the way. Although endowed with high intelligence, he did badly at school, barely managing to get through a second-rate college. Several early jobs petered out. An early marriage lasted three months, then ended in divorce. A second marriage, some time later, was worse. His new wife was unable to bear children, and the marriage was unsatisfactory in most other respects, but he stayed with it out of a sense of guilt. Constantly plagued by the wish to leave her, he nevertheless stuck it out for more than five years. At one point he was so infantile that he asked his mother for permission to break up the marriage. Finally, he fell in love with another woman, which gave him the strength to go off on his own.

The third marriage proved to be a very happy one. In his work he now began to blossom, and for the first time in his life acquired a sense of real competence. Everything would have gone well if it were not for the anxiety spells, and other physical symptoms. At first he tried to cope with these by blaming it on the environment, which led him to move around from one city to another. By the time he had reached his eighth city he had had enough, recognizing that it must be something in him.

Eventually the liberation period in therapy was replaced by one in which various anxieties manifested themselves, which led him to become very angry with the therapist. But again because of the extended experience of positive feeling he was able to work out the negative transference.

In the analytic honeymoon, the problem for the patient is the transition from mother to father, the important growth step of the Oedipal period. In many cases, a similar constellation exists. The mother becomes too clinging, making it perilous for the child to leave her. Sometimes, the storm raised by the mother faced by the prospect of the child's growing up reaches tornado proportions. The children react by various compromise formations. They are not so severely traumatized that they could not leave home at all; in that case they would be hospitalized sooner or later. But their growth is stunted in a number of different ways. The men are held back in their business or professional development; the girls make poor choices of mates.

In analysis, the therapist restores the growth process of childhood by becoming the silent permissive parent whose major concern is to let the child reach whatever potential he or she could reach. Any interference at this juncture would be interpreted as a return of the possessive mother. Attention, care, interest *without interference,* prove to be the decisive factors. If the patient makes mistakes, goes too far in this direction or that, hurts himself in one way or another, it makes no real difference; the mistake is soon corrected. What is vital is the genuine permission to the patient to have a growth experience in which the primary goal is its benefit to him.

By contrast, in many cases that turn out badly, the therapists make a variety of mistakes in the honeymoon period. All could be summed up as inhibiting the growth process all over again, as the mother had done in childhood.

Father, uniformly weak or absent, could not stand up to the domineering mother either. The result was that the patient repeated the neurotic relationship with the mother rather than move on to a more wholesome constructive relationship with some extra-familial figure. When the therapist tries to benefit from, or take credit for, the growth of the patient, what is being repeated is manipulation of the child by the mother.

In most successful cases, the patients are relatively young, in basically good shape, with every reason to hope for a bright future. They are held back, as they soon realize, by severe internal problems that stem from childhood. In effect, the therapist says to them: "You have everything to look forward to; just free yourself of your childhood." They are able, for the period of the analytic honeymoon at least, to concentrate on the internals, rather than to waste endless hours, as more disturbed patients so frequently do, on the harm that is being done to them by one external source or another.

These cases direct attention to the central role of *hope* in psychotherapeutic improvement. The patient's sense of hopelessness is traced to his battles with his parents; he sees that once these battles are overcome, the struggles of the real world are much easier and more rewarding. By concentrating on the internal conflict, the feeling of hopefulness, paradoxically, is repeatedly strengthened.

The paradox stems from the fact that the confrontation of the inner enemy leads to a successful conquest. This in turn provides a basis for feeling that future inner conflicts can also be overcome in the same way. By contrast, if the patient is convinced that the problem is an external one, he acquires relatively little sense of control over it, since it is not up to him to determine when external dangers will threaten again.

Just as the early good experiences with mother provided a basis for hope which reappeared in later life, the analytic honeymoon builds a similar basis. Even when, as is usually the case, there are many ups and downs before a final satisfactory outcome is reached, the patient is sustained by the memory of the early days, when all problems seemed to yield as if by magic.

The clinical phenomenon of the analytic honeymoon is a potent reason for preferring the standard technique with the average neurotic adult. As early as 1905 Freud laid down criteria for successful psychotherapy that still hold up: age range 20–50, in good health, reasonably intelligent, problems not too crippling. Developmentally, these patients suffer from a severe Oedipal conflict (although in the light of our modern knowledge they have other conflicts as well), which has been formulated as the difficulty in making the transition from the mother to the father. The standard technique (the one described in detail in this work) allows these patients the greatest opportunity for growth. Variations of this technique, even though they may be more suitable for other types of patients, are contraindicated and even harmful for such a patient. Again, the points must be emphasized that technique must be stated in terms of goals and that technique must be adapted to the needs of the individual patient, not the reverse.

Although neurosis has many facets to it, in one sense the basic struggle is that between the positive feelings and the negative ones. The neurotic may best be thought of as a person in whom suffering, for inner psychic reasons, predominates over pleasure. This trait stems from an emotional climate in childhood in which the parents stressed suffering more than anything else. When such a person enters therapy, and goes through a period in which he can release all kinds of pleasure, including the enjoyment of new experiences he had never dreamed of before, it has a truly liberating effect on his psyche. Through the actual release of positive feelings over a long period of time, the patient learns that an entirely new attitude toward human relationships is possible. This, too, engenders a great feeling of hopefulness.

Finally, some comments are appropriate here about the healing power of love, a topic that will be discussed at a number of points throughout this book. The analytic honeymoon is in every sense of the word except the physical a love experience between analyst and patient. The patient not infrequently expresses it in so many words. While the therapist as a rule does not verbalize it, because such verbalization would be misunderstood by the patient at this stage, he often has the same strong love feelings for the patient. It is these love feelings, which the patient senses, that provide the drive behind the rapid improvement. If by contrast a patient feels that the therapist has no great use for him, or dislikes him, or even hates him, and it is really true, then the effect is crushing.

In supervision, where the therapist is freer to verbalize his feelings about patients, one is surprised over and over again to see that the patients who do well are those whom the therapist likes, while those who do badly are those whom he dislikes. For historical reasons hatred of the psychiatric patient is the normal attitude in our culture. The therapist, whatever his original professional background, must come to grips with this cultural attitude. It might even be said that the degree to which he overcomes it will be the most important determinant of his professional success as a therapist.

The love of the therapist for his patient, important though it is, is not the only factor in improvement; in addition there is his capacity for understanding. But love alone can produce remarkable effects at times. The success of faith-healing through the ages, such as it was, probably came from the capacity of some faith-healers to impart this love to their patients. Today, especially with schizophrenics, the ability of the therapist to sustain a warm accepting feeling about the patient over a period of years is the most significant factor in their improvement.

When to this love is added understanding, a real analytic transformation of the character can result, even in the most deteriorated of personalities. But understanding without love proves to be of little value for the average patient. The analytic honeymoon should be used to strengthen the therapist's conviction of the importance of love.

SUGGESTIONS FOR FURTHER READING

Few special papers have been devoted to the phenomenon of the analytic honeymoon. See references for the previous chapter.

CHAPTER 5

The Erotic Transference. Other Forms of Positive Transference

He: How charming you are beloved!
　　How meet for the pleasures of love!
　　Your tallness suggests the palm tree
　　　With your breasts its clusters of dates
　　Said I: "I must climb this palm tree
　　　And clasp its graceful branches."
　　Your breasts will be as vine clusters
　　　The bouquet of your breath as quinces
　　The taste of you like the finest wine
　　　That slides down the gullet smoothly
　　Gliding over the lips and teeth.

She: I belong to my beloved
　　　His desire is for me alone
　　Come away then, my beloved!
　　　Let us go into the country,
　　Lodge in one of the villages
　　　And start at dawn for the vineyards,
　　To see if the vines have budded
　　　Their blossoms begun to open
　　And the pomegranates are in bloom
　　　There I will give you my love.

Solomon: *Song of Songs*

Within the positive transference four subforms can be distinguished: the erotic, the homosexual, the dependent, and the moderately positive. Each merits extended discussion.

THE EROTIC TRANSFERENCE

Since Freud was a man, the earliest form discovered was that of a woman patient with a male analyst. The opposite, that of the male patient with a woman analyst, is equally common.

With the discovery of the erotic transference Freud took a decisive step forward. Historical research has shown that Breuer, with his famous patient Anna O., was too perturbed to continue when she told him that she had fallen in love with him. Freud was faced with a similar situation when, as he tells us, a woman patient got up from the couch and threw her arms around him. But instead of withdrawing, as Breuer had done, he used the incident to further his theory of psychic functioning.

The erotic transference may, like any other libidinal manifestation, have almost any dynamic meaning. It may be a bid for reassurance, a cover-up of hostility, an expression of penis envy, an oral-incorporative wish, a defense against homosexuality, or any and all of these at different times. The goal in therapy is to break through to the biological desires; for this purpose all the dynamic pregenital factors have to be thoroughly analyzed until they no longer play a significant role.

It is not possible to tell in advance what meaning erotic feelings may have, or to equate different patients merely because they display similar behavior. Each person has to be understood in terms of her own background and life experiences. There can be no doubt that the mechanical application of any formula, no matter how correct it may be as a general proposition, is the most deadening of all approaches to psychotherapy. The patient must be viewed as a human being in a human situation. Likewise, the childhood origin of any erotic manifestation, whether oral, anal, phallic, or other, has to be worked out individually in each case.

An intense erotic transference is often extraordinarily difficult to handle. The reason is its demanding character and its extreme unpredictable variability. Here are two clinical examples:

> Susan was a 22-year-old girl recently released from a mental hospital. She had been hospitalized a number of times since the age of 12, and had made a number of suicide attempts.
>
> Shortly after she started treatment she fell violently in love with the analyst. He was the most wonderful man in the world, and the most marvelous thing that had ever happened to her. The therapy was being conducted on a twice-weekly basis; on the days when she did not come she wrote the analyst passionate love letters.
>
> After several months of this, the feelings of despair began to come back. She felt her love was unrequited. She started a love affair with a young boy; this did not satisfy her either.

Finally, she terminated treatment abruptly. Before saying good-bye, however, she revealed that she was going to make a profit on the therapy now. Her mother had been paying for one session; she was not going to tell her that she had stopped, and would continue to collect the money.

Several months later she wrote to say that she had submitted to electric shock.

Mary was also 22 when she began treatment. Her therapy proceeded less dramatically than that of Sue's. She formed a strong positive transference, but the erotic aspects were repressed for a long time.

After some years of analysis, the sexual feelings became very strong, although still to some extent unconscious. Her life centered more and more around the analyst's office. Apart from her work, she had few friends. She would walk from her home to the analyst's office, a distance of about three miles, arriving several hours early. The time before the session was spent in the waiting-room or washing her underwear in the bathroom. When sexual interpretations were given to her she would giggle hysterically, like a little girl.

While the transference was most difficult to work through, the case had a much more favorable outcome than that of Sue. She was able to leave home and establish a relationship with an older man, the first sustained heterosexual relationship of her life.

The dynamics of these two cases are similar: an intense attachment to the therapist who represents an infantile figure. Still there is one vital difference: Sue's love suddenly turned to indifference and despair; Mary's persisted in much the same form for many years. Theory is really at a loss to explain why one patient goes through a radical reversal of feelings, while another does not. Mary in her outside relationships showed the same kind of ambivalence that Sue showed toward the analyst, yet Mary for some reason did not bring it into the transference. It is true that the demands that Mary made (staying in the waiting room and bathroom for hours) could be met, while those of Sue (sexual gratification) could not. Yet in every case it is not so much the demands that are made as the patient's capacity to handle reality that plays the decisive role.

In the management of the erotic transference three principles are of cardinal value. First, the patient's guilt about her sexual feelings should be reduced and, if possible, eliminated; sexual desire per se is healthy, though it may lead to undesirable consequences, much as hunger may induce overeating and obesity, yet appetite for food remains normal. Second, and paradoxically, the capacity for libidinal gratification should be increased rather than decreased. For excessive desire usually goes along with a lack of satisfaction; to use an oral analogy again, the chain smoker does not enjoy his cigarettes as much as the person who is able to savor every puff. And third, the patient's image of love must be clarified; she must be helped to shift from an infantile to an adult kind of love. Each of these points merits further elaboration.

1) Reduction of Guilt

The patient must somehow work through to the feeling that if she has sexual desire for the analyst it is the most natural thing in the world. This is done by systematically analyzing the fantasies surrounding sexuality.

A very common fantasy connected with sex is that of "seduce and reject." The patient expresses a sexual feeling for the analyst. When asked what would happen after sex, she says, Then I would leave. One patient put it in the form that if the analyst actually had sex with her it would prove that she was psychotic and would therefore require immediate termination of treatment.

A woman whose sexual transference was expressed in seductive actions and allusions denied over a long period of time any conscious sexual feelings. Finally she came in one day with a dream:

"I am standing looking out of the window. You [the analyst] come up behind me and take me around to give me a kiss. I turn around, say 'that ends that' and walk out."

The dream brought out the concealed sexual dynamics. This woman, who had a history of considerable promiscuity, much agitation, and depression, including one suicide attempt, had on a number of occasions acted out this pattern of "seduce and reject" with a number of men.

It is instructive in fact to see how the transference fantasy boils down much of what was acted out in her life. On one occasion, a previous lover called her after a lapse of several years, saying that he wanted to resume the relationship because he was so unhappy with his wife. She invited him over to her house while her husband was away, had sex with him in her own bed, assuring him all the time how wonderful he was and how grateful she was that he had come back. Spurred on by this acceptance he then began to call her again. But this time she was never available. She never said no outright, leading him to believe each time that she would see him soon. But there was no soon. By this time she was in analysis, and the revenge process was shortened by the awareness that it was getting her nowhere; otherwise it might have gone on for years.

It is important in this and similar situations to interpret the hostility as the consequence of sexual frustration, rather than the sexuality as a cover-up of hostility; the latter interpretation would make the patient feel more guilty.

Many therapists, because of their own countertransference problems, react to the strong sexual desire of the patient in a way which does the patient more harm than good. One frequent form this takes is to diagnose the patient "schizophrenic"; actually the therapist is only doing what the layman does, covering up his own fear by saying to the other person: You must be crazy to do a thing like that.

> Arthur, in strong transference to a therapist of the same age as his mother, had an overt sexual dream about her: they were in bed having sex. Then the therapist's husband came between them. The therapist, trained to believe that Oedipal fantasies exist only in schizophrenics in outright form, wondered in supervision whether the patient were cracking up. Shortly thereafter the patient was "seduced" by a girl who described herself as promiscuous into a trio, two men and a girl. The therapist was now convinced that he was going psychotic, losing all controls. Actually, she had led a rather restricted sex life herself, and was frightened by his display of lack of inhibition. The dream and the trio experience both proved to be valuable material in furthering the patient's libidinal growth.

> A group therapist had a group of six patients, one of whom was an older woman who developed an intense crush on him. Once or twice at the end of the session she would brush up against him before he could step out of the way. He described this as "schizophrenic" behavior.

There is no doubt that the intense erotic transference makes enormous demands on the therapist, who often finds it difficult to maintain the analytic process with undisturbed equanimity. Yet this is precisely what has to be done to be of most value to the patient. What the therapist has to concentrate on is the consequences of the erotic feeling, not the feeling itself. If these consequences do harm, as is so often the case, that fact must be brought out. The patient is only too ready to cry *mea culpa* and again be made to feel guilty about his libido as in childhood; the analyst must insist that a healthy wish can lead to guilt-laden fantasies.

2) Increase of Gratification

It is a truism that a patient's story cannot be accepted at face value; it is for this reason that the most common analytic phrases are: "What comes to mind," or "Tell me more about it." Only a full exploration of the sexual feelings can disclose what is really going on. As a rule, such a full investigation brings out that the patient does not enjoy sex very much. Sometimes the patient is really sex-starved and the analyst is an available man. More often, however, the patient finds something seriously lacking in her sexual experience, and tries to cover this lack by a sexual fantasy with the analyst.

> At one point in her analysis Rachel developed a strong erotic transference. She wanted to have sex with the analyst. When the full fantasy was unraveled, it turned out that she wanted to have sex on the office floor. When the analyst wondered why she would fantasize having sex in such an uncomfortable place, she was able to talk more about her fear that she would never experience real gratification with her husband or with any other man.

In spite of decades of intensive education, analytic experience still indicates that the average woman in our society still suffers from marked problems of frigidity. The woman who talks most freely about sex seems to contradict this statement, yet closer investigation reveals the same conflicts. Here are several instances.

> Shirley came to treatment saying she knew she'd soon be thinking about an affair with the analyst. She'd been having affairs for twenty years, even though she was married and had three children, and experienced full satisfaction with her husband. As the therapy proceeded it turned out that she had been fantasizing affairs, not having them, and that her husband enjoyed the sex act immensely, while she did not.

> Ruth had a long history of "free" sexual affairs from the age of 17. Yet at 22 she married a man who suffered from severe premature ejaculation and in addition was afraid to touch her body; sex with him was a most frustrating experience. A strong sexual transference developed; the most persistent fantasy was one of lying naked with her head on the analyst's stomach. In the course of the analysis

one striking fact emerged: it was painful to her to masturbate, or to have a man touch her clitoris. When this was more fully analyzed, her lack of gratification in the many sexual affairs became apparent. Eventually she divorced her husband and married a man who provided much more sexual gratification.

Frigidity is for the most part corrected readily enough in analysis. Even "sector" therapy, which concentrates exclusively on the sexual problem, can sometimes take care of it. Masters and Johnson also report that in their work with subjects an increase in sexual satisfaction was experienced, though they do not attribute it, as a dynamic psychologist would, to the increased permissiveness given by the authority figures. Ideally, the woman should reach vaginal orgasm.

3) The Meaning of Love

The decisive factor in the resolution of the sexual conflict is the clarification of the meaning of love. The promiscuous wish, which arouses so much needless guilt in people, especially women, is but part of the broader growth towards satisfying love relationships.

Most patients come into analysis with some history of love that turns out to have been infantile in character. It is essential to help them shift from a neurotic to a normal concept of love.*

The analysis of the transference provides valuable insights into the meanings of love and sex to the patient. It is here primarily that she learns of the neurotic character of her loves, and is enabled to go beyond it.

> Carole had an intense erotic transference. The analyst was the most remarkable man in the world, she could not live without him, and she loved him. Yet, the very next session she came in, refused to take off her coat, and said: "I have one question to ask you; if your answer is not right I am leaving immediately."

Here her sharp ambivalence and omnipotent wish to dominate the other person came out most dramatically. This reminds us once again that in the management of any erotic transference a great deal of time must be spent analyzing ambivalence. As with hostility, it is important to keep the stress on the positive aspects of love. It is not true that because she issues an ultimatum today she did not love yesterday. Rather, the love feeling begins to weaken because the analyst

* For a fuller discussion see Chapter 1.

is seen as an infantile figure who will punish her for getting too close.

In our society some degree of sexual frustration is inevitable; probably the same is true of any culture, though anthropologists rank ours pretty high on the scale of sexual unhappiness. When the person has reached the stage of true love feelings, sexual frustrations diminish considerably but do not disappear entirely. For example, there is for the woman the unavoidable clash between her sexual and her maternal feelings. At the same time, the growth toward love leads to the least amount of sexual frustration consonant with the good life.

The recognition of love allows the patient to place her feelings about the analyst in proper perspective. Ultimately she sees the analyst as he is in reality, a man who likes her and is devoted to her welfare. Within this framework sexual feelings on both sides are quite normal and cause no serious conflict.

A few words should be said about a countertransference problem which is so keenly felt by many analysts, a question brought up over and over again in technique seminars: If the patient is so eager to have sex with the analyst, why not gratify her wish? In his paper on "Transference Love," Freud [22] devoted several pages to a careful consideration of this question. It is clear from the detail and thoroughness of his discussion that he must have been tempted to accede on one or more occasions, refraining only because of his thorough knowledge of the countertransference. Occasionally, reports filter through of analysts who have had sex with their patients, so that a certain amount of empirical evidence is available.

As might be anticipated, gratifying the sexual wish has two consequences. First it turns the analysis into a love affair, thereby negating its long-term benefits, even if the short-term gains are sweeter. And, second, as a love affair it is no different from any other love affair— offering temporary pleasure but no deep inner change. It is also worth remembering that while the analyst might be well trained in his profession, there is no guarantee that he is equally well trained as a lover.

A third consequence is even more serious. As in any love affair, sooner or later one party, usually the woman, will push for marriage. If the analyst refuses, as is usually the case, the woman will feel doubly rejected, first because her lover turns her down, and second because her analyst in reality finds her unworthy of marriage. The results of this double rejection can be calamitous.

Since the analyst is in a parental position to the patient, sex with her is similar to incestuous relationships between father and daughter.

As with incest, the problem is partly the actual effect of the sex, and partly what kind of personality the father is to break the barriers in such a way.

In most of the cases that have come to the writer's attention, severe disturbance was noticeable in the analyst; this led him to act out his sexual fantasies with the patient. As a rule, however, the patients were neither benefited nor harmed; it was merely another affair. Here is one instance.

> Dr. T., a cardiologist most of his life, turned to psychiatry in his later years. He wrote a book about family problems, which had some temporary success, on the basis of which he set himself up as an expert in marital disputes. Actually he had had no formal training.
>
> One of his patients was a wealthy woman who fell in love with him. He told her that she was too good for her husband, that her son was being ruined by a rigid father, and that her erotic fantasies about him and other men were quite normal. He encouraged her to have a series of sexual affairs.
>
> One day Dr. T. told his patient that he was about to sail for Europe, and invited her to come along. He told her that he had a 60-year-old body, but that it could still perform creditably. She refused.
>
> After his return, the therapy was resumed. One day he called her, said that he was in a midtown hotel, and invited her to come over. When she arrived, he was there with another woman. He invited her to have sex *à trois*. Again she refused, whereupon he said: Maybe you don't like this woman, I can get another.
>
> Alarmed by this experience, she then consulted a friendly psychiatrist and told him the whole story. He revealed to her that it was widely known that Dr. T. was taking drugs, and strongly urged her to switch to another therapist. But she was intrigued by the situation and refused.
>
> Shortly thereafter Dr. T. committed suicide. The patient then stopped all therapy.

On the other hand it would be too puritanically moralistic to assume that all therapists who have sex with their patients are severely disturbed. Some pursue a doctrinaire theory. Others may have other reasons. In a recent journal article, one therapist reports on forty years of experience in which he has permitted and encouraged women to gratify any physical wishes they may have with him, including intercourse; he claims satisfactory results.[23] This, however, is a rare exception.

Even ordinary social contacts outside the therapeutic chamber may lead to wild fantasies on the part of the patient with a variety of undesirable consequences. It is also worth remembering that the therapist runs certain legal risks if he deviates too much from the customary procedure. Katz, Goldstein, and Dershowitz [24] report a case in which a psychiatrist had social contacts with a disturbed woman, and then dropped her. She sued for negligence and was awarded 6,000 British pounds.

While it is essential to be aware of the legal framework within which the therapist operates, it is also essential to be critical of that framework, especially in an area where change is so rapid, and the profession is in a position to contribute to that change. As the above case is reported, the psychiatrist took a more than usual interest in his patient, then dropped her. This seems technically inept. Why, however, his unusual interest should be considered to have harmed her, while termination did not, is part of the anachronistic attitude that the law takes toward such matters. In a sense it justifies paranoia and rewards abandonment. Of course the psychiatrist in the case seemed to be poorly trained, making remarks such as "That's transference" when the patient told him that she loved him. The fact that technical therapeutic rules, such as avoiding social contacts (not true in general of medicine), become legally binding is also a matter of considerable interest.

To act is one thing, to feel, another. Even though it is undesirable for the therapist to act out his attraction toward the patient, it is quite the opposite with his *feelings*. The more he is able to experience a genuine liking for the patient the more he will be able to help her. Because of the need to keep his feelings in check, the analyst often takes the path of least resistance, denying them altogether. This creates another problem for the patient, who in addition to feeling rejected for neurotic reasons is rejected in reality. The fact that the therapist's rejection is a neurotic defense mechanism to protect him against his own sexual feelings does not alter the matter; in this way the analyst does not differ from the father or other men whom the patient meets. Searles has stressed that even with schizophrenic women it is vital to give them the feeling, toward the end of the analysis, that they are realistically attractive to the analyst. He places particular emphasis on the analyst's freedom to react to his patients erotically, going so far as to state:

> Since I began doing psychoanalysis and intensive psychotherapy, I have found, time after time, that in the course of the work with every one of my patients who has progressed to, or very far towards,

a thoroughgoing analytic cure, I have experienced romantic and erotic desires to marry, and fantasies of being married to, the patient. Such fantasies and emotions have appeared in me usually relatively late in the course of treatment, have been present not briefly but usually for a number of months, and have subsided only after my having experienced a variety of feelings—frustration, separation anxiety, grief, and so forth—entirely akin to those which attended what I experienced as the resolution of my Oedipus complex in my personal analysis.[25]

Like the positive transference in general, the erotic combines residues from childhood with present-day reactions. To a certain extent the sexual responsiveness of the patient for the analyst is physiologically determined. As with all id material, there are contributions from the past and from the present. The task of analysis is to break through the neurotic fantasies to get to the healthy physiological reaction. However, as every analyst knows, this is a most formidable task.

THE HOMOSEXUAL TRANSFERENCE

Oddly enough, this important topic has been sadly neglected in the psychoanalytic literature. Perhaps the cultural conflicts surrounding homosexuality are still too strong for the analysts to consider the topic dispassionately. It nevertheless plays an important role in every long-term therapeutic encounter.

With a male analyst, almost all heterosexual men develop homosexual feelings in one form or another during the course of the treatment. The same observation seems to apply to women with female analysts. Where it does not appear, in many cases it is the result of some unconscious repressive maneuver on the part of the therapist.

> Dr. M. pursued the theoretical conviction that homosexual feelings toward him should always immediately be interpreted as a wish to be taken care of. Colleagues generally felt that he himself had an unresolved homosexual component, though he vigorously denied it. In clinical discussions he insisted that his patients rarely produced any homosexual feelings about him, unaware of the fact that he was unconsciously forbidding their expression.

While almost all heterosexual men develop some homosexual transference feelings in analysis, overt homosexual men as a rule do not.

This paradox requires clarification; it can help to explain many of the clinical contradictions.[26]

Homosexual patients themselves remain unaware of this lack of transference until it is called to their attention. If asked to reflect on it, and to try to explain it, they generally put it on a physical basis. They say: "You're not my type," or "You don't appeal to me," referring to the body build. The fetishistic component in homosexual attraction is quite strong and often they can go on at great length and in considerable detail to describe the kind of man that appeals to them. Many times, however, it is clear that the defenses of isolation and denial are prominent, since patients describe features in other men which are identical with those seen in the therapist.

Much is known of the psychology of the homosexual (cf. especially Bieber [27] and Socarides [28]). Clinically, the nature of the homosexual object is readily identifiable as a significant person from childhood. It may be the man himself, a brother, or the idealized father. For example, one man whose major homosexual period extended from the time he was 18 until he was 25 was attracted only to men between the ages of 18 and 25. Another became homosexual in early adolescence, and sought out older, heavily bearded men. After he had left his father's home this man's ideal love object then shifted to a young, delicate, adolescent boy; i.e., himself. As is usual in such cases, interpretation of the nature of the love object met a vigorous resistance of intellectual acceptance and emotional isolation, which took a long time to work out.

In general, if a homosexual man is mature enough to enter therapy, there is some wish, however slight, to become more heterosexual, but without giving up the homosexuality. In the effort to become more heterosexual, the analyst is generally looked upon as a sexually permissive father who will allow him to have sex or even provide him with girls. For example, in the illustrative case (pp. 17–23) Jim dreamed that when he came to the office, a door opened and a beautiful girl walked out.

It could be argued that the denial of homosexual feelings for the analyst is caused by this fairly conscious wish to have him be the sex-approving father. But heterosexual men, all of whom of course also have some kind of libidinal disturbance, also cast the analyst in the role of sexual tolerance, and yet develop a variety of homosexual feelings about him. The mere desire to free the heterosexual libido can not thus resolve the contradiction.

It would seem rather that for the homosexual man there is a split in the love object, exactly analogous to the split in the heterosexual object for the average man. With some men it is permissible to have sex, with others it is forbidden. Of course, in terms of the heterosexual drive, the homosexual man displays *a fortiori* the classical split of women into "good" and "bad."

The heterosexual split is well understood as a consequence of the incest taboo: good women equal mother, bad women equal not-mother; mother has sex only upon compulsion by father. "Good" women do not have sexual desires. In groups men with this split often react with gasps of incredulity to expressions of sexual desire by women.

The homosexual split has basically the same root, only it goes further. As a rule, the forbidden man is father, with whom the patient could never identify. Not only are they unable to identify with father, often they are unable to substitute any other man in his place.

At a deeper level, the inaccessible father is the continuation of the phallic mother. The typical family constellation of the homosexual man is that of a phallic (what Bieber calls close-binding intimate) mother with a distant father. Developmentally, the boy is prevented from reaching father, first by the excessive restrictions placed upon him by mother, and second by father's indifference or hostility. In analysis this developmental lag is reflected in the splitting off of the analyst from the world of accessible homosexual objects.

Incidentally, the awareness of the split allows one to approach the therapeutic problem of the overt homosexual from a novel and, to the patient, surprising, angle; it becomes possible to interpret to him that he is afraid of homosexuality and thus to bypass, or at least minimize, the direct analysis of the homosexual acting-out which, as is well known, creates great therapeutic problems. Further, the emphasis on the fear of homosexuality relates directly to the transference situation, which is likewise of considerable therapeutic value.

Clinically, the homosexual transference may appear in one or more of three forms: direct homosexual fantasy about the analyst, acting out the homosexual wish, or a lack of desire for women. Each of these can be considered in turn.

1) Direct Homosexual Fantasy

Usually this comes out some time after the beginning of therapy. To the patient the fantasy is so frightening that it takes him some time to bring it out. When it does come out, it may be accompanied by the fear of "being a homosexual." Reassurance on this point is decidedly inadvisable; it is more important to continue the flow of fantasies that are now liberated.

Most of the fantasies center around the penis and kissing; anal fantasies are rare. This can best be explained as the revival of early feelings about the father, which involve either the wish to kiss him or the wish to play with his penis. These represent positive wishes toward the father, which is why they become part of the positive transference toward the therapist. The subjective feeling of intense shame about the transference reaction is directly traceable to the shame about the wishes for the father. Here are several case vignettes.

> Frank came into treatment because of a variety of anxiety symptoms (cf. p. 45).
>
> Shortly after therapy began, Frank in free association began to say that he would like to suck the analyst's penis. This brought back several memories. One was that as a child of about four one morning he awoke to find his father in bed with him, with father's penis between his legs. The other was a whole series of memories of homosexual experiences at puberty, which he had long since forgotten. Some of these involved sucking penises; a number involved rectal intercourse, particularly with an older man. As so often, the homosexual period was outgrown uneventfully, except that in his adolescence he saw himself as peculiarly self-defeating in his search for sex with girls. He also recalled how he had thought of himself as a girl for some time when he was a child; his mother had even sent him to a parochial school where most of the children were girls.
>
> The positive feelings in therapy persisted for a long time. The first part of his analysis was a true liberation experience.
>
> Together with the homosexual fantasies, now rearoused, went an increase in his heterosexual libido. Sex with his wife improved constantly. He was able to voice many heterosexual feelings about other women which had previously frightened him. There was no acting out of either the homosexual or the heterosexual fantasies.

> Omar, a 30-year-old painter, was the youngest of four brothers. He came to analysis because of generalized anxieties, together with discontent about his creative productivity.
>
> The initial transference was markedly positive. He unburdened himself of much material that he had never been able to relate to anybody else.

After the first few sessions came a persistent fantasy of sucking the therapist's penis. He saw it as big, adequate, much more powerful than his. On the whole his relations with women were unsatisfactory. There was marked castration anxiety, the continual feeling that his penis was too small to satisfy the woman, and some difficulties in sexual functioning. The thoughts about the analyst's penis were obviously compensatory fantasies for his own feelings of inadequacy.

Unlike Frank, Omar's childhood background did not include any homosexual play. Mostly his memories centered on the interminable bickering, including a number of serious quarrels, in his family, as well as the crushing fears which had bothered him all his life. The next older brother used to beat him up all through childhood, allegedly in a playful spirit, yet the memory of these beatings still lingered in him very strongly.

Together with the homosexual wish went the fear that the therapist would kick him out of therapy. This was but one of many fears of rejection. The fears of being thought homosexual by his acquaintances was also a powerful one, even though he had had only one passing homosexual episode in his life.

The homosexual transference material was of use mainly in interpreting his constant aggression, and his embarrassment about relating to women.

It is noteworthy that in both the above cases there was no pressure at any time to act out the homosexual wish. This is one instance of Freud's early observation that the neurosis is the negative of the perversion, or in more modern language, what is fantasized need not be acted upon, while what is acted upon inhibits fantasy. The homosexual wish here was also the wish to cling to a protective parent figure as a defense against crushing anxieties.

2) Acting Out

Sometimes patients who had never previously been homosexual begin to act out some of their homosexual fantasies during analysis. This represents an overflow of the libidinal feelings for the analyst, which become so strong that the patient cannot control them. This overflow may be accompanied by a conviction that he will end up a homosexual or it may not; usually not. As a rule it is again felt subjectively as uncomfortable, though all variations may be found.

Oliver, a 30-year-old civil service worker, came into treatment at the suggestion of a female acquaintance because he was so obviously shy with girls. In the early material he revealed a history of deep sexual frustration, and psychosexual regression all through his life. At 30 he was still a virgin. His fantasies were predominantly heterosexual, though on one occasion when he had been approached by a homosexual man he was tempted to accede. In childhood he had been a bed-wetter until the age of 16. This came out early, but later on he also mentioned that he had had bowel movements in his drawers until a relatively late age. Brought up on a farm, at one time he had attempted sexual contact with one of the animals.

In the first part of analysis, Oliver produced a number of blatant sexual dreams, usually where some vigorous male relative would take him off somewhere and introduce him to girls. When the therapist offered consistent sexual interpretations, he objected, saying Freudians have sex on their minds.

Unable to make sexual advances to girls, Oliver remained lost in his fantasies. Then a girl of his acquaintance, hearing of what had happened to him, offered herself to him, no strings attached. He accepted. This was the first of several brief sexual affairs with women.

Several months after the analysis had been in progress, he began to have homosexual fantasies about the analyst, chiefly thoughts of sucking his penis. This could not be correlated with any previous homosexual experience, but rather with the constant feeling that his penis was small and inadequate.

Once his sex life had started, his libido increased. In one period, when he had no sex available to him, he was approached by a man, whom he accepted. This started a series of homosexual experiences. Most were casual pickups, on trains, in bars, and the like. Several, however, were more serious. One was a stormy love affair, which he looked upon as one of the greatest things in his life. The partner, he stated, was physically very similar to the analyst; the transferential aspects of the love affair were interpreted. Still, he began to hesitate. Perhaps he really was a homosexual. His fantasies became increasingly homosexual. Chiefly, this was because of his disappointments with women.

During all this, the homosexual fantasies about the analyst continued unabated. The pattern of rejection by women followed by homosexual fantasy or action became more and more apparent. It was clear that the homosexuality was the reaction to sexual frustration, which in turn was tied up especially with a strong incestuous fixation on the mother and the younger of two sisters. Eventually the homosexual wishes gave way to a more gratifying heterosexual life.

In the cases of both Omar and Oliver, the genesis of a homosexual pattern is seen *in statu nascendi*. Both men were terribly frustrated

with women, though each for different reasons. In spite of the many
differences, a powerful incestuous fixation was close to the surface in
both. Some warm feelings for the father, faint though they were, also
existed in both, which probably stopped them from becoming overtly
homosexual; in Omar's case, the father was much warmer than in
Oliver's. The analysis was able to focus on the severe sexual frustration, tie it up with its childhood roots, and thus avoid the permanent
fixation on the homosexual defense. As long as the fantasies could be
brought into the therapeutic situation, they could be handled satisfactorily. This again shows that the average acting-out homosexual
is one whose fantasies of despair about a good relation with women
have been so deeply repressed that it requires deep digging to bring
them out into the open.

3) Lack of Desire for Women

In this version of the homosexual transference, the patient has no
homosexual fantasy, no acting-out, yet evinces a conscious aversion
or indifference to women. Dynamically, this kind of aversion is well
understood. It covers up the deepest kind of longing, yet it is not easy
to convert this into an interpretation which can be offered to the
patient. Many times there is a relationship with another man that is a
fairly obvious sublimation of homosexuality. Such a situation became
apparent in the following case.

> Roger was an 18-year-old college student who came to therapy
> because of a panic state in which he had called up his mother to tell
> her how frightened he was. He lived in the college dormitory, sharing
> a suite of two rooms with three other boys. One of these, Jim, was an
> especially close friend; with the other two he had no libidinal ties.
>
> In therapy, Roger presented an extraordinary kind of intellectual
> defense system. Happiness did not exist, he said, so how could the
> therapist get him to become happy? Let the therapist show him at
> least one happy person. Social contacts of any kind, except those
> forced upon him by his roommates, were almost absent. His time was
> spent working at school tasks, yet here he was doing poorly. Con-
> sciously, the only reason for therapy was to improve his school per-
> formance.
>
> About girls he said that he had no interest. He defied the therapist
> to prove to him that it would be good for him to go out with girls. As
> might be expected, he had nothing but contempt for his mother,
> whom he regarded as an irrational hysteric. His great ambition was
> to get as far away from his parents as he could.

Transference was of the indifferent kind. He denied any strong feeling about the analyst.

Some time after he started, the other two roommates moved out, and he was left with Jim as his only social contact, apart from his family and the therapist. Jim was a disturbed young man who because of inherited wealth decided that he need not go to school. Instead, he began a variety of experiments with drugs, relying on his knowledge of chemistry to manufacture some of the illegal ones (eventually he was caught). Roger, under his influence, then began to demand that the therapist administer drugs to him. When this was refused, he attacked the therapist as old-fashioned.

At one point, Jim began to explore DMT. He arranged to give a series to Roger. After one shot, Roger, frightened by the emotions aroused, discontinued. The therapist interpreted the DMT as acting out a homosexual experience with Jim; curiously Roger not only did not dissent but readily agreed. Next he demanded that the therapist give him DMT; when this was interpreted as a wish for homosexual contact, he again agreed, but still wanted it. A short while later, he came in with a transparent homosexual transference dream: "I go to a doctor for an examination. He wants to look at my rectum. At first I refuse, then agree." This dream, and its homosexual ramifications, were tied up with his lifelong fear of doctors.

After this, more homosexual material, including hitherto concealed transference reactions, came to the fore. The working through of these homosexual feelings led to an awakening of the heterosexual libido.

In the management of the homosexual transference, the first—and, in a sense, the major—requirement is that the patient should be permitted to bring out as much material about it as possible. Homosexuality is such a taboo topic in the current culture that most patients will shy away from it until there is no alternative. Yet, together with this taboo goes the constant fear on the part of millions that they are really homosexual. This fear, easily recognized as a secret wish as well, lies at the root of the ambivalent societal attitude toward homosexuality: on the one hand condemning it violently, on the other urging an attitude of laissez-faire toward it.

Once the homosexual material begins to come out, the therapist must sedulously avoid any superego interpretations which would force the homosexuality back. He must treat it like any other manifestation of the id, using it primarily to see how unnecessary defenses are built up against it. The manner in which homosexual wishes block the gratification of heterosexuality is particularly important. But the interconnections of homosexuality with aggression, friendships with the same sex, social shyness, creative outlets, and many other aspects of the personality are equally important.

Biologically, homosexuality is a stage in development. It arises in early childhood toward the parent of the same sex, often toward siblings of the same sex; later, in pre-adolescence, toward like-sexed peers. All of these are stages that the normal individual outgrows, but on which the neurotic fixates. By keeping this framework firmly in mind, the therapist can help the patient outgrow the homosexual fixations.

SUGGESTIONS FOR FURTHER READING

In spite of the central importance of the erotic transference, it has been sadly neglected in the literature. Freud, "Observations on Transference Love (1915)" (*S.E.* Vol. XII) has an excellent discussion. R. Fine, "The Erotic Transference," *Psychoanalytic Rev.* 52, 1965, Spring, considers the question fully. See also E. Rappaport, "The Management of an Eroticized Transference," *Psychoanalytic Quarterly* 25, 1956, 515–529. Greenson's (*op. cit.*) treatment of the topic is surprisingly brief (338–341).

For the homosexual transference, see R. Fine, "A Note on a Transference Manifestation in Male Homosexuals," *Psychoanalysis and the Psychoanalytic Review* 59, 1960–61, and W. Stekel, *The Technique of Analytical Psychotherapy* (New York: Liveright, 1950), Chapter IX.

CHAPTER 6

Positive Transference (Concluded). Negative Transference

My characters are conglomerates of various stages of culture, past and present, bits out of books and newspapers, scraps of humanity, strips torn from old Sunday clothes which have become rags, all patched together as is the human soul.

A. Strindberg: *Miss Julie*

THE DEPENDENT TRANSFERENCE

This is perhaps the most common of all transference phenomena, especially since the passive-dependent personality is such a phenomenon of our times. To some extent, dependency is inevitable in any therapeutic relationship. The term "dependent transference," however, should be used only when this dependency reaches a point where it interferes with therapeutic progress. Five types of clinical phenomena can be subsumed under this heading: requests for advice, requests for reassurance, inability to grasp explanations, lack of improvement, and inability to leave treatment.

1) Requests for Advice

To the naive outsider, the therapist is one who dispenses wise advice, so that it is not surprising that many patients come in with the same image. It takes a while to get the patient used to the idea that he will receive primarily understanding rather than advice. Many dependent patients protest strongly against this structure; they continue to demand specific detailed instructions on how to meet their life difficulties.

Some clarification is in order here on why the analyst refuses to grant the patient's request. Advice may be sought on a variety of minor and major problems. If the problem is a minor one, say, whether to see a certain movie or not, or wear one dress or another, it is clearly more important to see why the patient should need a professional to guide him in such seemingly trivial matters. If the problem is a major one, for example, whether to undertake a marriage, or to enter a certain occupation, the patient has usually requested advice from many different sources, and is still unable to make up his mind. More than other people, the analyst knows that the decision will not resolve the person's conflicts, but merely push them back to the next dilemma that comes up. Hence, in most major decisions it is not really possible to give sound advice. The therapist must once again realize that his major contribution is therapy.

A rather typical situation was that in the case of Esther, a 21-year-old girl who had begun to have a sex life, with great inner turmoil resulting. She demanded advice constantly on how to outwit her mother, so that the latter would never know what was going on. Esther was an extremely dependent girl, who had been tagging along with strong figures, beginning with an older brother, as far back as she could remember. At the same time, this outward submissiveness was accompanied by an inner defiance, expressed in such symptoms as constipation, lack of appetite, and self-sabotage whenever she came close to success.

In the battle to conceal her sexual activities from her mother, one decision after another had to be made, on each of which she plaintively and insistently demanded advice from the therapist. First, there was the question of whether she should have it at all (although she had had sex before therapy); upon analysis this covered up among other things an extensive petting experience at 13. Then came the question of where and how to cover up for her time. Next the problem of contraception had to be taken up. Out of fear, submissiveness, as well as an unconscious wish to have a baby, she had used no precautions; fortunately, she did not become pregnant. After much discussion and consultation with a gynecologist, who recommended pills, she bought a diaphragm. The next problem was where should the diaphragm be kept? If her mother found it in her room, it would be awful; that alone would not be so terrible, but her mother would tell her father, and that would be horrible. Father might have a heart attack, or even die of the shock. For a while she asked her boy friend to hold the diaphragm for her, but this proved impractical. She hid it in an article of clothing, always fearful that mother might discover it.

Sure enough, the mother did one day come across the diaphragm "by accident," as she was looking through her daughter's closet for "something." This produced some anxiety, but less than that connected with the anticipation of the discovery. Mother was initially shocked, asked for a special appointment with the therapist, which was later cancelled. After some thought, mother became reconciled to the idea that her daughter was having sex. This whole episode passed. But then came a new set of fears about mother. Now Esther wanted to move out on her own; again, many requests for advice covered up her extreme dependency. After the demands for advice had been analyzed over and over again, she was able to come to grips with her lifelong dependency.

In this case, as in so many others, the advice is tied up with dependency which in turn is locked with anxiety in a vicious circle. The dependent person is afraid of any independent step; this leads him both to question what he does, and to look for a strong figure on whom he can lean. In real life, dependent people usually find such strong figures, but at the cost of much suffering. In the therapy this attempt is repeated. The therapist, alert to what the patient is trying to do, does not fall into the trap.

Incidentally, it is in cases of this kind that poorly trained or unscrupulous therapists can take advantage of helpless patients. If the therapist does take over, prescribing every one of the patient's actions, the patient is initially quite grateful. But the result is merely a further prolonged dependency which is all the more difficult to sever. Any benefits that result from such authoritative therapy are usually transference improvements rather than signs of any inner growth toward maturity.

2) Requests for Reassurance

These are the patients who repeatedly ask whether they are all right, whether they will crack up, whether they will ever get better, and so forth. The questions may come sporadically, or they may be so insistent that they take precedence over anything else.

By and large, in intensive therapy, reassurance is avoided for the simple reason that reassurance does not reassure. The reason for this must be sought in the psychodynamics of the situation.

When the patient asks for some specific form of reassurance he is filled with a number of anxieties, only one of which is coming out through the question. If he is given a simple yes-or-no answer (in practice it must always be yes) he does not have a chance to ventilate the other anxieties that continue to plague him. Furthermore, questions almost always cover up some associations, and it is these associations that the therapist wishes to allow to come into the open. Production of material remains the primary goal throughout.

Two questions come up with particular frequency: "Will I get better?" and "Am I going crazy?" As with all therapeutic matters, both of these must first be approached in terms of the transference.

"Getting better" has many different meanings to people. As a rule the patient's goals are not those of the therapist, one of whose tasks it is to give the patient a broader perspective on his life. Thus, if the question of getting better is discussed more fully, this discrepancy can be brought to the fore. Then the educational process enters, leading the patient on to newer and broader goals.

Further, the feeling of lack of improvement can have many different meanings. One is an embodiment of the feeling of discouragement about life, which the contemporary happy-go-lucky attitude toward society tends to repress. Yet, as religions have known from time immemorial, people need some outlet for their sadness. The discrepancy between the rewards promised by our culture and the actual rewards achieved is almost always great; the more disturbed the individual, the greater the discrepancy. This leads to unhappiness and frustration, which must find an outlet somewhere. Many times the question about getting better can best be handled by a remark that it is good for the patient to express some of the discouragement that he feels.

> Frank (cf. p. 63) came in session after session saying that he felt a little bit better each time. After a while he himself noticed that he seemed to be overdoing this bit. Eventually the denouement came, when he entered upon a period of depression. Now all the previous gains seemed to have been wiped away with one fell swoop. He began to ask whether he would ever get better. The question was used to help him to clarify his goals in treatment, so that he could become realistic about what he could achieve in life, and what he could not. Underneath the depressive feeling about therapy lay an infantile omnipotence wish for a restoration of early childhood bliss, the major manifestation of which was the wish to separate himself from everybody else to live on an isolated rural farm.

The question about "going crazy" must likewise be handled

dynamically, by inquiring into the patient's image of craziness. In this approach the therapist is buttressed by his knowledge: first, that when a psychosis is impending, it does not come out in this way, and second, that almost always crazy means "something bad" to the patient, which he cannot further verbalize. This something bad often is some forbidden impulse, such as an outburst of aggression, or a release of hidden sexuality. When treated in this way, the id material is gradually brought to the light.

Gloria, from the very beginning of treatment, frequently wanted to know whether she was going out of her mind. She was a 25-year-old girl, with a most pathological childhood history, mother killed when she was a child, moved from one home to another for many years, never staying in one place more than a year before she was 15.

To go out of her mind had a number of different meanings. As a child she had always had to display the extreme of outward obedience, in order to please the family that she happened to be living with at the time, no matter how much she was seething with anger inside. It had gone so far that she could remember no anger toward anybody. A great deal of hidden resentment toward the analyst came out during this stage, particularly the feeling that he was some kind of crook or sexual maniac.

The other meanings of going crazy related first to her deeply repressed sexuality, which had precipitated her coming to treatment. Because of the encouragement offered by the therapy, she was able to sustain a sexually satisfying affair for the first time in her life. This made her feel so enormously guilty that she was constantly seeking reassurance from all her friends and acquaintances that she was not a bad girl.

In addition, going crazy involved the fantasy of staying home with her new parents, giving her a chance to have some kind of normal childhood again. There had been an actual "nervous breakdown" some eight years prior to therapy, during which she stayed home, ate a lot, watched T.V. all day, and was unable to function in any mature capacity. This went on for some six months. The wish to repeat this regression was strong.

In other areas, the request for reassurance often involves a reaffirmation of the patient's dependency in some undesirable way. For example, many patients will attribute great medical wisdom to the therapist, whether he is a physician or not, and will neglect physical problems because they are "psychosomatic." The therapist must frequently insist on a medical consultation with a qualified specialist to help the patient handle the symptom more realistically. The same in other fields. If a legal matter comes up, it must be taken up with a lawyer. The dependent patient would like to have the analyst be doctor, lawyer, therapist, banker, employer, and everyone else. By turning back the various questions about reassurance, the analyst helps the patient handle life's problems on a more realistic level.

3) Inability to Grasp Explanations

Some patients exhibit their dependency by a perpetual inability to grasp psychodynamic explanations. Intellectually, of course, they are quite competent; it soon becomes apparent that their analytic blindness has emotional roots. Sometimes these patients show considerable ability to assess the motives of other people, yet fail completely with themselves.

Dynamically, the obtuseness is secondary to the gains derived from being dependent. Their main concern is whether the analyst will accept their dependency; the interpretations are entirely secondary. At times, it may also have a spite meaning: Whatever you tell me I won't listen to you, much as the defiant child handles his mother's commands.

This category merges with several others described, so no further discussion is necessary here.

4) Lack of Improvement

Paradoxically the lack of improvement may be a manifestation of a positive dependent transference. It is literally true that many patients would rather not get better than give up the analyst. Once more it becomes clear that all the transactions observed in the analytic process can only be understood in the light of the transference reactions.

As a rule there is some change for the better which the patient ignores, but many times there really is no change over a period of time. In these patients there is an overwhelming fear of separation which usually can be traced back to over-destructive or over-possessive parents.

5) Inability to Leave Treatment

It has frequently been observed that many patients find it difficult to leave treatment, some of them continuing for years without apparent benefit, others improving consistently during treatment, but falling back as soon as the support of the therapist is gone. Some critics have seen this as a harmful consequence of psychotherapy, forgetting that therapy merely crystallizes trends which appear in other life situations as well. Dependency is a universal problem.

Historically, it was only gradually that the dependency needs of the patient came to the fore. At first, and for a long time to come, the problem was viewed medically or, at best, from some intellectual point of view. Only when repeated attempts to cure the symptoms failed because of recurrent lapses into the old or similar conditions did attention focus more and more on the transference, and the concomitant dependency gratifications.

Neurotic illness, or distance from the analytic ideal, can be evaluated in terms of the patient's attachments to the objects of early infancy. These early attachments of course are all highly dependent; indeed, in infancy the dependency is biologically determined. A number of authors have seen in the prolonged dependency of the human child, which goes far beyond anything else seen in the animal kingdom, one of the major roots of man's propensity to neurosis. The human being does not relish giving up a libidinal position; to make him do so often requires a considerable amount of skill and tact. If, on top of that, the parents unconsciously infantilize the child, the dependency is doubly solidified.

It is no wonder then that so many patients become extremely dependent on their therapists. In essence, this dependency does not differ from that in other human relationships. The major difference is that the therapist, aware of what is going on, does not exploit the dependency, but tries to help the patient get over it. Sometimes unscrupulous or poorly trained therapists consciously or unconsciously exploit the patients who become too dependent on them.

Two technical questions related to dependency are encountered with special frequency: the number of sessions per week, and planned separations from treatment.

With regard to the number of sessions, this is one way in which the dependency of the patient can be given normal gratification. He wishes to see the therapist as often as possible; let him do so—it has distinct therapeutic advantages. The idea that the greater frequency will make him more dependent does not seem to be borne out by actual experience. If anything, it could work the other way around as well. There is a formidable amount of material to be chewed through in intensive psychotherapy; more time cannot do any real harm.

With regard to the proposal that the dependent patient be given more time off from the analysis, the same observations hold. It would appear that little happens inner-psychologically outside of therapy, so that a separation in and of itself is merely an interruption. Some have gone to the other extreme, undertaking massive therapy for long periods of time, as in the marathon group. But for the dependent patient no amount of concentrated time, no matter how marathon, is enough.

In general, when the patient becomes too dependent, the only real cure for it is to analyze the dependency needs in all their various aspects, dynamic, genetic, interpersonal, and so on. This can only be done after a satisfactory transference has been established. Thus, the therapy proceeds by first allowing the patient to become dependent on the therapist, and then tracing the various roots of the dependency to help him overcome the problem. The alternative, outside therapy, is lifelong dependency, often in spite of the most extreme misery.

Countertransference problems in the dependent patient are apt to be quite strong, varying with what happened in the therapist's own past. He may conceivably derive some unconscious pleasure from the dependency; to some extent this is true of every therapist. If he did not seek this kind of unconscious pleasure, he would scarcely enter the profession or, having entered it, would not be likely to stay in it too long.

To derive pleasure from the dependency is not in and of itself a problem. Inherently this is a sublimation of the parental feeling, the ideal kind of countertransference (cf. Chapter 11). What creates a problem is, as in the analogous parent-child situation, the abuse of the dependency by the therapist. This may take various forms. If the therapist derives too much enjoyment from the dependency he can unconsciously infantilize the patient, in pretty much the same way that the parent does to the child. If the therapist cannot tolerate the dependency he will regard the patient as "very sick," and resort to a variety of undesirable therapeutic measures to counteract the "sickness." In one sense this is part of the history of psychiatry; as has been emphasized throughout, to regard the patient as a "sick inferior" being is part of the basic non-analytic countertransference which the well-trained person has to get over in the course of his own growth. In these cases the therapist must continue to analyze his countertransference as vigorously as the patient analyzes his transference. Here are a few case vignettes.

Martin, a tall, good-looking young therapist of 30, repeatedly had the experience that young girls assigned to him in the clinic would fall in love with him. In his own life this had happened, too, yet in spite of his attractiveness he had had considerable difficulties in relating to women. Marriage, deferred until relatively recently, had turned out badly. Unconsciously, his need was to reject women in accordance with the usual Oedipal constellation.

Sylvia, a 22-year-old married woman with a small child, after being assigned to Martin, promptly fell in love with him as predicted. Her transference followed the customary pattern of the erotic variety: longings for love, coupled with demands that could not be gratified, wish to terminate because the therapist was too cold, working through this wish. She of course did not know that Martin's countertransference was quite a problem too. At first, he resented her because she did not come up to his cultural expectations; this was part of his antagonism to his mother, who was "nothing but a housewife." He was bitter at the thought that Sylvia, as a result of her therapy, would end up "nothing but a housewife."

Sylvia's transference could be worked out because she was in therapy. But Martin's countertransference was not at that point available to any analytic scrutiny. There was no alternative but to switch the patient to another therapist.

Fred, a man in his 60s, had never had any children. His patients, as he frankly told them, took the place of children, and he lavished an extraordinary amount of care and attention on them. When he came to supervision much of what he was doing was establishing a social relationship rather than a treatment process. He would read stories to them, tell them anecdotes from his previous life, enter actively into their life problems, and in many other ways act more as a friend than as an analyst. At first the patients reacted positively to this approach, as is generally the case. But soon an impasse would result, which he did not know how to handle. It was only when enough impasses had piled up that he applied for further supervision.

MODERATE POSITIVE TRANSFERENCE

A fourth variety of the positive transference is one where the patient has moderately good feelings about the therapist, not going to the extreme in any particular direction. When transference reactions come up, the patient shows the capacity to analyze them without undue pressure to act them out in some harmful way, or to fall into some excessive regression. Admittedly, this is a kind of transference rarely seen, yet its delineation remains theoretically important.

In this kind of transference, erotic, homosexual, and dependent feelings do come up from time to time. But the patient has the ability to bring these feelings to consciousness, trace their childhood origins, look at them objectively, and work them through in the course of time. The transference reaction itself need not, and should not, be analyzed until towards the latter part of the treatment.

Concomitantly with this transference goes a minimum of resistances. Here again it is clear why transference and resistance are so closely allied; the strongest resistances arise because infantile transference wishes have to remain ungratified.

Since resistances are at a minimum, the emphasis is strongly on dynamic material all the way through. Fantasies, dreams, life history material are brought up, correlated, and pulled into a coherent whole by the cooperative efforts of analyst and patient.

It could be said immediately that patients with such a transference do not come in with any particularly severe problem. Their distance from the analytic ideal could be said to be at a minimum; sometimes, they have even benefited from the writings of analytic authors before ever coming to therapy. The childhood background is usually one of a stable family with the sexual disabilities that are normal in our culture. Often it is the intolerable sexual frustration that brings the patient to treatment, and the treatment concentrates on this area more than on anything else. The sexual problem most often is a genital one, the pre-genital components being at a minimum. The relationship here is similar to that of the analytic honeymoon, with the exception that the transference does not assume the violent or regressed character that so commonly succeeds the honeymoon period. Here is a case vignette.

Norma, a 27-year-old secretary, found herself involved in an unhappy marriage, primarily because of her sexual conflicts. Her husband had little libido, and when he did she often suffered from pain during intercourse.

To all outward appearances the home environment was exemplary. The parents were happily married. They had never quarreled, to the patient's knowledge. Both were active outgoing people, although the mother had a tendency to be a nag. There were two children, both of whom again outwardly made good adjustments.

In addition to the usual cultural fare, the parents provided her with a satisfactory sex education. In fact, the major sources of trouble in this girl's life were those inherent in the family structure itself; her parents could scarcely be faulted for any act, overt or covert.

Because her marriage was unhappy, Norma began a love affair with a co-worker, which was sexually extremely gratifying. However, the guilt feelings aroused led her into therapy.

In therapy the transference was moderately positive throughout. No extreme erotic or dependent or hostile feelings ever appeared; these feelings did arise, but were always kept within bounds. The dynamic material centered around tracing the sexual conflicts to the Oedipal situation. Oral and anal problems never appeared. With the gradual resolution of her Oedipal difficulties she was able to terminate the unhappy marriage, experiment for a while with a number of lovers, and eventually make a happy marriage. No severe resistances ever came up in the course of therapy.

THE NEGATIVE TRANSFERENCE

When the patient is continuously or over a long period of time hostile to the therapist, the transference is *negative*. The hostility may alternate with positive feelings, or with indifferent ones, or it may be the only feeling manifested by the patient throughout the therapy.

If the hostility is too extreme the patient either never comes to therapy or leaves after a very short time. So, in practice, experience is limited to the manageable negative transference. This means that with ambulatory patients there is always a predominant, underlying, positive transference; the self-selection process has weeded out those who hate the analyst too much.

However, the unmanageable type must also be borne in mind, especially for those therapists who deal with hospitalized patients. Paranoid patients in particular, under the influence of persecutory delusions, may become so violent that they present a real danger to life or limb. There are a few cases on record where psychiatrists have been killed by delusional patients. Few as they are, they indicate that clinical caution in hospital situations is always advisable. In office practice, unless the patient is acutely paranoid, the danger of a violent assault can be ignored.

Negative transference and resistance are related but still different concepts. In negative transference the emphasis is on the hostility of the patient to the therapist; in resistance the stress is on the manner in which the patient fights treatment. Clearly there is some overlap. Actually, in all cases of resistance the transference is negative, while when it is negative it is a major form of resistance. However, there are many instances of resistance where the transference appears to be positive; the negative feelings can only be inferred. Hence, resistance covers a broader range than negative transference.

Sometimes the anger comes out as a direct frontal assault. This is quite threatening to the patient, and he may break off treatment either because he is fully convinced that his anger is justified, or because he is fearful of the retaliation from the therapist that he is sure will follow upon his outburst.

Here are a few clinical examples.

Fritz, a 38-year-old heir to an immense fortune, came to analysis with a proposition: the trustees of his estate had the right to give him a large portion of the inheritance outright if they considered him mentally fit. If the analyst would go to court and testify that he was fit, he would give him a large sum of money.

Inquiry revealed that Fritz was homosexual, alcoholic, had twice been hospitalized for schizophrenia, and had married a gold-digger who separated him from half of his allowance. All these facts had made no impression on him.

The analyst suggested that he try analysis, without any commitment about a court appearance. Reluctantly, Fritz agreed. But in the fifth session he came in and let loose at the analyst with everything he had, calling him a Jewish pig, a Freudian quack, a liar, humbug, etc. He then disappeared, and was never heard from again.

Dr. Theodor Reik relates the story of a patient who said to him: You are not Theodor Reik. The patient was so convinced that Dr. Reik was an impostor that he wrote to the U. of Vienna, where Dr. Reik had obtained his degree, to verify that he was indeed the man. The University replied that its records had been lost during the war. Triumphantly, the patient said, "That proves my case," and left treatment. The refusal to admit the genuineness of Dr. Reik was clearly a concealed wish to destroy him.

Ronald, a 16-year-old boy, was brought to treatment by his mother, who noticed that it had been many years since he had had any friends. He came to therapy reluctantly, the ostensible reason given to him being that he would get some vocational counseling for his future career.

In therapy he was extremely difficult. When asked a question, he would take almost an hour to answer. E.g., when asked what his mark had been in algebra, he said: What is algebra? To clarify this point took the remainder of the session, when he would finally answer. Most often he expressed the feeling that the therapist was no good, so that he saw no point in coming. Sometimes he accused the therapist of deliberately releasing smoke to poison him, or of concealing microphones to "get the goods" on him.

At one point, the therapist felt it essential to see the mother. Ronald objected violently, but the therapist insisted. When the mother came, Ronald began to call up during the hour. He called so persistently that the therapist had to take the phone off the hook to be able to conduct the interview.

After this, Ronald began to call on the phone to annoy the therapist. He would call at 7 A.M., say "This is Christopher Columbus," and then hang up. Sometimes he would not say anything, merely calling 15 or 20 times an hour. Finally the therapist had to tell him that he would stop the therapy if Ronald did not discontinue the calls. At first Ronald said blandly, "How do you know I'm the one that's calling?" Then he asked, "Suppose I do it after I've left?" The therapist replied that if it became necessary to protect his practice, he would have to turn the matter over to the authorities.

Although he had previously been completely negative, the therapist's firm stand calmed him down considerably. He gave up his direct attack, and became much more cooperative in the therapy.

In all the above cases, the anger at the therapist is mixed with great feelings of despair. It is important to allow the patient to confess his feelings of despair. When that can be done, he is more likely to derive therapeutic benefit. This was possible here only in the case of Ronald.

A most important manifestation of anger is its constant projection to the therapist. He is seen as critical, disinterested, antagonistic, disapproving, ready to throw the patient out, and the like. The one thing that the patient consistently denies is that the therapist may be a dedicated practitioner who is trying to help him get better.

In such cases, it is a good idea for the therapist to say: Is there anything I have said or done to give you that impression? Sometimes the patient will mention something of a trivial nature, such as starting a few minutes late, or taking time out to answer the telephone. But usually there is nothing that the patient can put his finger on, so that the question helps him to focus on the anger welling up in him.

Rusty had a dream that he was having sex with the therapist's wife when the therapist walked in and asked him to stop. For some time after this, the therapist was seen as stern, ungiving, repressive, angry, and the like. Analysis of this sequence helped Rusty become aware of his anger, which had always been handled by a strong reaction formation.

When anger remains unrecognized, it is often turned against the self, which is why in so many of the instances cited there is a mingling of anger and despair. The projection of anger to the therapist, followed by its reintrojection as a criticism, is the same dynamic mechanism that led to the growth of the superego in childhood. Hence, the consistent analysis of the patient's anger toward the therapist leads to a modification of the severity of the superego.

In the management of the negative transference, it is important to allow the patient to express his anger, not for cathartic reasons, but as a way of working out his superego problem. As the patient comes out with his anger, and discovers that there is no retaliation, he learns that the therapist is different from his parents, and is therefore wrongly being looked upon as a superego. When this is repeated over and over again, the superego is sufficiently modified to allow a greatly increased amount of pleasure in living. Eventually, the patient will see less and less reason for getting angry, since he will be dealing more and more with reality, less and less with his superego.

It is important not to get involved with the patient in any kind of argument. Anger feeds on anger and, if it is allowed to continue, it can only lead to a rupture of the relationship. If the patient is too insistent, sometimes the only alternative is to change the subject.

The management of the negative transference is far more difficult than that of the positive. First, the therapist must help the patient see the ways in which his anger is coming out. Then he has to give him a chance to ventilate some of the anger directly in the analysis. Then the anger has to be traced to its childhood origins, as well as tied up with other aspects of everyday functioning. Repeated confrontations may be necessary when the patient insists that he is not angry, or is angry only because it is so fully justified. It is part of the work which demands an almost inexhaustible amount of patience over a long time.

In ordinary life, no one likes to have people angry at him. So the countertransference problems that arise in this area are considerable. The therapist must understand the anger witout reacting to it. Sometimes the therapist, made angry by the anger, destructively tells the patient that he is incurable. Such a statement represents an unpardonable therapeutic sin.

The duration of the patient's anger is a matter over which the therapist has little control. Sometimes it passes quickly; at other times it may last for months or even years. In those patients who constantly use the analyst as a whipping-boy for their anger, the release of hostility is important to their sense of well-being. If they cannot find it with the analyst, they cannot find it elsewhere, with a progressive worsening of their symptoms.

Since all human relationships are ambivalent, it is sometimes thought that some hostility must be released in the course of every long-term analysis. Some therapists even try to elicit the anger, on the grounds that it's bound to come out sooner or later, so why not now? This is a mistake. It does not do justice to the enormous variability found among human beings. Some patients are angry from the very beginning, remaining so until the end. Others are positive, then negative, then positive again, and so on. Still others may go through months or years of therapy with hardly any show of hostility. Nor is it to be assumed that the hostility is necessarily repressed. There may be such an inherently good rapport between patient and therapist that hostility is absent; this happens when there is an extended analytic honeymoon (cf. case of Caroline in Chapter 4, pp. 41–43). Here, as elsewhere, it is best to avoid excessive dogmatism. Dynamic inactivity remains the rule for the analyst in the beginning. Anger should be handled when it occurs, but its manifestations remain highly variable.

If the therapist deliberately provokes the anger, as some recommend, it is deprived of its therapeutic usefulness. For then the patient can justifiably say, "You did it; anybody would get angry under those circumstances." Unprovoked fantasies remain the best material for analytic work.

If the anger is too great, or if it is improperly handled, the result is an *abrupt premature termination*. This is by far the most important aspect of the negative transference in the early stages, and remains a threat, though in considerably diminished degree, throughout.

Some studies [29] have estimated that in non-analytic therapy somewhere between thirty and sixty percent of the patients drop out after a few sessions, but even in analytic therapy, which is much more clearly formulated, both theoretically and technically, the percentage of drop-outs remains high. In a world as full of anger as ours, many people remain unapproachable, no matter what the therapist does.

In one sense, the entire range of technical devices, especially in the early stages, is geared toward keeping the patient in treatment. Whatever other differences they may have, analysts are in general agreement that quick therapy is not in a position to alter character structure to any meaningful extent. When quick therapy is espoused, as with Alexander and French, the goal is a compromise symptom removal rather than a thorough restructuring of the patient's psyche.

Throughout the early stages, the patient maintains a goodly amount of anger that may surface with little provocation, resulting in abrupt termination. For this reason, it behooves the analyst to proceed with great caution until he is sure that a really good relationship has been established. In the great majority of cases, this occurs after the *first treatment crisis* has been overcome. To this topic we now turn.

SUGGESTIONS FOR FURTHER READING

Most of the literature on negative transference is combined with that on resistance. See references for Chapter 14. Some particularly useful papers are: N. Haak, "Comments on the Analytical Situation," *Int. J. Psychoanalysis* 38, 1957, 183–195. S.Nacht, "Technical Remarks on the Handling of the Transference Neurosis," *Int. J. Psychoanalysis* 38, 1957, 196–202.

The most extended discussion of negative transference is still W. Reich, *Character Analysis* (New York: Orgone Institute Press, 1949). For a perceptive re-evaluation of Reich's contribution, see R. Sterba, "Clinical and Therapeutic Aspects of Character Resistance," *Psychoanalytic Quarterly* 22, 1953, 1–20.

CHAPTER 7

The First Treatment Crisis

But I, that am not made for sportive tricks,
Nor made to court an amorous looking glass;
I that am rudely stamp'd, and want love's majesty
To strut before a wanton ambling nymph;
I, that am curtail'd of this fair proportion,
Cheated of feature by dissembling Nature,
Deform'd, unfinish'd, sent before my time
Into this breathing world, scarce half made up,
And that so lamely and unfashionable
That dogs bark at me as I halt by them . . .

And therefore, since I cannot prove a lover,
To entertain these fair well-spoken days,
I am determined to prove a villain
And hate the idle pleasures of these days.

Shakespeare: *Richard III*
(Duke of Gloucester)

In the first part of analysis, the most significant manifestation of the negative transference is the *first treatment crisis*. As a rule, it comes at the end of the analytic honeymoon, perhaps some three months to one year after the beginning of treatment. Positive feelings shift to negative ones; hate replaces love.

The word "crisis" is used advisedly; it is a real crisis in the therapy. Above all, it threatens the continuity of the therapy; if it is not resolved, the patient will leave treatment.

Beginning therapists often have an unholy fear of the outbreak of a "latent" psychosis in their patients. In the great majority of instances, this fear is unwarranted. It is true enough that psychotherapy induces a regression; indeed, without regression no therapy is possible. But this is quite different from the outbreak of a psychosis.

As an empirical rule, it may be assumed that the regression in therapy will not go further than anything previously experienced in the patient's life. That is, if he was at one time psychotic (in the strict clinical sense) it may break out again; but if he had never been psychotic before the onset of therapy the chances are very slight that it will happen now. Much more acute is the possibility that he will terminate abruptly. This occurs if the first treatment crisis is not handled properly. It is such a strong probability that the entire theory of therapy in the early stages centers around it.

There are many reasons for the first treatment crisis. It represents the other side of the honeymoon coin. Everything that goes on in the honeymoon stage may sooner or later come to be felt as a source of intense frustration. Catharsis, yes, but I've had enough of that—give me more relief. No punishment—why not? How can a human being exist in this analytic void? And so on with every other feature of the honeymoon. As in marriage, after a certain point a harsh reality enters the picture, which forces people back to earth.

To a considerable extent the shift from honeymoon to crisis derives from the cyclical character of superego functioning. Where at first the analyst was seen as a benign superego—approving, listening, comforting—now he becomes a harsh taskmaster, disapproving, not listening, offering no real comfort. Every patient projects his superego to the therapist, and reacts accordingly. The cyclical character of the superego is in turn a reflection of the alternate praise and punishment that were used to discipline the patient in childhood.

The crisis may take a variety of forms, though all culminate in abrupt termination. Usually the patient acquires some fixed idea which becomes a *casus belli*. Sometimes he mentions it, sometimes he does not, because it is so realistic to him. One of the advantages of the fundamental rule is that the patient is thereby forced to produce revealing material which helps the analyst overcome the treatment crisis.

When the fixed idea cannot be resolved, the patient adopts the typical childhood attitude towards any fear—run. It is this that produces the crisis; the patient wants to run, the analyst wants him to stay and reflect on his fears.

If the therapist is prepared for the crisis, he will subordinate all his efforts in the early stages to preparing for it; only after the crisis has been passed can a deep relationship be established. When the therapist is prepared he can offer reasonable explanations for what the patient is going through. If it is properly handled, the crisis can usually be overcome. But no therapist should be blind to the fact that some patients will leave no matter what he does. No one has yet succeeded in curing all the people who come to him for help.

If the therapist is not prepared for the crisis, it is all the more disastrous when it does come. Then he does not know what he is fighting. Taken by surprise, he is left with a real feeling of helplessness.

This is why the early stages of therapy must be handled especially carefully. Mistakes are more costly at this stage than at any other. The bland assumption that the patient is in too strong a transference to show any resistance is soon contradicted by harsh reality. The therapist must operate on two levels: first, he must handle the material that the patient brings to him with some appropriate response, even if it is only a "um hmm"; and second, he must trace underneath the surface production the vicissitudes of transference and resistance that are being manifested by the patient.

As a rule it is wise not to disturb a positive transference in the early stages. Even if the patient attributes magical power to the therapist, that can be taken up later on—not in the beginning. What he should prepare for is the inevitable disappointment when the patient discovers that the analyst is not a magician.

Any signs of negative transference should be handled immediately. If the patient is persistently late, or if he dislikes certain things about the office, or if he expresses direct annoyance with the analyst, these feelings must be explored right away. If they are left to one side, their force will soon accumulate to a point where they are out of reach.

The expression of hostility by the patient toward the analyst is usually accompanied by a sense of relief, unless the hostility is too intense. The therapist, by adopting a neutral, relatively passive role, offers the patient no real cause for anger. Hence, when it does come up he is in a position to trace it to its childhood roots, or to explain it in terms of present-day dynamics.

Barry's first treatment crisis came after three months of therapy. Up to that point, he had been extremely positive about the analyst. In a previous treatment situation, the analyst had suddenly dropped him as a patient, and he was afraid that the same thing would happen here. On the whole, he felt very positive, but there were occasional signs of negativism, such as the insistence that the blinds should be drawn during his hour because otherwise somebody might see him on the couch.

One day he came in to announce regretfully that this would be his last session. The analyst was honestly puzzled by what could have caused such an abrupt change. He explained that over the weekend he had met one of the analyst's other patients, and it was impossible for him to be in treatment with an analyst who was also treating an acquaintance of his.

By now, enough was known of his dynamics to bring this reaction into better focus. He had always been an isolated individual. In analysis, he wished to maintain this isolation, yet he was already aware of what it had cost him in terms of human happiness. Putting all these facts together helped him to understand his angry reaction, and he remained in therapy.

In theoretical terms, there are three major reasons that account for the sudden shift from positive to negative transference. These reasons are close enough to common sense to be usable as interpretations in the appropriate situations.

1. *The superego reasserts itself:* Things begin to go too well; unconsciously the patient looks around for some punishment.

2. *The id becomes too threatening:* In spite of all the reassurances offered by the therapist, open and implied, that the new impulses cropping up are perfectly normal, it is too good to be true. This is related to the first; the superego cannot be dismissed so lightly.

3. *The relationship has become too close:* Since our society is based on a great deal of distance, when people get too close, the intimacy is frightening. At first, the patient reacts with enthusiasm to the new intimacy, but then he begins to question it, especially since the therapist does not share much knowledge about himself.

In order to put the first treatment crisis in proper perspective, it is helpful to see how others close to the patient resolve or have resolved their problems.

If the relatives of the patients are examined more carefully, they turn out to choose one of three major solutions: conflict-laden dependent relationships, constant preoccupation with psychosomatic complaints, or some form of severe pathology such as mental retardation, homosexuality, or overt psychosis.

It is against this background that the choices of the patients must be viewed. Every individual tends to imitate the models set for him by the early family environment; if these are the solutions that he sees, then they tend to exert the strongest pull on him in later life.

Once the patient enters therapy, he embarks on a new kind of solution to his problems, radically different from anything that he has ever known before. Like everything new and different, this is also frightening. So, after the initial liberation, the old doubts begin to return. The superego reasserts itself; that is, the pressures of the parental imagos, banished for a while, return in full force. A struggle ensues between the new kind of life and the old. If the first treatment crisis is successfully overcome, he moves on to something new. If it is not, he returns to conflict-laden dependencies (unhappy marriage, in most cases), somatic preoccupations, or more severe pathology.

In the initial stages of treatment, the goal is to establish a relationship, nothing more and nothing less. Everything is subordinated to that goal, because any alternative is seriously dangerous to the patient's mental health. Gradually, the therapist must acquire the inner conviction that there is nothing in life that is more important for the patient than his therapy.

A typical instance occurred in the therapy of Stuart, a 37-year-old salesman whose first three months in treatment with Dr. K. were an analytic honeymoon. Suddenly Stuart was fired from his job. He was considering a number of possibilities, most of which would have taken him away from New York, thus terminating his therapy with Dr. K. The therapist, unsure of himself, did not place sufficient stress on the desirability of having Stuart remain in treatment with him. Stuart took a job out of town; follow-up could not be determined.

Further perspective can be gained on the first treatment crisis by examining some patients who refuse to come to treatment at all, even though they are obviously in dire need of it. First some case vignettes.

Roberta was the 50-year-old mother of Sam, a 19-year-old who came to therapy because he had been expelled from school. In supplementary interviews it was discovered that Roberta had used extreme punishment on her son all through his life, frequently beating him quite severely. At one time she had broken his knee, which took several months to heal. Even during therapy, whenever he disobeyed her she would discipline him by cancelling one of his two weekly sessions.

In relating her life history she told of one younger brother who had been hospitalized with schizophrenia since the age of 13. She would constantly inquire whether her son was schizophrenic and should be hospitalized.

No pressure could induce Roberta to accept therapy. On the contrary, she insisted that she was the very model of what psychologists were trying to accomplish. At one point she reluctantly agreed to consult someone about the situation; thereafter she would say,

whenever reproached, that she was in treatment too. It turned out
however, that this was a fabrication; she had seen another man once
and stopped.

Horace, a 40-year-old businessman, was involved in a fairly typical marital conflict. His wife, who had been in therapy for a long
time, felt neglected by him. He would rarely consent to have sex
with her, even though she pressed for it quite often. There was no
exchange of romantic feeling. On the contrary, he would constantly
berate her, telling her that she was a mental case, that she was no
good, that she did not know what she was doing, etc. When she
asked him for a divorce on several occasions he replied, "You go
get it, it's all your fault." In several supplementary interviews with
the therapist, he insisted that all the problems lay with his wife. His
only trouble was that she was so impossible.

Both cases have one major factor in common: blaming others for
their troubles, rather than looking into themselves. In many such
cases it could very well be called a clinical paranoia; in others it is
milder, though in the same general direction. When the blame is
shifted to another person, the individual sees no reason for intro-
specting about his problems; in practice this is the hardest kind of
patient to treat, regardless of what technical diagnosis is given.

When the therapist is handling a patient who is faced by this kind
of situation, as a rule the goal of treatment must be altered somewhat.
To a considerable extent the patient's feelings about the impossible
pressures created by his environment are justified. Many times these
patients come in with the statement that they must be pretty bad to
arouse such reactions. After a while they begin to see how disturbed
the other person is. But since the close relative remains unapproachable, the only realistic solution eventually is to leave. It is in these
cases that children leave their parents, and impossible marriages break
up. But the patient, who is usually quite masochistic, is frightened to
adopt this way out. Instead of focusing on the inner conflicts that lead
to the constant friction, the therapist has to help the patient find out
how he got into such a dilemma or, in the case of children, why they
are unable to break away from it.

Many patients come a few times, then stop; an examination of
these cases should also throw light on the problem of the first treatment crisis. Here are some examples.

John, a 40-year-old surveyor from Ireland, had moved around all
his life, unable to find roots anywhere. One of a large family, he had

never felt close to anyone at home. An early ambition to study medicine had to be abandoned because of lack of money.

In desperation John called an analytic institute and asked for help. After a few sessions he was offered a job as surveyor on a road-building crew, his usual kind of work. Because of the job he left treatment; he never reapplied at the Institute.

Mildred, an attractive girl of 28, had led a pretty rough life. One of three children, she felt quite distant from her entire family. At about 20 she emigrated from a European country to the U.S. Out of sheer loneliness she entered into a number of sexual affairs. Always careless about contraception, she had had no fewer than four abortions. Two were done by midwives under primitive conditions; after one she almost died. Once she aborted the fetus when it was fairly well formed; she went to the priest to confess her sin, who advised her to baptize the fetus. Finally, she gave birth to one child, even though the man refused to marry her. She was quite proud of her child, a boy, whom she looked upon as her major possession.

When she habitually failed to come to work, her boss suggested psychotherapy. She came a few times, but then created insuperable difficulties in arranging appointments and paying the small clinic fee. For some time she would call on the telephone, speaking for hours if given the chance. Finally her demands became so insatiable that they could not be met. She left treatment.

In the above cases the patients show either a narcissistic withdrawal or demands for a kind of dependency which simply could not be gratified under these circumstances. They differ from the previous patients, who do not come to therapy at all because someone else is to blame for all their misfortunes. Instead, the patients who leave after a few sessions tend either to feel hopeless about their condition, or to rely on some infantile form of dependency gratification. The hopelessness as a rule derives from a wish for a dependency situation that cannot be gratified.

Sometimes the hopelessness is masked by a demand for quick results. If no great change is effected within the first few sessions, the patient complains that this kind of therapy is a waste of time. Some of these patients come from a socio-cultural environment where, if gratification is not immediate, it can never be expected to come. But others have such a horror of interpersonal intimacy that they use one pretext or another to break off.

In the handling of the first treatment crisis, time plays a significant role. If the crisis comes too soon, little therapeutic effect has been achieved, so that it becomes difficult to get the patient to stay. Interpretations also have to be cast in general terms, such as you are afraid to reveal yourself, because of the lack of more specific information. Many stratagems can be tried, but it is well to remember at this point that in many cases the patient is going to leave regardless of what the therapist does.

In the average successful case, the crisis comes somewhere between three months and one year after therapy has begun. With these patients a good deal of the background is known; very often an analytic honeymoon has been in effect for quite a while, and even without a true honeymoon there has been a considerable amount of relief because of the therapy. Under those circumstances, it becomes much easier to work out the resistances. This is one important reason why the positive transference should be permitted to flourish for as long as possible; resistances will come up in due time—the therapist need not force them.

Apart from abrupt termination, attention should be drawn to several other forms that the first treatment crisis may take. These fall into two general categories: The patient may use some alibi to mask his unwillingness to continue, or he may get involved in outside activities that endanger the therapy.

Alibis may range all over the place, and must be treated with understanding and tact. Perhaps the most common is the complaint that the patient does not have enough money. If suitable inquiry has been made in the first session into how the patient intends to pay for the therapy, assuming that the method is not obvious, then this problem need not arise. The principle holds that, at the beginning of therapy, it is important to make sure that the fees are within the patient's economic competence.

Even experienced therapists may become careless in this regard. Dr. J., a physician, applied for analysis because he wanted to shift his specialty. He was accepted at a three times a week rate, at the usual fee, slightly reduced for professional considerations. A few sessions after he started he revealed the real reason for coming: in medical school he had had a severe anxiety episode that forced him to withdraw for a year; recently, disturbing developments in his life made him afraid that this episode would be repeated. At the same time he confessed that the fee, though customary, was way above his head. His medical practice was in extremely poor shape; he was a general practitioner who charged $2 and $3 per visit. An offer to reduce the number of sessions to concentrate on the immediate practical difficulties was rejected, as was the suggestion that he switch to a therapist who could see him at a lower fee. The therapy was discontinued.

On occasion the patient may raise such difficulties about the hours offered to him that it becomes clear that deeper reasons are involved. If necessary, the patient must be confronted with the reality of what he is doing, but as a rule it is wiser for the therapist to make every concession possible about hours, in order to avoid the direct conflict with the resistances too early. Sometimes patients will also use extraneous considerations to cover up the first resistances, such as raising the question of whether a non-medical analyst is suitable for their condition, after they have already started. Some sophisticated patients at times bring up the question of theoretical orientation; they want the therapist to be a Freudian, or a member of the Washington School. Usually this covers up some other feeling; in the popular mind a Freudian is one who talks about sex, while a Washington School analyst does not. It is best to get at what the patient is really after, and to avoid sterile theoretical discussions.

Nowadays, some patients even try to control the modality of their treatment; e.g., by asking for group therapy rather than individual, or the reverse. Many patients who request group therapy from the beginning do so after some disappointing experience with an individual therapist. But it is better to try to work out the failure in individual therapy, often with a switch to another therapist, sometimes focusing on what is going wrong with the current therapy, than to switch posthaste. Control of the situation should always remain in the hands of the therapist, who should have enough expertise to handle whatever comes up.

Sometimes the first treatment crisis involves a change in the transference that manifests itself outside the therapy rather than inside. This can take two forms: either the patient is dramatically better, or he is dramatically worse.

When there is a sudden improvement leading to termination it is known as a *flight into health*. This paradoxical phrase rests on the knowledge that a symptom change is not a character change, so that any improvement has to be evaluated in relation to the total functioning of the individual. The process of therapy is long and arduous; everybody gets to realize this sooner or later. Many patients, especially those whose underlying pathology is ego-syntonic, shun the laborious task of probing into themselves, content instead with some superficial change. In some cases this resistance operates on a conscious level. "Who needs it?" one patient used to say. More often it is rooted in deep unconscious conflicts.

Wilma, a writer for a large firm, suddenly found it difficult to get her work done. She would sit staring into space, holding her pencil in her hand for hours at a time, unable to get anything down on paper. This symptom brought her to an analyst.

Inquiry revealed that she had many other problems. Unmarried at 35, she had only one tenuous relationship with a man whom she saw perhaps twice a month. Up to a few years before, she had spent all her free time with her father. When her father died, she began to drink rather heavily. She lived with a younger sister with whom she was in intense rivalry.

It soon became clear that Wilma wanted mainly to show her superiority to her sister, who was in deep analysis, and to get over the immediate symptoms. In about ten sessions she was back at work, writing fluently. The deeper problems of alcoholism, latent homosexuality, and withdrawal from men, were untouched. It was a typical "flight into health."

Since the neurotic equilibrium in her life had been restored, she terminated treatment.

When the patient seemingly gets worse in the early stages, this too must be understood dynamically in terms of whatever is happening to him. The worsening may mean that the therapeutic regression has gone too far. Or there may be some basic lack of understanding between therapist and patient. Or the patient may be acting out some aggression he feels toward the therapist. The principle remains: Behavior can be evaluated properly only when the underlying dynamic meaning is exposed. Here is an instance.

David, a 30-year-old civil service worker, came to therapy in a panic. He was afraid that he was going crazy, and asked if hospitalization were not the best way out. The therapist suggested that he come in every day for a while, which he gladly accepted.

In therapy it turned out that there was a great deal of mental illness on both sides of the family; the worst fears arose in relation to his own mother, who had been hospitalized for many years. His wife's mother had also been in hospitals on and off for some time.

The transference quickly turned into an analytic honeymoon.

Buttressed by his positive feelings about the therapist, David made rapid strides. The panic subsided, his work went much better, and he began to face the real conflicts in his life.

For various reasons the intense 7 day a week pace could not be kept up indefinitely. When the therapist suggested cutting down to six sessions, David readily agreed. That evening in a fit of rage he threw a burning pot of coffee at his wife, scalding her severely. The loss of the mother-therapist, even for one session a week (the therapist was a woman) was still too hard to take. Again the question of hospitalization was brought up, this time by the wife, who was frightened for her life. Fortunately, the crisis could be worked out satisfactorily, without interrupting the therapy.

Therapists frequently get into trouble by ignoring the first treatment crisis. At this juncture, as at other critical stages in therapy, special measures may be necessary to keep the patient in treatment.

SUGGESTIONS FOR FURTHER READING

See references to Chapter 8.

Resistance. Direct Confrontation

This working through of the resistances may, in practice, turn out to be an arduous task for the subject of the analysis and a trial of patience for the analyst. Nevertheless, it is a part of the work which effects the greatest changes in a patient and which distinguishes analytic treatment from any kind of treatment by suggestion. From a theoretical point of view one may correlate it with the "abreacting" and the quotas of affects strangulated by repression—an abreaction without which hypnotic treatment remained ineffective.

Freud: "Remembering, Repeating and Working Through." 1914.

The above quotation from Freud, from the paper in 1914 that summed up his previous thinking on the topic of technique, has become the cornerstone of all subsequent analytic work. Since that time psychoanalysis has meant and still means the analysis of resistance.

No psychotherapeutic endeavor is ever carried out without a varying amount of resistance. The term itself is somewhat misleading, because it carries the implication of some antagonism. It would be more appropriate to regard resistance as an essential part of the character structure, although the kinds of resistances offered will vary from one person to the next, and even within the therapy of one individual will vary from one period to the next.

Resistance may be defined as any action or attitude on the part of the patient that impedes the course of therapeutic inquiry. Resistances and defenses are identical; what is called defense in the character structure is called resistance in therapy. It is because defenses and resistances are merely two words for the same phenomenon, that all therapy must be carried on in the face of some resistance.

In his 1926 book, *Inhibitions, Symptoms and Anxiety,* Freud offered a metapsychological classification of resistances into five types.[30] The first three are ego resistances. These include 1) repression or defense methods used by the ego to ward off unconscious material that would arouse anxieties; 2) transference resistances that aim to avoid memory work by keeping a new enactment of all the situations in the transference alive; 3) the epinosic gain—resistances due to the gain through illness; 4) superego resistance, where guilt and self-punishment tendencies are powerful, as a result of the conflict between the superego and the ego, or more correctly to an excessively harsh superego, this is also called the "negative therapeutic reaction"; 5) the id resistance that lies behind the whole working through process. This metapsychological classification has not proved to be of much practical value.

Another approach to resistances is to list the defense mechanisms, projection, displacement, reaction, formation, repression, and so forth, and to see how they become manifest in therapy. This is usual, but again tends to remain on the theoretical side.

Greenson classifies resistances according to their sources, fixation points, types of defense, diagnostic categories, and ends up offering a practical classification in which he distinguishes ego-alien resistance from ego-syntonic resistances.[31]

All of these theoretical classifications, while useful, are difficult, especially for the beginner, to translate into a direct therapeutic benefit. What seems to be of most value is to describe resistances as they come up in the actual analytic encounter. Such a description will be given in this and the next two chapters. Our concern is with the *phenomenology* of resistance more than with its metapsychology.

A simple, practical classification of resistances divides them into those in which the patient simply refuses, for one reason or another, to comply with the basic requests, and those in which the resistance is of a more subtle nature. The analyst asks the patient to do three things: to come at a certain time, to speak everything that is on his mind, and to pay a certain fee. Later, a fourth request is inserted, when the patient is asked to lie on the couch. Even though these requests are of a relatively simple nature, patients will defy them in a variety of different ways. This presents the first approach to resistances.

More subtle are those resistances where the patient seems to be complying with the requests, but fights the therapeutic method in one way or another. Examples of such resistances are an overemphasis on reality, a demand for reality gratification, a sense of hopelessness, excessive regression, or acting out.

DIRECT REFUSAL TO COMPLY WITH INSTRUCTIONS

Abrupt premature termination, the most blatant of all resistances, has already been discussed at length under the heading of negative transference (see Chapter 6). It remains a danger throughout the entire course of therapy, though it becomes increasingly less likely as time goes on.

The more usual refusals to abide by the instructions center around the three main requests made of the patient—time, talking, and fee —and, later, the fourth—the couch.

1) Lateness

Persistent lateness is not at all uncommon. Generally, the patient is expressing a mixture of despair and anger. Why come on time, when the therapist is not going to do anything for me, anyhow, is the message he is trying to convey. More elaborate fantasies may be involved as well, which should be brought to the surface. Like any other major transference manifestation, the meaning of the lateness must be pursued until it becomes clear to the patient.

Sometimes patients who come late demand that they be given the full time allotted to them. If the therapist has a busy schedule, this is impossible, and the request should be refused forthwith. However, even if a therapist has time available, it is unwise to lengthen the session to make up for the missed time; that would be a manipulation rather than analysis. It is almost always more important to impress upon the patient that his refusal to keep the agreed-upon schedule has some deeper meaning.

The extreme of this position is adopted by patients who for one reason or another are unable to come to a session or do not want to come, then call up and ask for another session. It is wise for the therapist to adopt the rule here that any sessions missed will be charged for, unless there is valid reason. At times it is even best to charge for the session, regardless of the reason. Therapeutically, this has the effect of focusing squarely on the transference situation.

A word of caution must be inserted here: So many forces may combine to interfere with appointments that lateness should not be interpreted until it has become a clearly definable pattern. When it is pointed out to the patient, there should be no doubt that it has occurred over and over again. Here are a few typical case illustrations.

Lyle, a student in analytic training, was almost always late to his appointment. There was always an alibi, usually a good one. His own patients (he was in medical practice) had held him up, there was an emergency, what was so important about five minutes anyhow, etc. Once he came in half an hour late and announced angrily that he was not going to waste any time discussing his lateness; the trains simply had not run on time.

After plowing through many alibis, it was possible to uncover the dynamic fact that at bottom he saw no reason to be analyzed and that he was doing it merely to comply with what he knew to be the official requirements of the profession. Underneath this lay a deep feeling of hopelessness about his life. Unhappily married, he had made an adjustment by setting up a relationship with a mistress who would alternately kick him out and beg him to come back. He really could not see any way out of his dilemma; to leave his wife would do too much harm to the children, besides, he did not want to marry the girl friend. So there was nothing to do but work out other people's problems. As this was brought out over and over again through the persistent discussion of the lateness and other material, the analysis began to acquire a deeper meaning for him.

Rachel, a 25-year-old married woman, was always ten minutes late for her sessions, even though she lived within a ten-minute walk from the analyst's office. For a long time she angrily brushed off any attempt to explore the lateness; what does the analyst care, it gives him extra time to do whatever he wants to do. Underneath this, of course, lay the reproach that he did not really care about her. Eventually, this was seen to be tied up with a sexual fantasy. In the time away from the office, before the session, she could indulge in florid sexual fantasies, either about the analyst or about some easily identifiable substitute. When this finally came out, the feeling that she could never find any real satisfaction in her sexual life could be brought to the fore and analyzed.

Duke, a wealthy businessman in his forties, came to treatment originally only for a few sessions, to resolve a marital conflict. After some preliminary discussions, he accepted the idea of analysis three times a week.

For quite a while, Duke was late more often than not; occasionally he would cancel altogether. That he had to pay for all this missed time did not bother him at all. In fact, when the matter was brought up, it eventually became clear that his attitude was: I am paying you, so what difference does it make? He strongly denied that the analyst could have any human feelings about him.

In his life, Duke was accustomed to buying people. Impotent with his wife, he had found a mistress who had milked him for many thousands of dollars. But since he was obsessed with the fear of being abandoned, he did not care about what he had to pay; anyhow, he could cover up his feelings with the rationalization that since he was so wealthy, the money did not mean anything.

Thus, the lateness covered up a deep sense of despair about being able to achieve a gratifying human relationship without paying for it. As this was brought out over and over again, he began to develop warmer feelings for the therapist. When his mistress's demands became too exorbitant, for the first time he was able to say "no" without being panicked by the thought that she would give him up. Together with this new feeling of worth, he began to come on time.

In the analysis of Robert, a 35-year-old student in psychoanalytic training, time did not become a problem until a certain stage in the analysis was reached when he felt himself severely rejected by the analyst. His character structure prevented him from bringing out this feeling except in disguised form. He began to come about five minutes late for every session. When this had been observed for some time, it was pointed out to him. He replied that he had built up the urge to have a cup of coffee at the corner drugstore before coming to the session and invariably erred about the time. This was further pursued to the point where the fantasy came out that the analyst should really have provided him with a cup of coffee. Robert's giving himself his own coffee was similar to other life experiences. His father was a barber who had suicided when Robert was 6. Beginning early in adult life, Robert began to give himself his own haircuts, a practice which he was unable to break until he had been in analysis for some time. His mother had brought him up on an enema schedule; again, as an adult, he began to give himself a long series of enemas. The persistent lateness was a part of his character pattern of denying the rejection and doing it for himself.

An unusual situation was presented in the therapy of Elliot, a 22-year-old student who originally came because of an unhappy engagement. More precisely, he had become engaged to a girl without wanting to do so, and suffered through six months of torture before he could bring himself to tell her that he did not want her. It was noted in Elliot's analysis that he came at precisely the right time. This was so unusual that it was called to his attention. He then explained that actually he came an hour earlier, and would walk up and down in front of the analyst's building, keeping his eye on the corner clock all the while. This corner clock, on top of a bank, registered the time every minute. He had calculated that it required exactly three minutes to get from the corner to the analyst's office. When the clock registered three minutes before the appointed hour, he would immediately come up to the office.

The production of this material led to some important new insights into Elliot's personality. He had pretended to be completely indifferent toward the analyst and the whole analytical process. He came because he had problems, such as a broken marriage, and certain obsessional rituals, but in reality, he cared nothing about the analyst; this was just a technical procedure that he was going to use as long as he had to. The analysis of his time pattern made it clear that he was blocking off any admission of tender feelings for the analyst, just as he had the compulsively defensive need to block off tender feelings for people in his environment.

2) Talking

In complying with the request to communicate, the patient may do so in many different ways. Everything that he does or says is of some significance. What is of particular concern here are the resistances involved with the request. These resistances may be either withholding material or the more striking case of prolonged silence.

Withholding material is one of the most striking examples of a powerful transference resistance. The patient knows that in order to be helped, he must say freely what comes to mind, yet certain facts or feelings are concealed for fear of what the analyst might do. This fear involves a projection of his critical superego to the therapist, who is then unconsciously seen as critical or disapproving.

In the famous case which has been called The Rat Man, Freud, at one point, asked the patient for a picture of his girl friend. This aroused such a strong protest from the patient that he was ready to quit treatment; eventually his feelings were worked out.[32] At another point the patient concealed for some time his suspicion that Freud was related to a certain Freud in Budapest who had committed one of the most notorious crimes of that day. Here his hostility to Freud (he's really a robber in disguise) comes to the fore. These instances are typical; what the patient withholds is either self-damaging in his eyes or will offend the therapist.

Often enough, the material withheld is of a sexual nature. But with surprising frequency, it is found that almost any kind of material can be withheld, once it has acquired an unfavorable cathexis in the patient's unconscious. Such a procedure is one way of making the unconscious conscious. The patient learns that what has been horrifying him so long need not be so horrifying to another person.

> Bryan stated a number of times that there was one thing he could not bring himself to tell the analyst. In spite of pressure from time to time, he would not reveal what it was. Finally, after several hundred sessions, he brought it out: he had never in his life brushed his teeth. First the therapist had to help the patient understand why this was withheld; it fitted in with his image of himself as a dirty little boy. One of his symptoms in childhood was having bowel movements in his pants, which always made him feel ridiculous in the eyes of the other kids. Once this secret came out, the image built up as a child could be discussed more directly, and the necessary changes brought about.

When material is consciously withheld, what is important is not the secret, as such, but what forces make the patient hold on to the secret with such tenacity. This fits in with the general principle: Interpret resistance before content. Through the consistent analysis of this resistance, considerable insight is gained into the patient's character structure.

> For several months Lyle would not reveal the name of his girl friend, with whom he was carrying on an illicit affair. As a rationalization, he insisted that the therapist was only human, and that he could misuse this material, though when this was gone into, he could not say exactly how it could harm the girl or him. What did come to mind was a memory that when he was about 20, he went to a dance hall and met his father there, who asked him not to say anything to mother. It also appeared that much of his life had been lived saving up for future pleasures; he would suffer 50 weeks of the year if he could only have two weeks in which he could be really happy. Withholding the girl friend's name was thus merely part of a broader pattern of viewing life as a burden punctuated by a few secret pleasures.

Anytime that a patient has secrets they must, of course, be approached tactfully, since an absolute demand that he reveal everything could be too much for the patient's ego to take. Once a therapist bears in mind that why the secret is kept is more important than the secret itself, he should be able to work out the practical details.

Many patients screen and color the material produced no matter how hard the therapist tries to get them to disclose everything. With these patients, it is wise to ask from time to time: "Is there anything which you haven't been able to mention lately, for any reason?" When this is answered in the affirmative, the resulting material may be very productive.

> Roger, an 18-year-old boy who kept to himself a good deal, was asked at one point routinely, "Is there anything you haven't been able to say lately?" It turned out that he had a dream which he would rather not talk about. Eventually he did; the dream brought out some homosexual material which the patient had deliberately been avoiding for quite a while (see p. 67).

Prolonged Silence. This is one of the most puzzling of all resistances, since every patient knows full well that he can only get better by talking. Yet there are patients who may be silent for really prolonged periods. A case was once presented to a psychoanalytic society in which a patient had been silent for two years. While this is quite extreme, it is not so unusual for patients at some stage in their analysis to be silent for one or two sessions. A symposium published in the *Journal of the American Psychoanalytic Association* in 1961 presented a number of cases in which silences had been quite lengthy.[33]

Unlike the previous resistance, this kind of silence is not so much a conscious withholding as a frank admission of despair. What good would it do, the patient is saying, in effect, even if I told you everything? Such feelings of despair come up from time to time during every analysis and should be thoroughly explored whenever they do surface.

> Dr. Y., who was in intensive analysis five times a week, would invariably spend at least one of the five hours asleep on the couch. After such a session, he would leave thoroughly refreshed. These sleeping sessions, were, he once said, the most fruitful of all, because they represented the only time of the week when he could find complete relaxation. This man was a drug addict who was in constant fear that he would be apprehended by the authorities for breaking the law and equally fearful that he could not give up the drug without the most serious consequences.

A colleague reports the case of a man who was silent for two ses-

sions. At the end of the second session he finally blurted out: I love
you.

In understanding these puzzling experiences, it should be borne in
mind that the structure of the therapy centers around the establishing
of a relationship and clarifying the resistances that the relationship
(the transference) goes through. If one or two sessions are spent silent
or asleep, they can be most revealing of what is going on in the patient's mind. Here again it becomes clear that intellectual insight is a
secondary factor in the whole therapeutic process. The curative factor is a growing awareness of what the patient is doing to the therapist
which, in turn, is a reflection of what he is doing with other people.

Freud suggested that whenever the patient is silent, he has some
thought about the analyst which he does not wish to reveal. This is a
good empirical basis on which to proceed. The despair felt by the
silent patient is that there is no hope of ever reaching a meaningful
interchange with the therapist; this despair can be based on a variety
of dynamic factors, such as heterosexual or homosexual desire, anger,
dependency, and so on.

3) Fee

Since money plays such a crucial role in our culture, it is no surprise
that it also plays a significant part in the resistances in psychotherapy.
Certain general precautions should be observed by the therapist. The
fee should be fixed at a level that the patient can afford. If the patient
cannot afford the therapist's fee then he should be referred to another
therapist who will see him at a lower rate. It is a serious mistake to
require a patient to pay an excessive portion of his income for analytical help. This depends on many factors, including the experience of
the analyst and the particular needs of the patient. With some patients,
particularly suicidals and masochistic personalities who function
poorly, it is essential to see them as often as possible, preferably five
days a week. With others, however, the experienced analyst can often
get better results on a once or twice a week basis than the less experienced one on a five times a week basis. The resolution of this question must always be made on the basis of a variety of practical considerations.

In general, whatever method the patient chooses to pay for the
therapy should be considered satisfactory, but running up any large
bill over a period of time should not be permitted. This invariably
interferes with the course of the analysis.

At a later stage in the analysis, the question often comes up of whether the fee should be increased when the patient has had some improvement in his earning capacity. In general, a majority of patients have an increase in earning power after some time in therapy. The same principles, however, apply as before. An increase in fee may be warranted, but should be requested only if it can be met with reasonable comfort within the patient's means.

Within these limitations, the patient's refusal to pay the fee agreed upon can have a variety of different meanings. Usually, as in other life situations where people show an excessive amount of financial dependency, the unwillingness to pay is an indication of a wish to be taken care of. The patient is making a parent figure out of the therapist, and is unconsciously or sometimes quite consciously asking him to take care of her. Here are several clinical examples:

Nina, a 28-year-old clerical worker, came to therapy because she felt that her emotional conflicts were interfering with her ability to get married. In spite of several opportunities, she had been, as yet, unable to marry. After a short period in therapy she began to create difficulties about payments almost every time that they were due. It had been arranged to make payments by the month. At first, this was agreeable, but later she began to rebel against it.

Nina was the youngest of three children. The next oldest sibling was eight years older. She had been babied throughout childhood not only by her parents and older siblings, but also by other members of the family. She frankly admitted that she "could not manage money." Analysis revealed that there had been many financial difficulties in her life. She liked to be good to herself, even at one time having an answering service for her private needs when this was entirely beyond her means. On a number of occasions, she had given checks to other people that bounced. Several times, she was in debt to a number of her friends. In the long run, she always managed to pay her debts but only after a considerable battle had been fought. The refusal to pay the analytic fee was coupled with a strong resentment toward men that came out in this disguised fashion. Although she bitterly resented the consistent analysis of her refusal to pay on time, the material produced proved to be very illuminating.

Al, a 40-year-old teacher, likewise showed a tremendous resistance to paying the fee agreed upon, although it was easily within his means. It appeared that he did the same thing with money in other life situations; for example, he had simply neglected to pay his Federal income taxes for several years in a row, thereby creating a most difficult situation for himself. Al was the second of three siblings. The oral nature of his character was strongly apparent in a variety of different kinds of material.

Not infrequently, money is used as an alibi to break off treatment because the patient is too embarrassed or too shy to bring up the real reason. In these cases, the therapist can do little more than discuss the reality situation as carefully as possible with the patient; however, since the average therapist in private practice does not conduct the same kind of inquiry into the patient's finances as a social agency, he is at a loss if the patient deliberately conceals or misrepresents his assets. In general, a direct attack on the money problem is less fruitful than a probing into the dynamics of what creates the difficulty. Here are several clinical vignettes.

Herman wanted to start analysis with Dr. M. In the first session, Herman related how he had had sex with his sister-in-law when he was 17. Dr. M. pointlessly inquired: "Do you feel that that was ethical?" Herman did not continue with Dr. M., the ostensible reason being that he had only a fixed sum of money at his disposal, and Dr. M. wanted some assurance that he would not put any time limit on the therapy. Later, Herman went to another therapist who did not raise these questions. Although the fee was the same as Dr. M.'s, no problems arose in connection with the second therapist.

Myron, a 27-year-old freelance artist, came for help because of depression and a block in his creative functioning. He had enough money to pay for several months of therapy.

Although it was extremely difficult for him, Myron was determined to make a living by selling his paintings rather than by some irrelevant occupation. He just managed to scrape through, but the analytic fee was of course a problem.

In this dilemma Myron asked if he could pay for part of the fee with one or more paintings. This is a request often made by artists. Although it interferes with treatment in some ways, the alternative of forcing the patient to work for the analysis interferes in other ways. In this case the analyst agreed.

In about a year the depression lifted, Myron was relating to women again, and he felt that he was back on a constructive course in life. The therapy was terminated, although it was clear that at some future time much more should be done.

Myron stayed away from therapy for a number of years. During this period he had a one-man show, during which a psychiatrist approached him to inquire about his life. He turned this into a fantasy that the psychiatrist esteemed him so highly that he was willing to analyze him without fee to let him develop his genius. Obviously this was the unverbalized fantasy which could not be brought out in the earlier therapy.

Some five years later, when difficulties with his wife were particularly disturbing, Myron returned to another therapist for further work. This time he recognized the need for change, and was willing to pay for it directly.

If a patient at any point in therapy has no visible means of paying for the therapy, it is important to inquire how he expects to handle the financial problem. This will provide good insights into his ability to handle reality. Sometimes, patients who rely on magical methods of dealing with the world simply have to be told point-blank that they must come to grips with the real problem before they can make any further progress.

The question is often raised about the situation where someone else pays for the therapy. Here there are two common instances: one is where a child's therapy is being paid for by a parent, the other is where the wife's therapy is being paid for by the husband. Problems differ in each case.

When the child's therapy is being paid for by the parent (we are talking here of a child who is a late adolescent or an early adult), it is essential to pay adequate attention to the person who is financing the therapy. Otherwise, treatment may be broken off abruptly without any further ado, especially when the patient is making progress of a kind which the parent disapproves of, which is all too often the case. Sometimes it is necessary to tell the parent point-blank: I will accept this case if you pay for the therapy and do not involve yourself in it in any way. If the parent then refuses, the therapy should be terminated. If the parent accepts the condition, then the child (usually a late adolescent) has the absolute assurance that nothing he communicates will get through to the parent and that he can continue as long as is reasonably necessary. A not untypical case is the following:

Orville, a 19-year-old boy who had flunked out of college, was being seen therapeutically twice a week. He was involved in terrible fights with both his parents, especially his mother, who was also markedly disturbed. His mother had actually fabricated a story that she was going to therapy, when she was not really doing so. In the course of the fights, the mother, at one point, told the boy that if he did not obey her, she would cut out a session. When this was made known to the therapist he laid down the condition that the mother should not interfere further with the therapy. This condition was reluctantly accepted, and the case could proceed satisfactorily.

A different situation arises when the husband pays for his wife's therapy. Here again many times the husband will demand only that kind of improvement that fits in with his view of the world, while any other is seen as a worsening of his wife's condition. It is always possible to lay down the condition that the husband should not interfere in any way with his wife's therapy, but it is not possible to stop the husband from terminating treatment when he sees results that run counter to his neurotic demands. This type of situation presents practical difficulties of the most severe kind. When it does occur, it is wise to look about for some way in which the wife can finance her own therapy, perhaps through her own family or some part-time job that will keep her independent of the husband.

4) The Couch

Not infrequently a good many resistances arise in connection with the use of the couch. Sometimes patients will refuse outright to lie on the couch. One patient insisted on lying on his stomach; when pressed for a reason he said he just felt like it. Some will alternately lie on the couch and sit up. Others will even use the couch as a resistance, afraid to face their feelings about looking at the analyst directly. Many other variations are encountered.

In general, the couch leads to a regression, which the therapist must be sure that he is able to handle. This regression involves the release of hitherto forbidden impulses; whether the patient will be able to handle these impulses, and how, depends on the strength and structure of his ego.

A rare instance of direct defiance of the therapist in connection with the couch occurred with Elliot, a 22-year-old student who absolutely refused to use the couch under any circumstances. He demanded that the therapist prove to him, preferably by means of valid statistics, that patients who lie on the couch could be shown to get better more quickly than those who did not. No interpretation could deter him from his persistent battle of the couch, reinforced at times by superficial reading of some analytic authors who labeled the couch a "rigid Freudian dogma." One day he even came in and threw his coat on the couch (another peculiarity of his was his refusal to hang the coat in the clothes closet provided for patients) saying: "Now I've used the couch." When this was interpreted as a sign of contempt, he argued vociferously that it was really a display of good feeling on his part.

Elliot's fight against the couch ran parallel with constant fighting in almost every area of his life. His greatest delight was to pick his instructors to pieces. On dates, he would like to take the girl bowling, give her a few pointers, then show her how badly he could defeat her. The continual analysis of his anger slowly brought about an emergence of positive feelings for other people.

SUGGESTIONS FOR FURTHER READING

The literature on resistance is enormous; it makes up the bulk of every discussion of technique. Nevertheless, the greatest part of it remains unsystematic. Still basic is Freud, "Remembering, Repeating and Working Through (1914)" (*S.E.* Vol. XII). The relevant portions of Greenson (*op. cit.*), Glover (*op. cit.*) and Fenichel (*op. cit.*) are all excellent. W. Reich (*op. cit.*), in spite of his one-sidedness, is still instructive.

H. Kohut, "Panel Report: Clinical and Theoretical Aspects of Resistance," *J. Am. Psychoanalytic Assoc.* 5, 1957, 548–555, presents a variety of viewpoints. See also R. Loewenstein, "Some Remarks on Defenses, Autonomous Ego and Psychoanalytic Technique," *Int. J. Psychoanalysis* 35, 1954, 188–193 and J. Lampl-de Groot, "On Defense and Development," *Psychoanalytic Study of the Child* 12, 1957, 114–126

On silence as a resistance see R. Loewenstein, "Some Remarks on the Role of Speech in Psychoanalytic Technique," *Int. J. Psychoanalysis* 37, 1956, 460–468, and Symposium in *J. Am. Psychoanalytic Assoc.* 9, 1961, especially J. Arlow, "Silence and the Theory of Technique," *J. Am. Psychoanalytic Assoc.* 9, 1961, 44–55. See also R. Calogeras, "Silence as a Technical Parameter in Psychoanalysis," *Int. J. Psychoanalysis* 48, 1967, 536–558.

CHAPTER 9

Resistance: Indirect Sabotage

He who hopes to learn the fine art of the game of chess from books will soon discover that only the opening and closing moves of the game admit of exhaustive systematic description, and that the endless variety of the moves which develop from the opening defies description; the gap left in the instructions can only be filled in by the zealous study of games fought out by master players.

Freud: *On Beginning the Treatment* (*1913*)

INDIRECT RESISTANCES

Most patients overcome the more direct resistances described in the previous chapter in a fairly short time. However, a large number of more subtle or indirect resistances prevail throughout the entire analysis, and the careful consideration of these resistances consumes a large part of the whole therapeutic work. Again the classification offered here is phenomenological.

1) Overemphasis on Reality

This is by far the most common of all resistances. In one sense it may be said to be the core resistance of all, since it is common to every defensive process. The patient always insists that he is dealing with reality, while the analyst is always trying to help him to see that he is dealing with fantasy.

In Chapter 2 it was noted that the patient who responds best to therapy is the one who has the optimal guilt-fantasy combination. As long as the patient harps on reality, he cannot feel much guilt or responsibility for what is happening to him. Accordingly he becomes reluctant to bring up his fantasy material. Reality considerations must be overcome before he can be led to deal with his fantasies.

Depending upon the patient's life circumstances, the overemphasis on reality can take many different forms. In marital disputes, wife will blame husband; husband will blame wife. In parent-child controversy, again each side will blame the other. The therapist must go to great lengths to help the patient see that regardless of what the partner is doing or has done, he bears some responsibility for his troubles and that only by looking into himself can he have a happier life.

When this resistance is prominent, the therapist is often accused of being oblivious to the realities of this world. When this reproach is more carefully analyzed, it usually turns out that the real trouble is that the patient has not evaluated the reality situation properly.

> Al, a college professor, was refused tenure after he had been there for some three years. He went into a panic-like state, with the feeling that this was the end of the world for him. When people told him that it was not, he insisted that it was. Much of his time he spent ruminating on how he might have handled the various interviews differently so that he could get tenure. Eventually, he was helped to see that his severe reaction was all out of proportion to the reality, that it was really he that could not see reality, not the analyst or any of his friends or relatives who were trying to cheer him up.

In situations of this kind, the question often comes up of how far the analyst should go in his investigation of the reality situation. When technical knowledge is required, sometimes it is possible to acquire it, sometimes not. The therapist must build up a good deal of expertise to handle all kinds of problems that are not within his own personal knowledge, so that he can really help the patient distinguish what is reality and what is not.

When the patient harps on certain aspects of reality over and over again, it sometimes begins to take on delusional qualities; in fact, according to theory, this is precisely what does happen in the formation of a delusion. Thus in therapy when these reality questions are taken up, delusions are forestalled. In such cases, without therapy a psychosis might have been the eventual outcome.

An example could be taken from the fear of having a small penis. It is safe to say that almost every man in analysis suffers from the conviction that his penis is too small. This can be understood theoretically as the result of comparing his penis with father's in the formative years, and never getting over that fixation point. The small penis is also one way of expressing his fear that father has castrated him. Sometimes patients try to check on this by reality measures, such as measuring their penises or consulting their physician. This never changes the conviction. One man went to several physicians, all of whom assured him that his penis was of normal size. He asked one physician to give him testosterone; the physician agreed, although he said in advance that it was of no value. Even after the testosterone, the patient felt that his penis was too small.

In one sense, every resistance that comes up is connected with reality; the patient asserts that such and such is really the case, where the analyst takes a more questioning attitude. As this analytic questioning attitude is communicated to the patient more and more, he gets an increasing sense of mastery over his environment, coupled with a decreasing sense of compulsivity about his actions.

The argument is frequently brought up that, after all, the patient, who is functioning in the world, is not distorting entirely, but is seeing the picture realistically. This has also been applied to the transference, the claim being that the patient perceives some real aspect of the therapist's activities which should not be tossed off as a transferred reaction to his mother or father. It is true that a good deal of what the patient sees may be realistic, yet the distortion still holds for the way in which he sees it. An analogy may be drawn with a Swiss cheese. One person sees the cheese, another the holes, yet both are correct.

Larry, a homosexual man in his 40s, would quite often try to draw the analyst into a theoretical discussion of why society is against homosexuals. While agreeing on the senselessness of the methods the police use to capture homosexuals and prosecute them, it was still important to point out to Larry that his was a very one-sided view of the world. Heterosexual activity is also not condoned in our society, except within certain limits. And there are far deeper problems at stake than the societal attitude toward homosexuals. Larry, however, used this as a persistent resistance coming back every once in a while to the analyst's blindness toward the persecuting society. In one way, the homosexual binds his paranoia when he takes such a tack.

The consistent analysis of reality resistances also leads to a greater feeling of freedom of choice on the part of the patient. Where otherwise he would see himself with one or two implacable alternatives, neither of which could be of lasting advantage to him, now he sees the world in a much more expanded form. Sometimes it is wise to ask the question: What alternatives do you see for yourself? This question alone may open new vistas to the patient, who would otherwise bog down in self-pity or senseless reproaches about what might have been.

Not infrequently the reality resistance masks some deep-lying fantasy that can only be uncovered by persistent probing. What emerges is that the patient looks upon his fantasy as an essential part of the reality, whereas the therapist can help him to see it for what it is.

> Nina, an attractive girl of 28, was convinced that she was physically unattractive to men. The fact that she had lots of men after her, and had had since her teens, meant nothing. She was so convinced of her unattractiveness that she would not even talk about it. Repeatedly, however, she tied it up with the envy of other girls; if I were prettier, all the girls on the beach would look at me because I would attract the attention of all the men. With this addition, the homosexual penis-envy and exhibitionistic wishes could be brought to the fore. The deepest fantasy of all was her wish to be a man, so that no feminine body, no matter how built, could satisfy her.

At times the patient distorts reality to a marked degree; persistent analysis should then be able to bring out the distortion and clarify to what extent it is merely wishful thinking. In some cases a certain amount of ingenuity is necessary to make the reality clear to the patient.

> Evelyn worked in an office as a secretary. After some years there, she became convinced that one of the bosses was in love with her, proof of which was that he kept on staring at her all day long. Considerable attention was devoted to this man, since she had developed a real crush on him. Nothing seemed to move her, however, until one day the therapist asked her to draw a diagram of her office. From this diagram, it became apparent that while she could look at his office all day long, he could not look at her because his office door was closed. When this was brought out, she realized that she was the one who was doing the staring. Other voyeuristic habits came to light with this piece of analysis; for example, at night when alone in her room with nothing to do, she would stare at other apartments with a pair of binoculars she had bought for that purpose.

From the analysis of the reality resistances, it is gradually brought out that the patient's concept of reality is always distorted to some extent; loss of contact with reality can scarcely be maintained as a criterion of a disturbance because it occurs in every case. The differences are primarily matters of degree.

In this way, the therapeutic process helps to provide the person not only with new insights into his inner life, but also with new ways of perceiving the outer world. This is particularly true of the people in his life who, before therapy, are viewed as happy gods and are gradually made into unhappy mortals as he overcomes his blind spots. But it is also true of the inanimate world that surrounds the person all the time.

Daisy had a great need to move from one apartment to another all the time. Within a few years, she had been in half a dozen places. Each time she would find the new apartment delightful at first, then begin to pick it apart. When the therapist pointed out this pattern, she remonstrated that with his money, he did not have to live in the kinds of crummy places that she was forced to settle for. Interpretations of the apartment as symbolic of her body did not get far. But with improvement in her love life, she was able to be more appreciative of the apartment she finally chose.

A particularly difficult resistance occurs when the patient tries to pin down the exact amount of time the analysis will take. Most people know by now that intensive psychotherapy is a long-term process that frequently lasts for years. After some initial hesitation, most patients will accept this as a fact of therapeutic life, realizing in the meantime that they are grateful to have someone take a sustained interest in them over a long period. Others, however, will object to the duration strenuously, saying over and over again that there must be something quicker.

Many of the patients who pick on time as a resistance are expecting some magical solutions to their problems. Indeed, the image of time, like everything else, is subjected to careful scrutiny in the course of therapy. Children live in a world of magic; to them magical solutions are very plausible. The adult who is expecting something of that kind is holding onto the vanished world of childhood.

A particularly severe form of this resistance was displayed by Peter, a 26-year-old man, who entered therapy because of a deep dissatisfaction with life. Peter was a chemist who did research work, and he was accustomed to precise formulations. Shortly after he began, he demanded to know how long the therapy would take. This was handled in an analytic manner: no direct time was given, but inquiry was made into what time meant to him. One of his fantasies was a magical one that a woman would walk up to him on the street and invite him up to her room to have sex. There were other magical fantasies connected with his work which for that reason proved to be very frustrating since he was at a level where he carried out the orders of others rather than thinking up new ideas.

The question of how long the analysis would take was raised by him over and over again whenever some difficult period was reached and each time the answer proved to be unsatisfactory to him. Finally, he consulted another analyst and asked him how long it would take. This man estimated four to five more years. Hereupon, Peter quit treatment, deciding to resign himself to his miseries.

Time may be used as a resistance in many other ways. At the beginning of treatment, the patient may mask his disappointment by saying—it's too early, I can't expect much change yet. Later on, he may become increasingly angry because of the amount of time he has devoted to the process. In both cases, he is using this method of venting his spleen on the therapist.

Another time resistance, seen somewhat less frequently, is that the patient's schedule is so busy that he cannot spare the time needed for therapy. This, however, is too obvious a dodge and most patients quickly see through it as a way of covering up some deeper conflict.

In Elliot's case, a peculiar resistance came up when he demanded hours at a certain time during the week, stating that if he could not get those hours, he would discontinue therapy. Eventually convenient hours were arranged, after which the implied blackmail and his handling of the hours could be analyzed. Elliot was full of all kinds of resentment; one session he devoted the whole hour to tearing up a briefcase which he said he no longeer needed. The time was being used as another bludgeon; his relationship with his mother was, as might be expected, a highly ambivalent one in which he alternated between being her lousy brat and her spoiled darling. He was fearful of this ambivalence in other people, and defended himself against close relationships most rigorously because of it.

Some patients take advantage of the therapeutic situation, in which they know that the therapist will try not to get into arguments with them, as areas in which they can release all kinds of objections to the analytic process. They may pick on the time, the fee, the couch, the use of dreams, or any other aspect of it; what counts is that they can argue indefinitely, thereby avoiding their own problems.

Outside analysis, this attitude is known as logic-chopping or a sophomoric approach. And indeed it is most often seen among male college students, who use this opportunity to live out the Oedipal hostility to father.

> Roger showed an unusual resistance when, shortly after treatment began, he came out with a flat statement that happiness was not a proper goal in life. He did not want to be happy. In books, where he had spent much of his libido, people were never very happy (incidentally a fair criticism of the books that he had been given to read). Hence, he demanded of the therapist: "Why should I be happy?" This was handled by extensive discussion of man as a biological organism, what life is about, as well as the more usual analytic material about his parents and the immediate environment. Of his paternal grandfather he said: "Nobody could ever by the remotest stretch of the imagination refer to him as a happy man." Still, it took a long time to convince him that his rejection of happiness was part of the emotional climate of the family in which he grew up rather than a valid philosophical proposition.

It is a wise rule that one should never enter into an argument with a patient. If something comes up that seems to lead to a flat disagreement, it is better to avoid the topic for the time being than to slug it out.

> Dr. L., a psychiatric resident, was told by his patient, Jim, that Jim's I.Q. was higher than Dr. L.'s, whereupon Dr. L. asked to have his I.Q. measured. Triumphantly, he showed Jim that it was two points higher than Jim's. Shortly thereafter, Jim terminated treatment.

2) Unreasonable Demands

Many patients make all kinds of demands on the therapist even after it has been explained to them that it is not customary to accede to such requests in therapy. They may ask for theater tickets, or advice on how to get into school, or information on medical or psychological topics. Or the demand may be more specifically therapeutic, such as asking for extra time at the end of a session, or asking for more extra sessions than the therapist can allow. Patients soon learn what is permissible and what is not in any therapeutic situation, and if they wish to do so they can express their childish desires for some transgression of the rules. When these unreasonable demands are refused, as they have to be, the patient becomes angry and then says, in effect, "You see, you do not love me either."

Sometimes the therapist is strongly tempted to give in to the patient's demands, only to find that a new and more imperative demand will take its place. Balint has offered a distinction between the benign and malignant forms of regression.[34] In the benign form, the patient will be able to accept the rejections; in the malignant form, every gratification will be followed by a new demand.

> Wilton, a young boy suffering from hallucinations that people were calling him names, asked for permission to stay on in the therapist's library. This was granted. Then he asked that he be fed, clothed, taken care of and, in effect, supported. When this was denied, he became so difficult that he had to be rehospitalized. As a sequel, though, it is to be noted that after a two-month stay in the hospital in the course of which the acute psychotic symptomatology disappeared, the transference to the therapist remained very strong, and when he came back, progress was fairly rapid. Unfortunately an incurable physical illness nullified the effects of the psychotherapy.

Sometimes patients go even further and ask the therapist to lend them money. This would put the therapist in the position of the parent, an identification that he does best to avoid at all times. It is imperative to maintain an adequate social distance for therapy to be effective.

> Orville was a college sophomore who came to treatment because he had flunked out. One of his symptoms was to be a hail-fellow-well-met on the surface, yet almost devoid of friends underneath. As soon as he met strangers, he would begin to take familiarities with them which were quite provocative. At one point, his father refused to give him money; he then asked the therapist to lend it to him. This was refused. In his rage, he broke an ashtray in the therapist's office. He was asked to pay for it, which he did. As his need to become too familiar too quickly was analyzed and outgrown, his effectiveness in the outside world increased considerably. It was clear that the jovial, on-the-spot familiarity concealed a wish to have the other person become a parent to him.

One of the most important kinds of demands that patients make nowadays, especially in the past few years, is the *demand for drugs*. This is essentially a form of resistance, spurred on by physicians in articles in the popular journals that extol the virtues of drugs without really evaluating all the factors involved.

A real question arises here about how effective the various drugs in use are. Obviously, their effectiveness depends on the degree and nature of the patient's pathology. In practice, it is well to assume that once the patient is in psychotherapy, drugs, with rare exceptions, are an attempt to circumvent the pain involved in the therapeutic encounter.

Drugs involve some change in bodily feelings; hence the resistance involved in their use is that the patient wishes to give himself some kind of bodily feeling which, in some way as yet unverbalized, will clear up all of his problems. With this rationale, patients can find a fair amount of support and expert opinion, from the Reichians among the psychiatrists to the proponents of LSD among the psychologists. In the average case, it is sufficient to tell the patient that the profession considers these devices undesirable in a case such as his.

But often this is quite inadequate and the patient insists on seeing for himself. Among the college population, in particular, drugs are very easy to come by, and their use seems to be widespread. To the adolescent, the overthrow of authority represented by the drugs, the striking bodily changes, and the magical appeal may all mount up to an irresistible lure. With some patients, there is little danger in the drugs; they take marijuana or LSD or dexamyl, have a reaction, then go back to the therapy. But many get stuck on the drugs and have more adverse reactions.

Roger, a college sophomore, demanded to be given drugs, since his "analysis wasn't working." He was an isolated boy who had no physical contact with any other human being. This had been pointed out to him many times but his pattern changed slowly. Once in desperation, he took a form of LSD from a friend of his, and had the most extraordinary sensations. The therapist suggested that he was having a substitute homosexual experience, which surprisingly made good sense to him. From this point on, the demand for drugs lessened and the normal therapeutic work was even more effective.

Actually what is involved is a careful evaluation of the realities described by the patients. To arrive at this evaluation, the therapist makes judicious use of his general knowledge of human beings and of his powers of inference from the distorted material presented to him. A judgment is required of the therapist. If another person is really impossible, or the difficulties are too great, then the therapist has to help the patient to focus on why it is difficult for him to change the situation. If, however, the reality seems reasonably adequate, then it is necessary for the therapist to focus on why the patient gets lost in his complaints about a situation that realistically does not call for such an attitude.

Another unreasonable demand that is frequently made is that the analyst should directly intervene in the real life situation of the patient and change it in the direction desired. This differs from the previous resistance only in that the focus is on the life situation rather than some specific person. It need scarcely be said that such a demand cannot be granted, yet it may take up an extraordinary amount of time.

> Samuel was a gifted research worker in a rather obscure field. By virtue of diligence, ingenuity, and hard work, he made most unusual contributions to the field. This occupied his spare time over a period of many years until he had finally gained recognition from his colleagues. But he filled the analytic hours with incessant complaints that his colleagues did not recognize him, did not support him, did not give him the encouragement that he was looking for. It took him a long time to see that what he wanted from the analyst was direct intervention in the field, to change the attitude of his professional *confrères*. Finally, after this had been worked through over a long time, a period of many years, he was able to recognize that the kinds of appreciation that he did get from the field were really what could reasonably be expected.

Finally, mention should be made of those patients who engage in endless complaints about a reality situation, unconsciously or consciously demanding that the analyst change the situation, and yet upon deeper search, reveal that they would not really be satisfied with any change. Their unconscious goal is to be able to complain about the world, a compromise masochistic solution to their problems. This is a variation of the overemphasis on the release of feelings, a resistance that will be discussed in more detail below.

3) Copelessness: The Negative Therapeutic Reaction

No reaction is more puzzling, more disheartening when it occurs and more difficult to overcome than the feeling of hopelessness expressed by the patient after several months of seemingly effective therapy. A gifted patient of the writer's who displayed this reaction coined for it the term "copelessness," which adds the inability to cope to the feeling of hopelessness. It is an excellent term, which will be used from now on. Because of its characteristics, it is also known as the negative therapeutic reaction.

Jerome Frank [35] has rightly stressed the central importance of hope in all forms of therapy, analytically oriented or not. And even in learning theory, Mowrer,[36] on the basis of a reexamination of the evidence, has concluded that what the animal learns in the traditional conditioning experiment is the positive feeling of hope that some reward will be forthcoming, or the negative feeling that none will be there; thus here, too, hope is seen as a basic reaction in all organisms.

In intensive psychotherapy, this is even more true. To a greater or lesser degree, every patient has some feelings of despair about his life. He can only see the problems; the manner in which the therapy will get him out of them remains a mystery. It is the therapist who always has to maintain the perspective, to be able to see ahead well past the immediate discomfiture, and to the eventual resolution. In this foresight, his own hope for the patient often carries him along more than anything else.

Much is known by now about the negative therapeutic reaction. Its discovery by Freud in the early years of psychoanalysis led to the formulation of the superego concept. Freud noted that many patients who could verbalize all the explanations offered to them still came back over and over again with the same symptoms; he reasoned that there must be some inner force that prevents the utilization of the insights gained and he identified this force with the superego, the internalized voice of the parents. Since then, a great deal has been learned about how parents build up this sense of despair in their children and of the many ways it can be brought out in later life.

Daisy was a young girl of 19 when she came to treatment. Although she had been very bright in school, her father had explicitly told her that it was a waste of time. Whenever she undertook anything he would say, "What are you knocking yourself out for?" Her mother reiterated that she was just an ordinary girl, and that she should not try to do too much in life. It is small wonder that after some initial response, Daisy became convinced that her case was hopeless, and that she could not cope with it—a typical case of copelessness.

As in the case of Daisy, the negative therapeutic reaction is understood in terms of the crushing effect of the superego. Much as the parents told Daisy in so many words that she would never amount to much, now the superego tells her the same thing. Fortunately, the reaction here came after some therapeutic effect had been achieved, so that she was willing to persist in her efforts to get better. If the reaction comes too early, there is a treatment crisis, the patient leaves and nothing is accomplished.

In these cases, it is a wise idea to analyze the superego pressure before anything else. The patient is brought face to face immediately with the attempts that her parents have made to crush her, and with the ways in which she is repeating these in the therapy. After this pressure has been lifted, other interpretations will be more easily handled, but, until it is, the patient frequently comes back over and over again with the retort, "Yes, I see all that; what good does it do me?"

At first sight, it may not seem that this should properly be classified as a resistance, much less connected with the transference. Yet analysis of the reaction shows that this is invariably the case. What the patient is resisting is the appearance of positive feelings that were forbidden by the parents, and in therapy, these positive feelings are related to the therapist. Although an oversimplification, it could be said that the patient gets better through the positive feelings about he therapist, and is made worse by his negative ones. By insisting that he will never get better, the patient is unconsciously releasing some of his anger toward the therapist.

Feelings of copelessness have other roots in the childhood background. (For a good review, cf. paper on severe regression during analysis.[37]) In the case of Daisy, for example, the parents themselves were imbued with this sense about their lives. They fought continuously. Whatever love there was between them had disappeared a long time ago. Father, although quite ill, would never consult a physician—he was certain that the verdict would certainly be a sentence of death. Actually, his life might have been prolonged a number of years if he had sought out medical advice sooner.

Many parents are able to relate to their children only when they are young. Once they reach adolescence the threat of emancipation becomes so overpowering that constant fights between parents and child begin to come up. The adolescent, himself, is going through great turmoil; when the parent reacts by trying to crush him, the conflicts become even more intense. A child may, and frequently does, rebel; this is the environment that breeds addiction, sexual promiscuity, crime, and damaging activities of all kinds. In this dilemma, the parents frequently redouble their efforts to prove to the child that he is no good, until it becomes a self-fulfilling prophecy.

When the child is restricted too much, he often resorts to the weapon of revenge. From the earliest years, when the child deliberately refuses to eat mother's food, or go to the toilet when mother asks him to do so, revenge becomes an important drive. A child takes revenge on the parent by not performing well in the outside world, knowing full well that that is what the parent wants most of him.

Later in therapy, the patient tries to take revenge on the therapist by not getting better. This kind of revenge, paradoxical though it may seem, can become an enormously meaningful drive for some patients; in a few cases it has been driven as far as suicide, with the thought: "I'll show the world what a lousy psychiatrist (or psychologist) he is." When a human being becomes attached to a parent substitute in a masochistic way, the vicissitudes of his self-damaging activities may be, and often are, quite serious.

> Bryan, after much apparent progress at one point, bogged down in his therapy. In his associations, he was proving to the world not only that his therapist was no good, but that all therapists are no good and that therapy is a futile undertaking. Much of the time he spent in libraries hunting up the literature on drugs in order to prove to the therapist and to the world that drugs were better than talking. This resistance took a long time to work out.

> In the case of Belle, the negative reaction took the form of denying the improvement that had occurred. Belle had come to treatment with a variety of problems, among others, lack of orgasm. As her sexual reactions were analyzed, she began to have orgasms. At one point, when she was feeling very bitter about her life, the therapist commented that after all certain things had changed for the better, such as her sexual reactions. Her indignant comment was that she had always been able to have orgasms, even before therapy! The distortion here served the consistent purpose of denying to the man that he had the capacity to please her.

As the above example indicates, when the patient is caught up in a battle of revenge against the therapist any or all of the defense mechanisms may be used: denial, projection, repression, reaction formation, regression, or any other. Nothing counts except getting even.

Apart from the revenge factor in copelessness, the patient may be holding out some wish from childhood which cannot possibly be gratified. It is of the utmost importance to bring this wish to the fore, to help the patient to see that he is responding to a childhood misperception of his life rather than to adult reality. Here is a typical instance:

Molly, an attractive young lady of 24, came to analysis because of indecision about marriage and indecision about her life work. She was the younger of two children, the older being a brother. Her brother had always been favored, even though her abilities in many respects were superior to his. Although she was extraordinarily productive in dreams, fantasies, and childhood memories, after several months, she bogged down in a feeling of copelessness. Eventually, she left the therapist, to try it with several others. When two succeeding attempts had failed, she came back to the initial therapist.

At this point, the feelings of copelessness came to the fore, and could be analyzed more directly. In terms of her childhood, they had two striking meanings: one was the conscious fantasy all through childhood that she was going to marry her brother, and the second was the conscious fantasy all through childhood that she would grow up to be a boy. This second fantasy was so powerful that when her first menstruation came on, she spent the whole day crying, convinced that her life had now come to an end. The fact that the two fantasies, of marrying her brother and of becoming a boy, were contradictory made no real difference; in fact, they only contributed to the copelessness.

In other life situations, Molly's most persistent resistance was an overattachment to reality. In virtually every life situation she encountered obstacles that she could not overcome; she felt copeless. Actually, she was a competent, attractive girl who was making headway in her chosen career, and who had made a reasonably satisfactory marriage. The consistent analysis of her two major childhood fantasies led to a changed attitude toward the feeling of copelessness with her present-day environment.

At the point where feelings of hopelessness arise, many therapists are tempted to switch to some other technique, convinced that the standard analytic approach has failed. This is precisely what the patient is trying to get them to do. And this is exactly why it is so important to persevere and analyze the hopeless feeling in terms of whatever material the patient has brought up. The feeling that the patient arouses in the therapist is exactly what he is unconsciously trying to arouse in other people. His copelessness has a manipulative purpose, to drive other people away, and allow him to wallow in his misery. Yet there is always the other side of the battle in the patient, the urge towards mental health, which, as Frieda Fromm-Reichman never tired of pointing out, is found in everybody.

SUGGESTIONS FOR FURTHER READING

See references to Chapter 8.

For the negative therapeutic reaction see Freud, "The Ego and the Id" (1923) (*S.E.* Vol. XIX) and "Analysis Terminable and Interminable" (1937) (*S.E.* Vol. XXIII).

CHAPTER 10

Resistance: The Continuing Battle

Masks are arrested expressions and admirable echoes of feeling, at once faithful, discreet and superlative. Living things in contact with the air must acquire a cuticle, and it is not urged against cuticles that they are not hearts; yet some philosophers seem to be angry with images for not being things, and with words for not being feelings. Words and images are like shells, no less integral parts of nature than are the substances they cover, but better addressed to the eye and more open to observation. I would not say that substance exists for the sake of appearance, or faces for the sake of masks, or the passions for the sake of poetry and virtue. Nothing arises in nature for the sake of anything else; all these phases and products are involved equally in the round of existence. . . .

Santayana: *Soliloquies in English and
Later Soliloquies*

4) Transference Excesses

The transference itself is the strongest expression of resistance, yet it is also the ally of therapy. This contradiction is resolved only by recognizing that transference is beneficial when it remains within certain limits. When it passes beyond those limits, it becomes a powerful obstacle to progress. It must then be analyzed before anything else is taken up. This point has already been touched upon in the chapters on transference, so we shall confine outselves to a few more case illustrations.

Generally, the positive transference at some point becomes excessively erotic. At that time, any excesses must be watched.

A typical situation was presented by Jacqueline, a striking blonde in her middle 20s. Jacqueline had originally applied for treatment to a hospital because she had tried to kill her young child. With two successive psychiatric residents, she had formed such strong sexual transferences that they switched her, perhaps as a defense against their own sexual feelings. When she came to the clinic, she was assigned to a young male therapist. At that time, she was seeing a man whom she thought of marrying, but about whom she had many reservations. In the therapy, she again became excessively erotic, even to the point of lifting her skirts higher and higher. In one session, she lifted her skirt all the way to her thigh, alleging that she had to adjust her garter. When the therapist pointed out that this was an obviously seductive maneuver, she replied: "How could you say that; after all you're my doctor. You can't have any sexual feelings about me." Shortly thereafter, Jacqueline married the man she had been so hesitant about, moved away to another part of the state, and had to terminate therapy.

Kermit, a 35-year-old businessman, came to therapy because of continued dissatisfaction with his marriage. At one time, he, his wife and all three children were in therapy, but this went on only briefly.

Although he was assigned to a woman who was some twenty years older, Kermit immediately initiated a sexual transference. He would come in and say, "When do we fuck?" When the therapist inquired about what was going on, he explained to her that his mind was full of sexual fantasies all the time, and that he could think of nothing else to do with a woman. In a previous therapeutic encounter with a younger woman the same thing had occurred.

Kermit could not handle the sexual excitement, nor would he accept a referral to a male therapist. Eventually he refused to pay the fee, and forced the therapist to drop him.

Marilyn, a pert young girl of 23, initially had a somewhat negative transference to the therapist, who was of about the same age as her father. After several years this became positive, and sexual fantasies began to come out both directly and indirectly. At one point she began to date a series of men, and to insist on performing fellatio on them; whether they wanted it or not, she preferred it to intercourse. When the analyst inquired about this pattern, it turned out that she was quite consciously trying to seduce him by showing him how good she could be in bed. This was handled as a resistance to her own further growth, and after some time she was able to see that it was just as important to have the man satisfy her as it was for her to satisfy the man.

Sometimes a resistance that is unmanageable can be handled with an analyst of the opposite sex. This is one of the few cases where the sex of the analyst plays a decisive role. An illustrative case is the following:

Marie was a 19-year-old girl who had suffered from poliomyelitis in childhood, for which she had been hospitalized for several years.

In the course of this hospitalization, as might have been anticipated, she developed an enormously rich fantasy life. She was left with a mild handicap in her left leg. As a result, although she was a very pretty girl, before analysis she had great difficulty forming any relationships with boys.

In her first analysis, with a man, she soon developed a violent transference. She was madly in love with him and thought about nothing but him. At one point this reached a stage where she came to his office and in a rage about his lack of response began to break up the furniture in his waiting room. He could not restrain her, and had to call the police to have her carried off to a hospital. In the hospital she calmed down immediately, and was released forthwith.

The analysis then continued with a female analyst. With her none of the violent behavior was observed. The transference was ambivalent, though largely positive. Analysis could then proceed in the usual manner.

In the case of the *negative transference,* the danger becomes acute that the patient, because of the feelings of antagonism and antipathy developed towards the analyst, will break off treatment abruptly. Some examples of this have been cited in the chapter on the first treatment crisis. Because of the danger of abrupt termination, the hostility must be brought to the fore and analyzed as soon as it appears. If it is allowed to pile up too much, it becomes unanalyzable and the patient will simply stop.

5) Somatization

For many people in our culture it is much easier to express their problems in terms of bodily symptoms than in terms of psychological anxieties. When this occurs in the course of a therapeutic process, it becomes a source of resistance, sometimes extraordinarily intense in nature, especially since the symptom could conceivably—and sometimes does—have an organic basis. Somatic symptoms should be divided into two groups: those in which a physical examination is essentially negative, and those in which there are real physical findings, but these physical findings are best understood in the light of the psychopathological history. Both of these somatic manifestations may become resistances in the course of analytic therapy.

One essential caution must be observed by the therapist in handling this kind of resistance: before interpreting any physical symptom he must first have an assurance from a competent physician that the symptom in question is not essentially organic. In order to get this assurance, the patient must either go to a physician on his own or be referred to one by the therapist. Many patients are enthusiastically overpsychosomatic, and will interpret every pain as psychological; for these patients the therapeutic problem is to get them to go to a physician, or to establish a confidential relationship with a physician in which they can really find out whether or not their pains require medical treatment. Other patients will overemphasize the organic character of their symptoms and will question any kind of interpretation involved, suggesting that there could be a physiological element. Even when the physician tells the patient pointblank that the symptom in question is psychogenic, the patient will often doubt it. Sometimes he will go to another physician or a series of physicians until he finds one who will give him the organic diagnosis that he is looking for. While the therapist is not ordinarily in a position to evaluate the physician whom the patient chooses, he should bear in mind the general orientation of the practitioner when he makes his interpretations. In general, if the patient has a good rapport with the therapist, he will be able to accept the considered opinion of the psychotherapist after all the data have been assembled.

By now research has conclusively established the fact that a large number of complaints brought to physicians are psychological in character.

In the therapeutic process, the resistance may appear as an excessive number of consultations with physicians, an unwillingness to accept any kind of psychological interpretations, or even the termination of treatment and its replacement by some physiological approach.

6) Acting Out

Acting out is best defined as any damaging activity that interferes with the psychoanalytic process. It is clear from this broad definition that the borderline between ordinary action and neurotic acting out may frequently be a most difficult one to define with any precision. Nevertheless, in spite of the problems in theoretical clarification, acting out becomes one of the most important kinds of resistances that appear in the analytic situation.

Two kinds of patients may be differentiated, in each of which the acting out plays a different role: the impulsive and the inhibited. These two can be grouped most usefully in relation to the management of anxiety. In the inhibited patient, the capacity for anxiety is considerable, and he can tolerate impulses without immediately running to action. His difficulty comes about because he inhibits his action too much rather than too little. In the addicted patient (often referred to as the acting-out patient), the problem comes about because he is unable to tolerate any anxiety. As soon as he feels any anxiety he must rush to some course of action. In these patients, it is necessary to help them to tolerate some anxiety, and inhibit the action. Thus, in these two types of patients the therapeutic tasks are at exactly opposite poles: in the inhibited patient the problem is to release action, while in the addicted the problem is to inhibit it. They must therefore be handled differently.

In the *neurotic, inhibited* patient, the analysis proceeds up to a point at which the patient no longer can tolerate the crippling effect of his inhibitions, at which time his repressed wishes come to the fore and he displays a desire for action. Generally this kind of patient is caught up in a masochistic bind about his impulse life, which is maintained by an excessively harsh superego. Sometimes this impulse life is accessible in greater or lesser amounts of fantasy, sometimes it is almost totally inhibited. When it is accessible, the analysis proceeds more smoothly. Here are some common examples.

The main outlines of the progress of Dan, the 28-year-old scientist, have been described above in the chapter on the analytic honeymoon. Here some details can be added about the dynamics of his inhibitions with girls, and how he overcame them in analysis.

Prior to analysis, Dan had had a bad marriage, in which his sexual guilts were reinforced. Some years after the marriage, his wife became mentally ill. She was severely depressed, and constantly expressed the hope that she would die soon. (Later, after the divorce, she did attempt suicide, and eventually did die before she was 40, of an illness that was probably psychosomatic.) As part of her depression she began to feel that her vagina had a terrible odor, as a result of which she suddenly refused to have sexual relations any longer.

Disturbed by this refusal, Dan regressed to his previous pattern of seeking out prostitutes. However, an overpowering fear of venereal disease, against which his mother had vociferously warned him, prevented him from enjoying this outlet. At the time that he began analysis his sexual contacts were few and far between. There was however a constant fantasizing about sex. The analysis revealed a classical Oedipal picture. After the father's desertion, Dan's mother acted as if he would become her next husband. Unconsciously, Dan had accepted this role.

The incestuous tie was strongly reinforced by a severe traumatic period around the time of puberty. When the family moved to a new apartment, where Dan had a room of his own for the first time in his life, he began to suffer from terrible insomnia, which he had never experienced before. He became afraid that there was a man in the room who was "going to do something to him"; he could not specify more precisely what. In his terror he could merely lie in bed, hoping and praying that the strange man would not get him. Some time during the night he would screw up his courage, and make a dash to his mother's bed, where he could sleep the rest of the night with a safe feeling. No comments about this behavior were ever made by mother or son. Analysis made clear that the bogeyman was his father, whom he both feared and longed for. The threat of father's rage made the semi-incestuous experience with mother acceptable. He could recall how he clung to his mother's body, and eventually became conscious of direct sexual wishes for her.

In his teens he had been unable to date girls, unconsciously fearful of what both mother and father would do to him. Consciously, he could give no reason, except that he felt quite guilty about his liking for pornographic pictures and burlesque shows, which he thought no "good" girl would sanction. Even dancing was taboo to him because he would get an erection immediately, and was again frightened of what the girl would say.

The analysis quickly led to an examination of his inhibitions about girls. He saw that he was projecting the angry hate-filled mother to all women. Girls could want sex and enjoy it as much as he could, he soon discovered. The burlesque shows and the pornographic pictures were seen as voyeuristic fixations. Some anal habits that filled him with shame were brought out into the open; their analysis relieved the guilt further.

The first tentative steps towards girls were made through dancing. He realized that if he got an erection in a close dance the girl might enjoy it, rather than be repelled by it.

Then he began to try to experiment with sex. The first few girls he approached turned him down. On the one hand this reinforced his old feelings of guilt and inadequacy; but now through the analysis he realized that they too might be inhibited in this area.

Eventually he succeeded in having an affair with a woman some five years older. This led to other experiences, which also reinforced his self-confidence. Initially in these affairs he had some sexual difficulties, particularly premature ejaculation, but this cleared up fairly quickly.

The resolution of the sexual inhibitions took about a year, but it took much longer to consolidate the gains and go on to a love match and remarriage.

When Lucille, a striking 21-year-old redhead, came to analysis, she was caught up in a masochistic relationship with a man with whom she was living. She virtually supported him in full, allowing him to do whatever he wanted. Since his ambition was to be a writer, he did not work, but spent much of his time amusing himself or doing nothing. In addition, he suffered from severe premature ejaculation, for which Lucille took full blame, since she insisted that she was a "castrating woman."

This masochistic relationship was similar to an earlier one, at 18, when Lucille had married. In her marriage she had also supported her husband, a student, who suddenly left her for another girl when she became pregnant. After the birth of the child her husband refused to contribute anything for her support, even when ordered to do so by a court. Lucille refused to have him prosecuted, again feeling that she was responsible for his non-support and abandonment of the child.

Lucille was an only child. Her father had died when she was 8. Memories of him were not too clear, but she did feel that he showed her some affection, which mother decidedly did not. Mother, a devout Catholic, filled Lucille's ears with the sinfulness and danger of sexuality. After father's death mother never went close to another man.

In severe rebellion Lucille began to have sex when she was 13, but never with any enjoyment. Her role was to give the man whatever he wanted, not to get anything out of it for herself. Mother remained totally ignorant of what she was doing.

It was obvious that the sexual acting out, which had stopped long before analysis began, was a search for the lost father. She saw him as crushed and castrated by mother, and her affairs were all rescue operations to give the father-substitute the love he had never received from mother. At the same time by picking impotent and inadequate men she was also unconsciously playing the role of mother castrating father.

In the analysis one of the most striking revelations was the recovery of memories of her childhood unhappiness. She particularly recalled how up to the time of her father's death she had gone to bed every night crying. Neither father nor mother knew what was happening to her.

On the surface the conflict that kept her in the masochistic situation with both husband and lover was her feeling of extreme guilt about everything that she had done in life. It was only natural that the analysis should tackle this guilt at a fairly early stage.

An analytic honeymoon ensued. After about six months of therapy Lucille realized that her lover's weaknesses were not her fault. With this realization she came to the feeling that she was entitled to her share of pleasure in life. As a result she succeeded in moving away from him, toward men who could fulfill her needs. The analysis, a rather short one, terminated with her happy remarriage.

In both of the above cases the patients were immobilized by severe guilts going back to childhood. It is noteworthy that in both the strong positive transference resulted from identifying the analyst with the dead or absent parent, but this time a benign figure who gave them permission to enjoy life. These two cases moved quite well, but in many others the patient bogs down in masochistic dependent relationships which may last for years without his being able to break out.

A different situation arises with the *addicted* patient. Here, as mentioned before, the problem is to get the patient to tolerate enough anxiety so that the acting-out behavior (previously called perverse behavior) may be brought to an end or channeled along more constructive lines. It is essential for the analyst to recognize that the anxiety is so overpowering that a mere suggestion to change behavior will usually be of no avail. A long period of analytic work is necessary to bring the patient to the point where he can tolerate the anxiety involved. Here are some typical examples:

Dr. Y. was a 35-year-old physician, addicted to a derivative of morphine (cf. p. 103). Before coming to the present therapist, he had been to two other psychiatrists, both of whom tried to manipulate his taking the drug, but without result.

When he first came to the present therapist, guided by this previous experience, no position was taken on the drug. Instead, a regular analysis was undertaken. Dr. Y. made considerable improvement, and established a very strong positive transference. After about a year, he seemed to be ready to give up the drug.

At this point, a new resistance set in. Dr. Y. was convinced that the drug covered up symptoms of colitis and pneumonia, and that when he gave it up, these illnesses would appear. He was afraid to discuss this possibility with any friendly physician, and he did not trust the analyst's reassurance that this was a very remote possibility. Besides the fear of the masked illnesses, there were other fears about giving up the drug which he could not verbalize. These had already been traced back to night terrors in early childhood, but that was not sufficient.

There then ensued a period where resistance centered around the third-night anxiety. Dr. Y. could give up the drug for two days, but on the third day he became so panicky that he could no longer stay away from it. The working through of this resistance took almost a year. The analyst made attempts to manipulate the situation to confront the patient with his anxiety in order to find out what it was all about. (This was after a variety of interpretations going back to childhood had been exhausted.) The patient would agree, but back out at the last minute. For example, one time the analyst offered to let him sleep over in his home, in order to face the anxiety. Arrangements were all complete, with a physician on call to handle any medical emergencies that might arise, when Dr. Y. called it off at the last minute.

Several times, Dr. Y. had to be hospitalized. During these stays, he was forced to remain away from the drug. The consequences of abstention were primarily insomnia and anxiety, but the threatened illnesses did not appear. Nevertheless, the reality still did not reassure him. As soon as he was discharged from the hospital, he would return to the drug.

For some time, the analysis seemed to be going steadily downhill. Dr. Y. was warned that he would lose his license and eventually did, though it was restored later, after he had recovered. His masochism, evident in other areas of his life, seemed so profound that at times the analyst could only offer him the interpretation that he was trying to hit rock bottom. Resistances seemed almost insuperable.

After about six months, Dr. Y. was finally apprehended by the authorities for excessive use of the drug, and was given the choice of either going to prison or going to Lexington. He chose to go to Lexington. There he met a large number of hardened addicts. He was horrified by what he saw, and by the realization of what he had been doing to himself. One inmate who particularly impressed him was a man who had been in Lexington no less than 27 times.

When he was discharged from Lexington, Dr. Y. first switched to morphine. It was only then that he could free himself from the drug for any length of time. The analyst had made an agreement with him that if he could stay away for three months, he would be able to stay away for the rest of his life. The first voluntary withdrawal outside the hospital came with the help of a friendly physician and nurse who stayed with him for three days and three nights. The analyst also visited him three or four times a day. (He later married the nurse.) Once he was free of the drug, he went away for a while and lived through a terrible depression, in which life seemed totally meaningless. But he was able to snap out of it and eventually come back to his profession and a new life.

7) Excessive Regression

The process of psychoanalysis inherently involves a certain amount of regression on the part of the patient. For optimal results, this regression has to be maintained within certain limits. If it does not go far enough, the patient does not develop a transference reaction that is therapeutically manageable. If, however, it goes too far, the patient may present realistic dangers that endanger the course of therapy or even require its termination.

There is not too much that the analyst can do about the regressive process. Sometimes, quite often in fact, a recommendation is made that with patients who show a tendency to regress, "supportive" therapeutic measures should be adopted rather than just analytic. In the writer's experience, this serves to precipitate a regression even more often than a straight analytic approach. Many times, the effects of analysis with such a regressed patient cannot be accurately evaluated until a number of years have passed; the regression experienced in analysis has to be seen in the perspective of the entire psychological development. A case in point is the following:

Sally was a 20-year-old girl who had been in analytic therapy or analysis for a period of some five years. Originally, she had gone into therapy because she constantly ran away from home, could not get along with her parents, and was completely confused about her role in life. Analytic investigation revealed further problems going back to earliest childhood. For example, throughout her life, she was convinced that she was an angel with magical powers. At the age of 7, she was so sure she could fly that she jumped out of the window. Fortunately, it was only half a story up, so that the damage was slight. Her parents, as usual, were totally oblivious to the nature of her difficulties.

In each analysis, some progress was made, but no adequate resolution could be effected. The first time, when she was 15, she was seen every day by a psychiatrist, but refused to talk to him much of the time. Eventually, she went away to school and continued with another therapist.

When she first came to the present analyst, she was in love with a young man who apparently did not reciprocate her affections, at least to the same extent that she did. She was tormented by her love feelings, and continually threatened suicide. Analysis began at the rate of three times a week, but soon increased to six. At first, she seemed to make some progress, then there ensued a continual regression. She stayed home, cried all the time, could not do her schoolwork, could not function, and frequently threatened suicide, though no actual attempts were made. Eventually the suicidal threats became so serious that hospitalization was recommended. Since there were no available hospital beds in the area nearby, she was sent out of town, where treatment was continued with another therapist.

She remained in the hospital for about a year, eventually calming down. After release from the hospital she continued in school and when last heard from was making a reasonable adjustment to life in the light of her severe difficulties.

There are many cases, especially in acting-out personalities, where the regression is really a pseudo-regression, or in some respects, more correctly, a progression, though it seems like a step backward to the patient. These are the patients whose acting out conceals some profound anxieties. As a result of the analysis they are enabled to curb their acting out and face their anxieties more directly. When that happens, they often feel temporarily worse, because the previous outlets for the anxieties have been taken away from them. Also they intensify the regression to the point where they seem to behave on a more childish level than previously. All this is desirable for the course of the analysis, though objectively very difficult for the patient to tolerate. The resistance involves a demand that the anxiety should be done away with by some magical means, as had been the case in the past. When this resistance becomes very strong, the continuation of the analysis may be threatened, though it is often possible to work it out.

8) Excessive Emotionality

Analysis is for everybody, of course, a highly emotional experience. Nevertheless, even within this highly charged atmosphere, the patient must reflect on the interpretations and on the material that has been produced in order to get optimal results. Some patients find this kind of reflection extraordinarily difficult; they react with nothing but emotion to everything that is going on. This presents a special kind of resistance.

What is necessary with these patients is to help them to stand still for a while and look at their feelings rather than emote all the time. Sometimes they come to treatment with the mistaken conviction that catharsis is the only thing that is required. In other cases, they may verbalize insights, but the emphasis remains very strongly on the emotional release. Here are several illustrative cases.

Olive, a 30-year-old sculptress, came to analysis with the complaint that she was having an extramarital affair and could no longer tolerate the strain that this put her under. After a few sessions it became apparent that she had not been having an affair but had been fantasizing about it. Initially, therapy seemed to be going with great éclat. She produced an incredible variety of dreams, fantasies, memories, all with much primary process material laid out on the surface. She felt thrilled with the way the analysis was going. However, in all this she really acquired no insight into her life, but merely released a great many of her feelings.

After she had been in treatment for several months, the analyst advised her that he would be going away for his usual summer vacation. This produced a strong negative emotion. First she decided to take a week's holiday immediately. Then she decided to leave three weeks ahead of the analyst and come back three weeks after he had resumed his practice. The negative emotion was as strong and vociferous as the positive emotion had been. It had the same basis: There was no real insight, merely an outpouring of feeling. Where before the analyst could do no wrong, now he could do no right. Her girl friend gave her just as much insight as the analyst did.

After about a year and a half of analysis the patient actually did become involved in an extramarital affair, with a man who was close to the Don Juan of her fantasies. Once she had achieved this affair, even though quite consciously she hated the man, she felt that she had had enough and terminated the treatment.

In the case of Samuel, a 30-year-old research worker, there was an alternation of excess feeling and absence of feeling. Samuel's childhood background was most traumatic. Father and mother had divorced when he was about 2; even though he lived only a few blocks from father, he never again saw his father during his childhood. Mother kept up a constant diatribe against her ex-husband. Mother was also both seductive and extremely domineering, and she continued to bathe Samuel until he was well into puberty; in fact, he protested against the bathing only when he began to get erections. As late as adolescence he continued to have conscious incestuous fantasies about his mother.

With this background, it is not surprising that he demonstrated a pattern of alternatively showing strong feeling and repressing all feeling. Much of the time he spent during the hours recounting the threats that he perceived were being made against his advancement in his office. His fearfulness became so apparent that it was obvious even to him that he had mild paranoid tendencies. Nevertheless, he would come session after session and declaim about some new threat. It did not matter that the threats that had come up a week before had now disappeared; a new one was on the horizon and engaged his entire attention. So much of the hours were spent in releasing his fear and anger that somebody should threaten his fantasy world of security, that little else could be discussed.

Then again at other times he would break out in violent depressions. He would sob uncontrollably, feel despairing, even contemplate the thought of suicide. In his first marriage, after some years of happiness, he began to get more and more angry at his wife, and more and more threatened by her.

Eventually, this led to a long series of diatribes against her, similar to the diatribes against other threatening figures in the outside world, and eventually a divorce. With his second wife, he was again happy for a while, and then the old pattern resumed. This time, however, he had had enough analysis to realize that he was bringing on the disaster himself.

The major resistance shown throughout all this history of fears and threats was the demand that the analyst should somehow alter the real world, rather than that he should alter himself. When the analyst indicated that he could not do so, but could only help him to see what was going on, he would fly into a rage. However, the rage against the analyst could be contained within reasonable bounds so that the analysis could lead to a successful result.

9) Absence of Feeling

This is another fairly common resistance to the analytic process. The patient can intellectualize a great deal, can often verbalize all kinds of insights, but he feels little or nothing. Sometimes these patients have a strong positive transference, sometimes a negative one, sometimes an indifferent one. Whatever the transference, the problem is more one of allowing them to bring out their feeelings. When such an affect-blocked patient comes into analysis, it is best to concentrate on the feelings from the beginning. Here is an illustrative case.

Morris was the youngest of six children. He was totally unwanted; in fact his mother referred to him as the thirteenth abortion, because she had successfully aborted twelve times before he came along. Naturally, the other siblings were much older. The next older, also a boy, had beaten him up unmercifully all through childhood.

Before analysis everything Morris touched had resulted in failure. He lacked about ten credits to graduate from college. For a long time he had wanted to be an art teacher, but when it was discovered that he was color blind he had to give this up. At the time that he started analysis he was involved in unsatisfying office work.

With women there had been a few unhappy relationships. In the most recent he had been living with a bohemian girl, whom he admired for her lack of concern, which was in marked contrast to his persistent anxiety. However this girl had kicked him out after they had been living together for about five months, which Morris accepted without any protest, since he felt that she was far above him in every respect.

Several months after he had broken up with her, she called, asking to see him. At first he thought that she wanted to restore the relationship, but this was not the case at all. It turned out that she was pregnant by another man, and that what she wanted was for Morris to give her the money for an abortion, since she did not want to tell either him or her family. By this time Morris was in analysis, and could see how masochistic it would be of him to give her his entire cash reserve to save face, so he refused.

Apart from constant anxiety, Morris could feel virtually nothing. He never got angry, or excited, or felt much joy about anything. Life to him was one long series of onerous injunctions, which he was in duty bound to obey without a protest.

It quickly became apparent in the analysis that he was motivated primarily by extreme terror of his mother. Father had died a number of years before, when Morris was a little boy, but before he died mother had had him jailed for non-support. After this jailing she never desisted from telling people what a louse he was and how she had put him in his place. Typically, even after the jailing father went back to live with her.

A strong positive transference developed, primarily because the analyst was virtually the first person in his life who saw some good in Morris. He was encouraged to finish college, move on to a good profession, and relate in a more meaningful way to women.

The analysis was a long one. While it was on the whole quite successful, the affect block could never be completely broken. At one point he took up with a girl who had been through a Reichian analysis, which left her with the ability to vomit at will. She considered this a great triumph for the therapy, and urged Morris to try it too. But by this time he had had enough analysis under his belt to see how spurious her claim was, and instead induced her to go to a trained analyst.

Eventually, like Jim in the illustrative case, he made a compromise solution by marrying a girl who was unable to bear children, and suffered from some serious physical illnesses, including chronic gall bladder trouble. But he felt very happy with her. When he had occasion to contact the analyst several years after termination, he was quite happy with his life resolution. The fact that he could still never get angry at anybody bothered the analyst much more than it bothered him.

Patients who display no feelings in some ways have the most difficult of all resistances. The psychoanalytic process aims at the release of feelings; if the patient fights this release, all the interpretations in the world can prove to be useless. In these cases, the analyst must concentrate from the very beginning on the nature of the feeling life of the individual. To discuss intellectual content when there is no feeling attached to it is virtually useless.

As can be anticipated, many of these patients block off their feelings because when they break through they are so powerful. It can be expected that outbursts of fear, rage, and even intense excitement will occur and will frighten the patient enormously. In patients who do have such outbursts, the technical approach is to help them to become aware of the outbursts and of the measures that they adopt to ward them off. Usually the outbursts will break through on occasion, in spite of the patient's efforts to control them.

> A case in point arose with Elliot, a 22-year-old young man who was extremely argumentative and intellectualizing. It was obvious both in individual and in group therapy that he was enormously angry, yet he could not see his anger. One day as he was fooling around with his wife, he became acutely aware of the problem. He realized that he had no sexual desire for his wife. As usual, he blamed his wife for this, and went on and on about how it might be better to have an affair or to change wives, yet he could not bring himself to do it, especially since his wife was pregnant. One day he grabbed his wife, at first rather playfully, and then began twisting her arm, almost to the point of hurting her. At that moment he began to get an erection. This made him realize that he could get sexually excited only in response to anger. This realization sobered him at least to the point where he could discuss it more calmly.

SUGGESTIONS FOR FURTHER READING

See references to Chapter 8.

On acting out, see Symposium, *Int. J. Psychoanalysis* 49, 1968 and Symposium, *J. Am. Psychoanalytic Assoc.* 5, 1957.

A particularly crucial paper is L. Spiegel, "Acting Out and Defensive Instinctual Gratification," *J. Am. Psychoanalytic Assoc.* 2, 1954, 107–119.

CHAPTER 11

Countertransference: The Growth of the Therapist

In self-analysis the danger of incompleteness is particularly great. One is too easily satisfied with a part explanation, behind which resistance can easily keep back something that may perhaps be more important.

Freud: *The Subtleties of a Parapraxis* (1936)

Just as transference may be used in both a narrow and a broad meaning, countertransference may be used in the same way. In general, the broader meaning of countertransference will be referred to in the following discussion, with the narrower meaning a special case.

Just as the patient must re-think his entire attitude toward his "neurosis" and the whole therapeutic process, the analyst must do likewise. The analyst realizes, of course, that the patient is not sick in any medical sense, but suffers from difficulties in living. Since the patient is not sick, the therapist cannot look upon himself as a physician who is called upon to diagnose a cut-and-dried illness and to prescribe appropriate treatments. He must rather look upon himself as a human being who is listening to another human being, trying to help him out of his morass.

Looked at in this light, it has already been noted that the goal of psychotherapy for the patient is growth rather than cure. But what of the therapist? If he is not curing the patient, what is he doing? He is contributing to the growth of another human being. In this process, it is unavoidable—in fact, it is essential—that he should also experience some growth. Thus, it becomes desirable for him to reformulate his conception of his role to the point where he looks upon the entire therapeutic process as one that contributes to his growth as well as to that of the patient. Should he succeed in reformulating his attitude

140

toward therapy in this way, it would give him and the entire therapeutic process a totally novel cast.

Three instances from the historical development of psychoanalysis
may be cited to show how the consistent attempt to understand countertransference has contributed in rather surprising and unexpected
ways to the development of psychoanalysis as a form of therapy.

The earliest instance may be taken from Freud and Breuer.[38] As
is now well known, the process of psychoanalysis was first approached
by Breuer in the case of Anna O., an hysterical young girl whom he
treated from 1880 to 1882. Breuer reported the nature of the treatment and its results to Freud, who later elaborated his cathartic
method and eventually turned it into psychoanalysis.

Subsequent investigation has shown that the reason Freud was able
to proceed to an analytic approach, while Breuer was not, was that
Breuer could not control his countertransference, while Freud could
control his. It seems that Anna O. fell in love with Breuer. He was
a busy general practitioner, who was so unusually interested in the
case that he visited the young girl every day at her home. When he
noticed that she had fallen in love with him, he was horrified at the
thought of what might result, especially since he was a happily married man with five children. He immediately withdrew from the case.
He correctly perceived that in order to embark on such an undertaking he would have to revamp his entire mode of living.

Freud, on the other hand, relates that at one point in the cathartic
treatment of an hysterical woman, at the end of an hour, she got up
and threw her arms around him. Instead of being frightened away by
this demonstration, Freud subjected it to a careful analysis. It was
then that he developed his concept of transference and its concomitant, countertransference. Through the careful analysis of his own
contertransferences, he was able to keep his objectivity, thus remaining
in a position to see the patient's signs of affection and love as manifestations of a transference. He was neither bowled over by the demonstration of love, as some others might have been, nor did he dis-
miss it as inconsequential. He rather saw it as a manifestation that
was relevant to the very heart of the whole therapeutic process. It was
then that he was able to reformulate his entire thinking, and place the
central stress in therapy on transference and its related resistancees.

A second instance can be cited from the work of the psychologist
Jules Holzberg.[39] While teaching a course in abnormal psychology,
Holzberg hit upon the idea of assigning the students to attend one of
the nearby mental hospitals, rather than having them do the traditional

term paper. These students—juniors or seniors in college, with no previous background whatsoever—visited one patient one hour a week or so for a period of six months, later for a period of one year. Much to his surprise, Holzberg discovered that in the course of these visits, a significant effect was experienced by both the student and the patient. The patients felt that they had somebody to talk to, while the students felt that they had acquired a new and deeper approach to the nature of mental illness. Thus, the mere act of listening to a mental patient, without the usual cultural defenses of hostility, sarcasm, laughter, or derision, had a positive effect on the growth of college students.

In another recent paper, Merkle and Little [40] report on what they call "The Beginning Psychiatry Training Syndrome." The syndrome they refer to consists of a variety of anxiety reactions that appear in the psychiatrist when he first undertakes the practice of psychotherapy. He shows many overt signs of anxiety, including a variety of somatic symptoms: in some cases, these go so far that he feels virtually incapacitated to continue his professional work and is forced into a therapeutic situation of his own almost immediately. The authors ascribe the syndrome to the reaction to the attempt to help a mentally ill person out of his various dilemmas.

Several of the points that they make are quite significant. First, they report that the majority of psychiatric residents who undertake psychotherapy report a syndrome of this kind, in greater or lesser degree. Further, and this is highly significant, those residents who do not report anxiety reactions are the ones who eventually turn out to be the worst therapists. In other words, some anxiety at the beginning is essential to attain competence as a therapist.

The anxiety of course is merely a sign of the shaking up of the ego of the psychiatrist. When he takes this shaking up seriously, he reaches an entirely different level of development. If, however, he does not take it seriously, he remains an over-defensive technician who will do his patients little good.

The history of psychoanalysis has involved the extension of the process from the original hysterical and obsessional patients whom Freud treated to character disorders, psychopaths, schizophrenics, and the entire gamut of human disorder. It is quite clear in reviewing the history of the extensions of psychotherapy by a variety of psychoanalysts that a systematic understanding of the countertransference has been the primary tool in facilitating such an extension.

Freud himself, in developing the whole process, went through a profound transformation of personality, which has not been sufficiently appreciated in the literature. It was only after he had been treating patients for a number of years that he came upon a variety of countertransference reactions, which he handled by an intensive self-analysis. The French analyst Didier Anzieu [41] has pieced together this self-analysis from the dreams reported by Freud in *The Interpretation of Dreams,* the mass of autobiographical material in *The Psychopathology of Everyday Life,* the letters to Fliess, and other sources. He has shown conclusively how the whole experience left a profound mark on Freud, which in turn led to a revolutionizing of his therapeutic approach.

Today it has become axiomatic that anyone who wishes to practice psychoanalysis must undergo an intensive psychoanalysis of his own. This is a position that has been reached only after the disappointments of many years. It has repeatedly been demonstrated that the analyst cannot get the patient beyond the point that he is at himself. If he does not undergo any analysis or if he does not pursue his analysis satisfactorily, then he will repeatedly run up against blind spots in the analysis of his patients that he will be unable to overcome.

Just as the therapy of the classical neuroses was made possible by Freud's self-analysis, the extension of psychoanalysis to practically all human conditions has been made possible by the consistent deepening analysis of the practitioner. These extensions have been made possible by overcoming the fear of, or antipathy toward, the variety of problems that confront the psychotherapist. In the case of the delinquent, Aichhorn made a fundamental contribution by overcoming his fear of the delinquent's aggression. With the schizophrenic patient, Sullivan revolutionized the therapy by understanding his own emotional difficulties. In recent years, Searles, particularly, has documented with extraordinary honesty and clarity how the development of his therapy of schizophrenics went hand in hand with the advancement of his own personal analysis.

From a theoretical point of view, it is important to see why personal analysis and therapeutic skill go together. The growth process that is pursued in the personal analysis may be viewed as a development from hatred to love, a gradual overcoming of hostility toward one's fellow human beings. In the same way, the therapeutic process involves a consistent overcoming of hostility toward the patient. The mental patient in our culture is viewed with scorn, derision, and hostility. Every practitioner who comes into the field begins with these biases. The patient is thought of as "queer," "off his rocker," "crazy," "nuts," and so on. To be able to help him, the analyst must get over the culturally fostered feelings of hatred, and move toward an attitude of sympathetic understanding. Thus, in both processes, the personal analysis and the growth of therapeutic skills, the same psychological growth is required: from hatred to love. A practitioner who succeeds in fostering such a growth process is one who becomes the most effective in the long run.

This, however, immediately raises a knotty administrative problem. At what point in his analysis should the prospective therapist be allowed to undertake the help of other human beings? The image of the perfectly analyzed analyst who has resolved all his problems and then moves on to help other human beings has long since gone by the board. Rather, what is operative today is the image of the individual who has benefited sufficiently from his own personal analysis so that he can be objective about people who come to him for help. In line with this thought, the almost universal requirement of all analytic institutes is that the personal analysis should proceed to the point where the analyst's problems do not interfere with his work as a therapist. In practice, this means that in a short amount of time, after a year or two of analysis and the attainment of his professional degree, the analyst is then permitted to undertake therapy. This could hardly be otherwise, for if he were forced to wait until the termination of analysis, he would have to postpone his therapeutic career for a number of years.

Thus, the analyst starts to use therapy after he has been in therapy for a year or two; his own analysis continues while he is treating others. This means that he is approaching the growth process from two points of view: one in terms of himself and the other in terms of his reactions to his patients.

Another way of looking at this is to conceptualize the analyst-patient relationship ideally as the parent-child relationship. The wise analyst is in most essential respects similar to the wise parent. Then, in his own personal therapy, the analyst plays the role of a child, while in his therapeutic endeavors with others, he plays the role of a parent. The combination of these two roles, the need to separate them, and the need to work them out, play a significant part in his personal and professional development.

The manner in which the therapeutic experience can be used to further the growth process varies widely from one person to another; it is always possible and indeed necessary to view the therapeutic experience as one in which some growth must necessarily take place for the analyst.

Every therapeutic case is unique to some extent. The analyst represents some figure from the patient's past, which leads to a variety of transference phenomena. Every patient, however, also represents some figure from the analyst's past, which in turn leads to a variety of countertransference phenomena. Thus, no matter how great the technical skill of the analyst, ultimately it is the consistent analysis and understanding of the countertransference that provides the most secure foundation for satisfactory results. Nor could one expect it to be otherwise.

Although it is commonplace to observe that a variety of reactions displayed by a series of patients are all manifestations of transference, it is equally clear, though less commonplace to observe, that the variety of reactions displayed by a number of analysts are also manifestations of transference; that is, technically, countertransference. Nor could it be expected to be otherwise in a field that is so highly affected by subjective factors as psychoanalysis.

Anna Freud [42] observed:

> Years ago, in Vienna, we instituted an experimental technical seminar among colleagues of equal seniority and equal theoretical background, treating cases with similar diagnoses and therefore, supposedly, similar structure. We compared techniques and found in discussion—not only as Dr. Stone put it today—"that no two analysts would ever give precisely the same interpretation throughout an analysis," and more surprisingly still, that such uniformity of procedure was never kept up for more than a few days in the beginning of an analysis. After that, the handling of the material would cease to run parallel, each analyst giving precedence for interpretation to another piece or even layer. These differences in timing would influence the emergence of the next material and this, in turn, influenced the trends in interpretation. Even though the final results may be the same, the roads leading there were widely divergent.

In another significant study, Glover [43] tabulated the results of a questionnaire sent to the 29 analysts who were members of the British Psychoanalytic Association in 1938. There has scarcely, if ever, been a more cohesive group of analysts in the history of the science. All 29 of these people had either been trained directly by Ernest Jones or by persons trained by Jones. In spite of this extraordinary uniformity of background, a great divergence in various aspects of technique was noted. In the manner of handling resistance, transferences, childhood material, interpretation, reassurance, anxiety, even in such finer matters of techniques as the handling of fees, broken appointments, or taking notes during sessions, there were enormous variations.

It has long been known that the image of the perfectly analyzed analyst is a total myth. The analyst is a human being who has made more progress with his own problems than the patient, and has reached a stage where he is in a position to help others, because of his superior objectivity and knowledge. But he still has problems, some of them mild, some of them fairly severe. The notion that the technical procedures adopted by analysts under these circumstances would be the same, even though they are all taught to do the same thing, is equally a myth. There is scarcely any field in which the personality of the therapist is impressed on the treatment procedure as strongly as in psychoanalysis.

Nor is it even easy to find out what the analyst has done in his analytic hours. Some years ago, Kubie,[44] in a surprising research finding, disclosed that psychiatric residents who reported their cases to him at a seminar at Yale University did not do so accurately. When their reports on the sessions were compared with recordings obtained during the sessions, the widest divergencies were uncovered. In one case, a man who reported one interpretation was found to have given exactly the opposite interpretation during the session. It is clear from this, and from much other material, that the analyst not only handles the hour in a subjective way, but feels so defensive about his procedures that it becomes quite difficult for him to report them accurately to some outside observer, even when there is no judgment or significant evaluation involved.

Freud once commented that the technique that he had developed was suitable to his own personality, and that some other person might develop a different technique more suitable to his. Under these circumstances, it behooves every analyst to view the refinement of his technical procedures as part of his own growth process. In the course of analysis, he is bound to run up against the same problems regarding sex, love, hatred, identity, ambition, depression, elation, and so on, that he had to overcome in his own analysis. His attitudes toward these symptoms in his patients will inevitably be strongly colored by the degree to which he has overcome them in his personal analysis. As he intensifies his analytic work, penetrating into the conflicts of others, his own conflicts will be touched or in some cases re-aroused. If he takes the consistent position that the analysis that he does is also part of his own self-understanding and growth, he finds that it becomes a warm human undertaking, which is experienced as such by the patient.

Among the criteria for the termination of analysis, there has long been a demand set up for self-analysis after the formal analysis has been completed. Few people are in a position to maintain such self-analysis for any length of time. But one kind of person who is in an extraordinary position to make use of this opportunity is the analyst himself. In his analytic work he is continually confronted by a variety of irrational and transference reactions toward his patients that he must explore without anyone else's help. One criterion for determining whether the individual is ready to undertake analytic work is to decide whether he is in a position to single out these reactions and make use of them therapeutically.

There is understandably little literature on this topic. In a rare but stimulating article Maria Kramer [45] has described some of her own reactions after analysis. She suggested the name "auto-analysis" for this type of undertaking

The potential analyst first comes to grips with his problems in his own personal analysis. No other satisfactory method has ever been discovered. Personal analysis has become the cornerstone and the *sine qua non* for anyone who wishes to undertake psychoanalytic psychotherapy. Generally speaking it is more important and more central than any other aspect of the individual's training, though this does not mean that other aspects of training should be slighted.

When the transition is made from personal analysis to doing analysis under supervision, a problem immediately arises. The person who knows the therapist best is the personal analyst, who is as a rule continuing the analysis. Should the analyst begin his supervision with his personal analyst or should he go to some other person?

On this question, diverse attitudes have arisen in the course of the history of psychoanalysis. In the Thirties, a strong debate about this topic arose between the so-called "Hungarian" and "Viennese" schools. The Hungarian school felt that the analyst could be properly supervised only by somebody who knew him well. Most of his problems with the patients were considered reflections of residual problems he had with himself—countertransference problems. Therefore, the first analytic control ought to be carried out most usefully by his personal analyst. This first control analysis was seen as a continuation of his own analysis, with a new slant to it. His thoughts were turned toward his patient, and as he would develop these thoughts in working with his own analyst, he would analyze his difficulties with his patient, see his blind spots, and thus improve as an analyst. Control analysis was thus seen as a form of personal analysis, perhaps an advanced form in which more stress would be laid on bringing in select free associations about the work with the patient.

The opposite position was taken by the representatives of the Institute in Vienna. They thought that the personal analyst should preferably not control the first case of his candidate. The candidate should be exposed to different points of view and should work with a person who would teach him rather than analyze him. It was suggested that this control experience, rather than consisting of an analysis of his blind spots and countertransferences, should be strictly a didactic experience. The supervisor was to be strictly a teacher who would explain, correct, and direct, and he must use a didactic approach, without touching the affective problems of the beginning analyst. If such problems arose, they would be referred to the candidate's personal analyst, or he might be required to go back into further analysis.

Since that time, the situation has changed in several respects. First of all, the personal analysis is universally seen as a therapeutic analysis rather than a didactic one. The candidate must come to grips with his own problems and not merely because he is going to do analysis, but because he recognizes that, brought up in our culture with the kind of family and social conditions that prevail, as well as the instinctual demands that are basic to being a human being, he necessarily has developed conflicts that require analytic work. This personal therapeutic analysis now generally lasts a long time; five to ten years is no longer so unusual. To postpone the initiation of analytic work until analysis has come to an end entirely seems to impose an undue hardship on the potential analyst, as well as on the profession which, as usual, suffers from a shortage of manpower. Accordingly, the potential analyst is generally permitted to do work under supervision after he has been in analysis a relatively short period. Generally, in the more purist institutes, this work is called psychotherapy rather than psychoanalysis, but, as indicated elsewhere in this work, a really rational distinction between these two forms, except in those extreme cases in which psychotherapy is clearly nonanalytic, is difficult if not impossible to draw. Certainly, the patient does not draw any such distinctions, and would be horrified if he were told that he was being given an inferior form of therapy because his therapist had not yet finished his training program.

A second change that has occurred is the crystallization of the institutes, with a corresponding increased rigidity in the nature of the training process. American institutes have, by and large, opted to make the control analysis completely independent of the training analysis. However, there are large numbers of analysts who are trained outside the institutes and here the problem is by no means so directly resolved.

Where more flexibility is permitted (that is, outside the formal training programs or within formal training programs which are more flexible), it has often been found that the Hungarian point of view makes more sense. It is clear that the hesitations, doubts, hostilities, anxieties, or other reactions that the analyst has to his early patients have attached to them a great deal of shame and guilt. To expect a person rationally to reveal all his shame and guilt to another person who is in a position to judge him is surely unreasonable. On the other hand, if the first control is the personal analyst, all these reactions can be revealed with impunity. Accordingly, there is much to be said for the position that the first control should be the personal analyst. This procedure is still widely followed in less formalized training circumstances.[46,47]

SUGGESTIONS FOR FURTHER READING

A full review of the literature prior to 1953 is in D. W. Orr, "Transference and Countertransference: A Historical Survey." (See references to Chapter 3.)

The best extended discussion in available texts is in Glover, *op cit.,* Ch. VI.

General considerations regarding the profession may be found in: R. Greenson, "That Impossible Profession," *J. Am. Psychoanalytic Assoc.* 14, 1966, 9–27. L. Stone, *The Psychoanalytic Situation* (New York: Int. Universities Press, 1961). B. D. Lewin, "The Analytic Situation: Topographic Considerations," *Psychoanalytic Quarterly* 28, 1959, 455–469.

A trenchant critique is in T. Szasz, "On the Experiences of the Analyst in the Psychoanalytic Situation," *J. Am. Psychoanalytic Assoc.* 4, 1957, 197–223. Specific problems relating to countertransference are treated in: L. Altman, "Panel Report: Theory of Psychoanalytic Therapy," *J. Am. Psychoanalytic Assoc.* 12, 1964, 620–631. R. Spitz, "Countertransference: Comments on its Varying Role in the Analytic Situation," *J. Am. Psychoanalytic Assoc.* 4, 1956, 256–265. P. Greenacre, "Certain Technical Problems in the Transference Relationship," *J. Am. Psychoanalytic Assoc.* 7, 1959, 484–502.

CHAPTER 12

Countertransference: Some Common Problems

Regardless of how thoroughgoing a training analysis may be, it is just a beginning of an interminable process of self-analysis. This aspect of the training analysis, which has its personally protective as well as its professional value, has not been given its due emphasis in discussions of the first phase of training. An analyst may be confronted by any of his patients in any period of his professional life with one or another vulnerable area in his own personality. Healthy defensive systems and character traits are never completely immune to pressures which may be generated by work with patients, and changes caused by aging, fatigue, illness or other external events may increase the analyst's vulnerability to the challenge of a patient's demands. In self-defense, his resistance to these demands may bring about technical mistakes which are generally called countertransferences. . . . Or these challenges may stir up symptomatic responses which could disturb the analyst's balance between health and illness. Protection against these hazards of the profession is provided primarily by the training analysis and continued in the development of his self-analytic function during supervision.

> J. Fleming and T. Benedek:
> *Psychoanalytic Supervision*

Like transferences, countertransferences run the gamut of positive, negative, and indifferent. Since it may be assumed that the prospective analyst at the least has overcome his worst countertransferences, the discussion can be confined to the broad areas of positive and negative feelings.

1) Positive Countertransference

It is certainly true that by and large analysis proceeds best with a patient whom the analyst likes. It could scarcely be otherwise, since if the analyst has to suffer through years of treating a person he does not really care for, it is bound to be reflected in his attitude, in the intensity of his work, and in the sincerity of his interpretations. However, while positive countertransference is the most desirable attitude, just as the positive transference in the patient makes for the best results, it must be very carefully watched.

A temptation for most analysts is to love the patient too much, much as the temptation for most parents is to smother the child with affection. In large part as a reaction to this temptation, Freud laid down the rule of non-intervention in the patient's life. For technical reasons (the effect on the transference) it is desirable for the analyst to withhold whatever strong feelings he may have about the patient. But this is a far cry from not *feeling* them. When he feels too little, an undesirable situation is created, against which there has been a reaction in more recent years. The analyst should be a real person to the patient, but should not inject his personality where it is not to the interest of the patient.

In the attempt to be real, many analysts become involved in *over-identification* with the patient. As a result of this over-identification, they lose the capacity to be objective about the patient's dilemmas, injecting instead their own life experiences. This, naturally, can only do harm to the analytic process.

It is essential for the patient to have the feeling that the analyst is behind him in his life's endeavors. But it is not at all necessary or desirable for him to have the feeling that he gets approval for whatever he does, regardless of the consequences of his actions. On the contrary, it is essential that he should be able to take some constructive criticism from the analyst, when that is called for, and it is called for at many points in a long-term analysis.

A typical instance in which the over-identification plays a role is the analysis of marital disputes. When they come out, the analyst is apt to react to the patient in terms of his or her own marital difficulties, past or present.

Bob, a 36-year-old man, was in his second unhappy marriage. In his first marriage, his wife had become increasingly depressed in the course of time and had gone to an analyst. At one point, this analyst called in Bob to inform him that his wife seemed to be suicidal. When Bob came home, his wife pressed him to tell her what the analyst had said; after much hesitation, he revealed what had transpired. It is to be noted that at no point did this analyst recommend that Bob enter treatment. The wife, apparently staggered by this remark on the part of her analyst, then did attempt suicide. She was hospitalized briefly, and released. After her release, she separated from Bob, moved to another state, and never wanted to see him again.

Several years later, Bob met and married his present wife. When difficulties arose in this marriage, his wife induced him to go to an analyst. The second analyst, however, took somewhat the same line as the first. She was an older woman, who apparently found Bob an attractive younger man, wealthy, successful, and entertaining. She had such severe sexual hang-ups that when Bob used the word "fuck," which he did at least twice in every sentence, she would reproach him for using such language in the presence of a lady.

In this analysis, the therapist again took the tack that Bob's problem was basically that of marrying "crazy" women. There was a minimal amount of effort devoted to Bob's childhood background and his own psychological difficulties. Although the wife had a number of emotional difficulties, it seemed to Bob himself that the consistent interpretation that she was crazy made very little sense. Eventually this analysis failed too. Bob had to go to a third analyst to straighten out the mess that he was in.

Over-identification may play a significant role in many other life situations; for example, if a patient has great difficulty with authority figures, on jobs or in school situations, the analyst often takes his side in spite of the fact that such partisanship is inimical to his growth.

Most of the most important excesses of the positive countertransference occur in regard to the sex life of the patient. Inasmuch as part of the therapeutic encounter is always directed toward straightening out the sex and love patterns, the countertransference problems depend upon the degree to which the therapist has worked out his own conflicts in this area, as well as the way in which he has worked them out. Broadly speaking, there are five ways in which the countertransference may affect the handling of the sexual problems: a) having sex with the patient; b) over-encouraging the patient in sexual acting out; c) blocking off therapist's sexual feelings; d) blocking off patient's sexual feelings; e) blocking off discussion of infantile sexuality.

a) Having Sex With the Patient: This countertransference has already been discussed in the chapter on the erotic transference. A few more comments may be made here.

It is an open secret that more than one therapist has had sex with a patient who feels deprived. This cannot be handled by recourse to conventional morality, since the therapist ideally puts himself in the position of one who is trying to reform the conventional morality that leads to a world of neurotics. It must be treated as a purely therapeutic effort.

From the therapeutic point of view, the sexual encounter occurs more often between a male therapist and a female patient than vice versa. While it is going on, the patient is often contented with the arrangement; difficulties arise when the therapist wishes to break off or when the patient begins to make more demands. In this way, the sexual affair in therapy evolves in much the same way as an affair outside of therapy. When the male loses interest or is less attentive, the woman feels neglected and reacts strongly.

Therapeutically, the sex is just as undesirable as any other violation of the rule of abstinence. If a patient is given too much gratification, then the opportunity to analyze the fantasies connected with her action is lost. Furthermore, the wish for gratification may be so overwhelming that any further talking therapy is out of the question.

As has been noted, the therapist who gives way to his wish to have sex with a patient is usually suffering from rather deep-seated conflicts of his own. Much as in the case of the parent who commits incest with a child, the real trouble lies with the personality of the therapist rather than with the act as such.

Dr. C., a promising young psychiatrist, suddenly developed the idea that indiscriminate sexual relations between everybody would solve the problems of the world. He encouraged all his female patients to come to the sessions armed with contraceptive devices and would have sex with them almost every time. Some of his patients left and turned to other therapists. Others remained. In one case, the husband of a patient reported him to the District Attorney's office, but charges were quashed.

Eventually, Dr. C.'s disturbance became more and more apparent. From heterosexual acting out, he moved on to homosexual and to family orgies. This was rationalized by the contention that the problem in the early childhood environment was excessive sexual restriction, which should be handled by removing all barriers. Several times he visited families of patients and engaged in sex *à trois*.

Even this did not satisfy Dr. C. His depression and anxieties became worse. He had to give up the practice of psychiatry and return to general medical practice. Eventually his illness became deeper and deeper and he was hospitalized. Nothing seemed to help. After release from the hospital, he finally committed suicide.

In another case that came to the attention of the local psychoanalytic group, a therapist, after several years of treating an inhibited young woman, began having occasional sexual intercourse with her.

After some time, he tired of her and discontinued intercourse. When she objected, he advised her to go to a hospital. Instead, she left treatment with him. In the course of the investigation that was undertaken at her request, he decided to return to analysis. In his makeup, a powerful current of sadism was covered over by a strong reaction formation that led him to join all kinds of political reform movements. His faith in inner change was evidently much less than his faith in outer change. However, it is to be noted that no severe psychopathology was found in him, as in the previous case; with him it was more lack of training, and insufficient appreciation of his own inner forces.

On rare occasions, therapists have after beginning a sexual affair gone on to marry their patients. It is obviously difficult to get at the dynamics of such situations. At times, it seems to have worked out; at other times, it has led to further difficulties. In the last analysis, there is no short cut to making the unconscious conscious.

b) Overencouraging the Patient in Sexual Acting Out: The therapist, though he is able to control his own sexual feelings for the patient, may instead overencourage her to act out with other men. A fine line must often be drawn here, since sexual activity is as a rule one of the goals of therapy. The distinction lies between gratifying sexual activity and compulsive sexual conquest; the latter is undesirable, the former is desirable. In other kinds of acting out, the same subtle differentiations must be drawn.

Here however, differentiations are not so easy to make in practice. In discussion groups of analysts it frequently becomes apparent that what is acting out for one person is normal release of emotion for another. The meaning of sexuality in the therapist's own life plays a powerful role in his theoretical views on the subject.

A decisive question is whether the activity does the person harm or good. By and large, a counterbalancing principle may be invoked here. People who have a good deal of sex without permanent gratification do well to improve the quality of their sexual functioning rather than the quantity; conversely, people who have had little sex will often benefit from the mere experience, even if it produces no lasting satisfactions within this or that relationship. Growth is a slow matter and cannot be forced overnight.

A countertransference problem arises when the therapist pays more attention to his own needs than to the patient's. In general, this is the touchstone by which one can judge whether or not something is a countertransference. This is one more reason why the therapist needs intimate knowledge of his own motivations.

With the popularization of Freud's theories, a group of patients has come to analysis who seemingly do not have the sexual conflicts of the previous generation. They believe that sex with anybody, anywhere, any time is justified and is in fact a sure cure to everything that ails man. But they still come for help after they have tried this mode of release without success.

The reason why the mere acting out of sex does not solve the neurotic conflict is that it avoids the deeper meaning of the sexual activity to the person. Very often it fails to note even the surface problems that arise within the sexual activity.

> Dr. G., a young physician, was quite successful in having sex with the various young women whom he encountered, particularly nurses. When inquiry was made about the details of these encounters, it turned out that he had considerable difficulty ejaculating, a fact which had never been revealed before.

In his classic paper on wild analysis,[48] Freud notes the poor advice given by an Austrian practitioner to a neurotic woman. The patient, a 47-year-old widow, came to a physician, complaining of various anxiety symptoms. He told her (this was in 1910) that a physician in Vienna had discovered the causes of such illness to be sexual, and she had three solutions open to her: remarry, take a lover, or masturbate. Freud rightly pointed out that he did not mention the fourth and most important solution, psychoanalysis.

If a patient comes to treatment full of sexual inhibitions, the mere advice of the physician or other therapist that she give up her inhibitions will be useless or harmful. Therapeutically, the proper approach would be to examine what in her past life has made her so inhibited; in the course of this examination, at some point she will give up the sexual withdrawal, but the precise point is something that cannot be determined in advance.

> Dr. C., the physician mentioned above, before he began his own sexual acting out, was wont to encourage his patients to do so. Once he was consulted by a 35-year-old woman who told him she was a virgin. He prescribed a diaphragm and ordered her to find someone to have sex with her over that weekend. She did as told, but the ensuing anxiety was so great that she left treatment with him and went to

another therapist where she spent considerable time complaining about the moral laxity of the man who had given her such bad advice.

By contrast, another 35-year-old girl entered treatment with a story of an attachment to an older man who was out of the country. She had had sex only several times in her whole life, after her father died. Analysis revealed a strong fixation on the father, who had acted seductively toward her all through her adolescence. As the analysis of her attachment to her father progressed, she was able to break off with the man in the distant country, find suitable companionship here, including sexual, and eventually made a happy marriage.

c) Blocking Off Therapist's Sexual Feelings: This is by far the most common countertransference manifestation encountered. Young therapists are almost always terribly frightened that, if they have sexual feelings about the patient, they will do the case irreparable harm. Actually, precisely the reverse is true. If an attractive young lady comes to treatment, finds her therapist in reality cold and indifferent to her charms, her symptoms may, in fact, get worse instead of better. One of the major lessons a therapist must try to teach his patients is that there is a vast difference between a wish and an action. Sexual wishes are normal; sexual actions in a therapeutic situation are harmful.

Actually, young therapists reveal that they are bending over backward to hide true feelings. Unconsciously, one motive for entering the profession is that it does give access to sexual feelings that are otherwise kept secret, just as an unconscious motive for entering medicine is to be able to touch the body—again something otherwise forbidden. In his zeal to hide the sexual wish, the therapist leans to the opposite extreme and tends to become completely neutral. The patient often senses the unconscious hypocrisy and reacts negatively.

d) Blocking Off Patient's Sexual Feelings: This is another common countertransference mistake that goes along with the previous one. The therapist, anxious to avoid the implication that he is leading his patients down the primrose path, besides being unconsciously afraid that sexual material will excite him too much, calls a halt to any expansion of sexual feeling that the patient experiences. He can do this by direct or by indirect interpretations, or he can even do it by a statement to the effect that the patient is "acting out" too much. (It should be noted that the concept of "acting out," while of great value, is frequently invoked to confirm the therapist's prejudice rather than for valid scientific reasons.) A patient who regards the therapist's statements as on a par with religious doctrine, if she is in positive transference, will respond to any interpretation as a direct command. The result will be that she comes to feel guilty in situations where she should be pleased with the freedom of her actions.

Herbert was a therapist with an unsolved homosexual conflict. One of his first patients was a young girl who came to treatment with a classical hysterical symptom. Analysis revealed that this covered up various sexual wishes. When this was interpreted to the patient, she began to have sexual experiences with the young man whom she was dating. The therapist, rationalizing his actions by the statement that she was becoming "schizophrenic" ordered her to discontinue these experiments.

Sometimes, doctrinal prejudices are used to deny the sexual character of the patient's actions or wishes. The various reasons why there have been so many denominational disputes within the field of psychotherapy are beyond the scope of this book. But whatever the rationale offered, in practice, many therapists who oppose Freud use the theoretical opposition to blind themselves to the most obvious sexual material in their patient's productions.

Milton, a man in his 30s, had the most terrible fear of touching a girl's body. He suffered from premature ejaculation; the girls whom he chose as partners were invariably frustrated. He was in therapy with an analyst of the Horney School who kept on interpreting his fear of the woman's body in characterological terms. This did not help. When he finally went to another therapist, who discussed in specific terms the fear of touching a woman, its origins, its unconscious meanings in terms of mother and father, and so forth, the problem cleared up.

Of course, if the therapist himself has not come to grips with his own sexual difficulties, as is the case not too infrequently, he will not be able to handle his patient's sexual conflicts satisfactorily. Again, the decisive factor is the amount of growth that the therapist has achieved in his own life, not the theoretical school he adheres to. When growth is not completed, countertransference reactions mar the therapy.

e) Blocking Off Discussion of Infantile Sexuality: Not only the direct wish for sexual intercourse but the whole gamut of infantile sexuality comes under scrutiny in any intensive psychotherapy. Masturbation, incestuous wishes, homosexual fantasies, anal wishes, fel-

latio, cunnilingus, and so forth, are all there to be examined therapeutically in terms of what they have meant to the patient as well as
how they are being blocked off at the present time. In this process,
the therapist must have free access to his own experience in these
areas, as well as to his own conscious wishes about them. If he has not,
he is bound to lead the patient to repress some vital material.

In the early days of the writer's training, he was instructed to stay
away from incestuous material in the early stages since it could pro-
voke a psychosis. This was standard technique at that time. Once by
accident he asked a patient how close he had come to incest in childhood, and the answers that came out were most revealing, while they
did not precipitate any kind of psychotic episode. Since then it has been
routine practice to ask this question, and the consequences have been
excellent. One can only come to the conclusion that many therapists
have not worked through their own incestuous feelings sufficiently to
be able to handle them comfortably with patients.

> A 30-year-old man came to therapy because of blind rages and
> creative block in his painting. He had been through about a year of
> therapy with another therapist some years before, with relatively
> little effect. When asked in the initial session how close he had ever
> come to incest he replied: "Incest," and went on to relate how he had
> twice had intercourse with his sister while they were children. In the
> entire year of previous therapy this had not been brought up at all,
> perhaps because of the other therapist's fear that such highly charged
> material could have an explosive effect. The results of the revelation
> were excellent. The patient made a good relationship and went on to
> make a number of significant changes.

A third way in which excesses of positive countertransference can
harm the analysis is by making the patient too dependent. In effect,
the analyst in these situations never lets the patient grow up. The
countertransference here is similar to that of a smothering mother
who uses a variety of hypocritical rationalizations to cover up her
fear of allowing the child to grow up and leave her, which would make
her feel useless and abandoned.

The analyst may keep his patient dependent for various reasons.
He may relish the sense of power that he derives from running the
lives of dependent people, or he may cover up the deficiencies in his
own life by desperately holding on to others. Here are some clinical
vignettes:

Dr. S., an alcoholic psychiatrist, had a practice largely confined to patients recently released from mental hospitals. Almost all of them had a technical diagnosis of schizophrenia, which Dr. S. exploited to the fullest advantage. At times, when Dr. S. was extremely lonely, she would call up a patient at 1 or 2 in the morning and ask, "Don't you want to see me?" The patient, pleased and flattered by the interest shown by the psychiatrist, would go over immediately. Needless to say, this kind of treatment could not be kept up indefinitely, and patients would then experience a variety of terrible feelings of rejection. Eventually, Dr. S. herself was hospitalized. After release from the hospital she did not improve and eventually committed suicide.

The case of Dr. R. was much less obvious. Dr. R. had nursed a sick, dying wife for a period of many years, as well as a dying mother. Shaken by these two experiences, he had made a second marriage to an incredibly unattractive woman, devoid of either brains or beauty. It was a marriage that no one could understand.

One of his patients was a most attractive young girl, who was given to extreme anxieties, fits of depression, and temper tantrums. One of the patient's main demands was that in those moments when she felt horribly panicky someone should hold her. Nobody had ever really cared for her, and the only way in which she could believe that someone really loved her was if she could be held.

Dr. R. fell into the trap. He rationalized his treatment by saying that the patient was "schizophrenic" (which she was not). When she asked to be held, he held her, a procedure which obviously gave him a great deal of gratification in view of the deficiencies in his own life. He plied her with drugs, reassurance, suggestions, and a virtually total domination of her life. The patient in some ways felt grateful to Dr. R., but in other ways resented him deeply, because it was clear that she could not grow up under this kind of treatment. Eventually, she left, with a minimum of therapeutic benefit.

2) Negative Countertransference

Although the therapist is in a profession in which the goal is to help the patient who comes to him, it need scarcely be said that a certain amount of hostility may be present in varying degrees. The psychoanalytic observation that all human relationships are ambivalent applies to the analyst-patient relationship as well, and the ambivalence of the analyst must be subjected to careful scrutiny.

Three types of hostility in the analyst may be distinguished: First, where the basic hostility toward other people simply has not been overcome; second, where there are differential reactions to certain patients; and third, where the hostility is aroused by something that the patient has said or done. Each of these must be considered in turn.

a) Unanalyzed Hostility: Since the basic attitude toward the emotionally disturbed individual in our culture is one of repulsion or hostility, the professional comes into his work with this bias. As a rule it will take him several years of analysis to overcome the bias even to some extent. If the therapist has not had any analysis, or if the analysis has concentrated on some severe symptom not related to the total character structure of the individual, or if the total character structure of the individual has not been taken under scrutiny, then a good deal of hostility toward his patients will remain.

It is rare to find a therapist who will say frankly: "I do not like this patient," much as it is rare to find one person saying frankly to another, "I do not like you." The therapist, after all, is in a position where he has to pretend at least to the outer world that he has the best interests of the patient at heart. In this respect he is in the same position as any other member of the helping profession. Freud's comment may be recalled here, that the physician goes into medicine because of repressed sadism. To what extent that is so is open to question, but certainly it is one motivation which must be given full consideration. The wish to help in all the healing professions frequently covers over the wish to hurt.

Usually, the hostility of the therapist is covered over either by some diagnostic label, or by some unwise technical procedure. Since he does not like the patient, he says, in effect, "I do not want you to get any better." This is reformulated as, "You cannot get any better; you are doomed to be the way you are." Based on his assumption that the patient cannot get any better, the therapist will frequently resort to some uncalled-for technical procedure such as shock treatment, excessive drugs, or premature hospitalization.

Here are a few clinical examples:

Hobart, a 23-year-old young man, given to repeated depressions with suicidal content, was admitted to the psychiatric ward and assigned to Dr. W., a first-year resident. The young man's symptomatology went back to the illness of his mother, who had attempted suicide over a period of many years, had been hospitalized without any adequate results, and eventually died as a result of suicide. Hobart's depression was unusual in that it was not evoked by any disappointment in life, but seemed to be generated as a memory of what he had gone through with his mother. The attending psychiatrist had to impress upon the resident that this was an unusual case, but Dr. W., who had never had any analysis, was unable to comprehend the patient involved. His only concern was whether to diagnose him a psychotic depression or a neurotic depression. He combed his textbooks with a fine-tooth comb, searching out the pertinent discriminatory characteristics related to each diagnosis. In the meantime, the antisuicidal precautions were so weak that he even allowed the patient to keep a belt, which Hobart laughingly reported to the attending at a later stage. It was clear that Dr. W. was rather angry at the patient, who was unusual, and through his unusualness baffled the physician's reliance on textbooks. It was clearly a case where only a warm humanitarian empathic approach to the patient could have any results. Eventually Dr. W. was so angered by the patient that he wanted to send him to a state hospital, which would have had catastrophic results for Hobart. It was only through the intervention of the attending, a colleague of Dr. W.'s supervisor, that some sense could be made out of what had happened to the patient.

Dr. R., a 28-year-old psychiatrist, had gone through a serious depression herself in the course of her training, which necessitated hospitalization. Partly as a result of this experience, she had gone into psychiatry. However, her analysis was seriously incomplete, since she had concentrated only on getting over the worst of the depression.

One of her patients was a man in his late 40s who was in many ways similar to her father. This man, Jack, fell madly in love with Dr. R. Although an outpatient he would spend hours on end at the hospital, trying to gain a glimpse of her as she went through her rounds. Jack came from another city, where he had had an unhappy experience with his former family and their psychiatrist.

Jack had been married for many years to a woman with whom he had two children. When they were divorced, the children were put in psychotherapy. The psychiatrist advised Jack to leave the city and never see the children again. Jack complied.

It was understandable that Jack would fall into a severe masochistic dependent love transference with Dr. R. He followed her around the hospital; he would come to the hospital late at night. He bought lottery tickets, giving her half of the winnings if there were any. He sent her flowers. He took an apartment near the hospital, offering to let her use it whenever she wished, with or without him.

Dr. R.'s countertransference to all this love was one of extreme annoyance. Why did this man bother her so much? Why did he follow her around? Why did he send her flowers? Why was he so attached? And so on. She did not realize that she was expressing, in her feelings toward Jack, her general feelings toward her ex-husband and toward men. Instead of trying to understand the dynamics of the man, she spent her time with the supervisor arguing whether or not this man should be called "schizophrenic." Eventually her anger at the patient mounted to such an extent that she switched him to another therapist. This was most fortunate since, if she had not switched him, she could have done him more harm.

Diagnosis as a Countertransference: The uselessness of diagnosis as an approach to therapy has already been discussed at length in Chapter 2. Here, what we would like to discuss is the way in which diagnosis is used to conceal the hostile countertransference.

In former centuries mental patients, suspected of being "witches" or "possessed by devils" were probed with irons, tortured, thrown into the water, or otherwise lacerated until they died. In many cases they were simply put to death on the ground that they had poisoned or harmed some upstanding member of the community. The theory of the persecution of witches, if it can be glorified by such a name, stated that there were demons in certain people that could be exorcised and demons in other people that could not be exorcised.

This notion carried over to the concept of psychiatric diagnosis. There are illnesses from which the patient recovers—that is, demons that can be exorcised—and illnesses from which the patient does not recover—demons that cannot be exorcised. The latter, the illnesses from which the patient cannot recover, are generally grouped under the heading of schizophrenia (it may be recalled that when Bleuller first coined the term, he spoke not of schizophrenia but of a group of schizophrenias). The analogy was carried to the point where, if a patient who allegedly had schizophrenia recovered, the diagnosis was changed; he must have been either neurotic or had a manic-depressive psychosis. The only major point made about schizophrenia in Kraepelinian psychiatry was that it is a hereditary, incurable illness.

Although much has changed since Kraepelin, this image of the doomed schizophrenic, the man with a demon that cannot be exorcised, lurks in the background of all psychiatric thinking. The enormous difficulties that lie in the path of treating the schizophrenic are ascribed to the demons, rather than to the society, or culture, or the family, or other external circumstances.

Psychoanalytic psychiatry has built up a radically different view toward the schizophrenic; from its point of view, the schizophrenic is a person who has suffered severe rejection from a mother early in childhood. As a result of this severe rejection, the patient never manages to reach any kind of meaningful human relationships later on in life. Because of the ego weakness and its consequence, even when good relationships later are offered to the patient, he tends to reject them or to spoil them. It is only through long, patient treatment with an understanding practitioner that this underlying suspicion and hostility toward the world can be changed.

As has been mentioned before, the problem in the treatment of the schizophrenic lies in the first stage—establishing the relationship. Because of his history of rejection, his suspiciousness, his projections, his hostility, the schizophrenic makes it very difficult to establish any kind of relationship with a therapist. If the focus is on establishing a relationship, as is the case with the courageous and sensitive analytical therapists who have treated them, then eventually a relationship is established and the patient can be helped. If the focus is on attaching some diagnostic label to the patient, the result is literally to make the patient worse. Where we have a human being who craves warmth and interpersonal intimacy, he is given a harsh label and thrown into a hospital where he is met with coldness, rejection, and indifference. The very thing that he is most afraid of is given him in abundance. A more ludicrous and tragic situation would be hard to imagine.

It follows from a clinical point of view that the primary distinction should be between those who are willing to accept treatment and those who are not. Whether the patient is called "schizophrenic" or not is entirely beside the point. If he is willing to make a relationship and accept treatment, the rest can be handled in terms of the way in which he reacts to the treatment.

Once the patient makes the relationship, then it makes little difference what diagnostic label is attached to him. If the patient does not make a relationship, or does not make one readily, then the entire effort of the therapist must be devoted to establishing one. Again here, it makes little difference what technical label is used. What counts is the maneuvers that the patient adopts to avoid establishing a relationship. Thus, once more, the diagnosis is essentially irrelevant.

If a psychiatrist's treatment is pursued in accordance with the goals rather than in accordance with prescribed techniques, then all patients are amenable to treatment to a greater or lesser degree. The kind of treatment would vary not with the technical diagnosis, but with the kind of relationship that the patient establishes. If the therapist puts the emphasis in this direction, he can establish a warm, interpersonal, empathic contact with the patient, the kind that is most likely to produce therapeutic results. If the therapist interposes a diagnosis to salve his conscience, or to cover up his hostility, then a new barrier is placed between the therapist and the patient, and further difficulties are created.

b) *Differential Reactions:*

Differential reactions to certain patients may be based on hostilities in the analyst, because these patients remind him of figures in the past from whom he has not yet achieved total liberation. When the analyst notices these hostilities, he should engage in further self-analysis to find out why these figures from the past still haunt him. The patient, even though he or she may resemble someone with whom the analyst did have difficulties, is after all now in the position of a patient rather than in the kind of real-life situation that the analyst was involved in before. This, in turn, should help the analyst work out his previous hostilities. Here is a rather typical instance:

> Katherine, a 25-year-old girl, came to analysis because of depression and difficulties with men. In a previous analytic experience, she had found that the analyst could understand her without criticizing her in this way. At the same time, she had broken off the other analysis for external reasons.
>
> With the present analyst, she began with a tremendous amount of hostility. Nobody could equal her previous analyst. The present analyst, Dr. S., did not understand her, gave interpretations that were completely absurd. What she needed was someone to comfort her, to recognize her assets. Katherine believed that she was so extraordinarily attractive that all she had to do was walk into a room and all the men would admire her. She firmly believed that she had enormous capabilities, for example as a dancer, and if she had given herself a chance, she could have become a professional dancer of world renown.
>
> As the therapy progressed, Dr. S. found himself getting more and more angry toward Katherine. In self-analysis he realized that she reminded him very much of his first wife, whom he had divorced after years of bitter struggle. She was narcissistic, demanding of attention and praise, blind to her faults, devoid of insights. At the same time, he recognized that Katherine, although she was in many ways similar to his first wife, was now a patient and not a potential

mate. Yet he was unable to give Katherine any interpretations because of her extremely hostile reactions. All he could do was accept
her as she was. This proved to be an entirely novel experience for
him. He began to reflect on what might have happened if he had
accepted his first wife as she was. In the course of this self-analysis,
he achieved a greater sense of freedom and liberation from the hurts
of the past.

c) *Reactive Hostility:*

Finally, a good deal of hostility is often generated in analysts by
patients who attack them indiscriminately or by patients who do not
make any appreciable progress. The analyst feels frustrated in that his
efforts have met with so little success, and covers up his frustration
with a good deal of anger.

Beginning therapists lose many patients by bombarding them with
interpretations, whether correct or incorrect. A number of reasons
can be adduced for this kind of mistake which should be considered
mainly a manifestation of countertransference.

First of all, the analyst is still in analysis, usually, or often, in negative transference and blaming his analyst for not giving him the right
interpretations that would resolve his difficulties immediately. In reaction to this situation, he then becomes the good mother giving the
child (patient) the food that he has not been getting from his own
mother (analyst).

It is much harder for the analyst or patient to appreciate the non-
intellectual aspects of analysis—the warmth, the capacity to listen,
the constant readiness to offer encouragement and support, the intimacy, the chance to reveal things which haven't been revealed
before, and so on. The entire gamut of transference feelings is much
harder to appreciate from the point of view of the analysand than
from the point of view of the analyst.

Second, the analyst feels that he has to offer the patient something.
In a way, this ties in with the first point of not appreciating the significance of the non-intellectual factors in analysis. The analysand has
a hard time appreciating what the analyst is giving him. It is only
after he has had enough experiences of the kind where a patient says
after some time: "I don't know what you're doing for me, you never
say anything. But it sure helps me to come here," that he can appreciate the real nature of the therapeutic process.

Third, as a result of his theoretical training, the new analyst is full
to the brim with all kinds of profound knowledge of the psychological

processes. When material is offered to him, it is only natural that he should jump at it with all the information he has so recently acquired. What he fails to appreciate is that the most significant aspect of the analytic process is the production of material. It is only when enough material is produced that interpretation really has any actual value. The countertransference problem is one of shifting the emphasis from the analyst to the patient.

Fourth, the analyst does not realize that interpretation is seen as a criticism. He may baffle or antagonize or even confuse the patient. It does not matter if the interpretation is correct or not. In his seminars, the analyst has generally concentrated on whether the interpretation correctly gathers up what the patient is telling him. He fails to consider what the effect of the interpretation is on the patient. When the patient is still relatively new, the problem is one of establishing a relationship, and interpretation is experienced as a threat of rejection by the analyst.

While the net effect of interpretation is to drive the patient away, this is by no means always the case. Examples of abrupt terminations as a result of poorly timed interpretations have been given earlier, under the heading of first treatment resistance and the transference. But it also happens that patients will swallow inaccurate or inappropriate interpretations for a long time as a result of a masochistic personality structure, and will leave only when external circumstances are appropriate. Here are some clinical examples:

Jane, a 27-year-old editorial worker, went to therapy because of recurrent feelings of depression, and repeated unhappy love affairs with men. She did not know that the therapist was a surgeon who had gone into psychiatry without much real training. Jane was actually a verbal, cultured girl with a sufficiently strong ego, excellent analytic material. The therapist, instead of giving her a chance to bring out the data of her life, began to bombard her with certain one-sided and biased interpretations almost from the very beginning. Her first approach was that Jane had been raped by her father when she was a little girl. Jane had no memory of any such rape, but felt that if the psychiatrist said so there must be some basis for it. She therefore searched her memory for any material that could lead to such a conclusion. The psychiatrist said that she had derived this conclusion from careful study of the patient's dreams, not one dream in particular, but the whole pattern of dreams. Jane did not believe these absurdities, but still swallowed them. The other interpretation was that Jane's mother had tried to abort her—this also the psychiatrist deduced from dreams. This, too, Jane inwardly thought absurd, but outwardly accepted.

After some three years of this kind of "analysis," the psychiatrist one day suddenly decided that Jane needed religion. Jane noted that the psychiatrist had a strong religious attachment with statues of Jesus and other religious figures abundantly spread all over the house. This cause, which the psychiatrist pushed with great determination, came out of the blue. When the summer vacation came, Jane could no longer tolerate the situation and did not return. Typically she could not tell the psychiatrist directly; instead she wrote her a letter.

While there had been some relief from the depression, probably as a result of the situation, the therapy was very largely a waste.

Al, a 22-year-old veteran, was extremely anxious about his life. He met a fellow who was a student in an analytic institute, and who offered to take him on as a trial case. This friend, John, then became Al's mentor. He spent enormous amounts of time with him, sometimes as much as six to eight hours.

John took over Al's entire life. He would take him out to dinner, introduce him to girls, and so on. The "analysis" was based entirely on interpretations of free association. For example, Al had a recurring thought of shooting an arrow into the air, which John interpreted as a wish to have intercourse with mother. Another fantasy of shooting a gun at a stranger was interpreted as a wish to kill father. As long as John kept up the relationship, Al felt rather good. He was a rather weak, dependent kind of man who enjoyed the attention and support that he was getting.

Then John abruptly stopped the "therapy." Al almost collapsed and but for fortunate circumstances might have ended up with a brief hospital stay.

After the break-up with John, Al began to look for another analyst but, spoiled by his previous experience, he made all kinds of demands, which he knew in advance the analyst would not grant. Finally, one analyst made some concessions in order to begin treatment, which Al accepted. Once these concessions were past, and the treatment was continued on a regular basis, Al went into an almost violent negative transference which lasted for more than a year. It was only after the negative transference had been worked out that Al began to make a great deal of progress in his life. Eventually, the real analysis, since the first experience could hardly be called that, resulted in an outstanding success.

NONANALYTIC INTERVENTION

There are many situations where some intervention on the part of the analyst is called for. But there are equally as many situations where this intervention is motivated more by countertransference reactions than by the needs of the patient. Such measures as reassurance, supportive therapy, free treatment, drugs, shock, premature hospitalization, or other direct intervention in the patient's life should be used only with the greatest of caution, and only if the analyst is convinced on the basis of objective evidence that real analytic help will not be a benefit to the patient at that time. There are a great many instances where the analyst, because of his unconscious hostility to the patient, or because of defiance to his own analyst or to the profession, insists that the patient is untreatable, or untreatable by analytic means, and resorts to all kinds of measures that immediately make the situation worse. In by far the great majority of cases, analytic help is the kind that is most needed.

It is an essential part of the analyst's growth to realize that his own analysis is the most important experience in his life. The more this conviction is strengthened in him, the easier it will be to give his patients the only real help that he is in a position to give, true psychoanalysis.

SUGGESTIONS FOR FURTHER READING

See references to Chapter 11.

CHAPTER 13

The Learning Process in Psychotherapy

Bless me, whose deepest suffering,
deepest of human suffering, was this—
I could not be the one I longed to be.

A. Strindberg: *The Great
Highway*

It is obvious that psychotherapy is a learning procedure. Because of this, numerous attempts have been made to apply conventional learning theory to the process. These attempts have, by and large, met with little welcome from the more experienced, better-trained psychotherapists, for a variety of reasons. Primary among them is the fact that conventional learning theories arise very largely from animal experimentation and deal with concepts and procedures that are much too elementary for the complex activities undertaken in the psychotherapeutic process.

As a result, psychoanalysis and psychoanalytic therapy have had to adopt their own theory of learning, independent of what is more usually referred to as learning theory. The psychoanalytic concept of learning is based on actual clinical experience with the patients who undergo the process. Its basic concepts are the concepts described and used throughout this book—establishing a relationship, transference, countertransference, resistance, working-through, and so on.

At the same time, it is in order to subject the entire learning procedure to a more careful analysis.

In psychotherapy, problems are isolated, elaborated, and eventually change the person's pattern of behavior. Ideally, the learning procedure for any one problem goes through five distinct stages:

1. definition of the problem
2. elaboration of the problem in the present
3. roots of the problem in the past

4. insight—increased awareness of various aspects of the problem
5. change

Each of these will be considered in turn.

First it is essential to appraise the role of therapist and certain aspects of the relationship between the therapist and the patient, since it is this that gives the distinctive coloring to the learning process in psychotherapy.

Experience shows that the therapist is essential to the process. Self-analysis is at best merely an aid to the more formal procedure; in most cases it is totally ineffectual. The question is why the therapist is so important.

From the beginning of therapy throughout, the patient is expected to *produce material*. In this respect, as already mentioned, psychotherapy differs from all other learning procedures, since without this production of material, little or no learning can take place.

An apparent exception to this can be made in the treatment of psychotics; in many cases the analyst has to guess what the patient has in mind. But even there, the guessing is based on something that the patient has done or something similar that some other patient has done; there is an extrapolation from something that the patient offers the therapist, not a bolt from the blue.

A simple example may illustrate this point.

A young man had been given up by the previous psychiatrist because he could not "understand his gibberish." After a short time in therapy with the present analyst, he came in one day and would not talk. He walked around the room holding his fingers to his mouth, indicating that he was not going to say a word. The analyst was baffled by this behavior, and had no clue to what was going on. At this point, the patient suddenly handed the analyst a series of index cards, with notes on them. The patient was a student at one of the local universities, and these were apparently notes that were taken in his classes.

The analyst glanced through these notes and found one with a quotation from Lao Tse-tung, saying "Silence is golden." When he came across the quotation, he took a stab that the patient was acting out the idea that silence would somehow lead to a therapeutic success. At this, the patient said, "How did you know?" and began to talk.

Admittedly, it was a lucky guess on the part of the analyst, but even this lucky guess could not have been made without the help of the cards that had been offered to him by the patient.

The production of the material is important because of what is done with it. First of all, it helps to focus on what is crucially relevant. Second, it is a point of departure from which a start can be made, the most relevant point of departure, since it deals with what is uppermost in the patient's mind.

In producing the material, the patient becomes anxious in various ways. This anxiety can be broken down into two types: separation anxiety and castration anxiety (punishment anxiety, in more ordinary terms). For each of these anxieties, the therapist plays a specific role.

For *separation anxiety,* the therapist provides a long-term continuous relationship in which the patient can hopefully come to feel completely at ease. In this situation, as has been seen, many patients are overcome by a terrible fear of rejection which has no concrete basis, but is rooted in the patient's past. By actually interacting with the therapist, the patient brings the separation anxiety to the fore, and manages to overcome it or lessen it considerably. (Incidentally, this is a theoretical argument against brief therapy; in a brief encounter, the separation anxiety can never be handled properly.)

Separation anxiety is one of the most awful fears that face the human being. It is known now that in childhood, premature separation from the mother can lead to severe ego distortions—or if too early, to actual death. If the separation is prolonged in childhood, nothing short of therapy in later life will ever undo the harm that has been done.

As the individual grows and his ego becomes stronger, the capacity to tolerate separation becomes greater. In fact, from one point of view, the entire course of development can be viewed as an increasing separation from the mother and, still later, from the typical family set-up. But no matter how strong the ego is, separation is always a blow.

A parallel can be drawn between the way separation anxiety is handled by an adult and the way in which it is handled by the child. It is obvious that no infant can tolerate separation from the mother or some adult substitute for any appreciable length of time. The only "cure" is to provide some other person who will give the comfort, security, and physical care that are necessary for the maintenance of life and well-being.

The case is similar with the adult. While adults do pride themselves on their ability to tolerate separation, in reality they do not have the capacity that they assume they do. If an adult is rejected by a loved one, the reaction is to seek some other person or to defend himself by seeking no one; this process has a parallel in the child. The only real resolution of the problem lies in recognizing the infantile character of the separation anxiety, thus freeing himself to make adult choices. This freeing can only be done through the agency of some other person; in the analytic situation, through the agency of the analyst. This is another fundamental reason why the therapist is of such crucial importance to the entire process.

For *castration (punishment) anxiety,* a different rationale exists. Punishment is the holdover of the parents who punished or threatened to punish the patient when he was a small child. Now, this kind of punishment relates most directly to a child's instinctual manifestations; the process of socialization is one in which the child gives up various methods of instinctual gratification at the request of significant figures. This process is crystallized in the superego, which makes the person feel guilty about his wishes. Guilt is superego punishment.

The superego is the heir of the parents. It is formed in the interaction with other significant people, and can only be changed in the same way—that is, by interaction with others. Here again the therapist becomes a vital necessity. The patient projects his superego to the therapist; a consistent comparison of this projection with the reality of the therapist serves to break down the superego in the course of time.

> A typical example is Rachel, a 25-year-old girl who came to treatment with a variety of problems. As soon as she started treatment, she stopped masturbating. The therapist inquired why she had done that, to which she replied that it was a dirty habit and the therapist must look down on her for it. It took a long time to convince her that in this regard, as well as her sexual feelings, the therapist was quite different from her parents.

This leads up to a basic feature of every therapeutic process. When the patient becomes aware of some impulse, such as masturbation in the above example, he tends to feel guilty about it. This guilt is overcome by the therapist's more permissive attitude. However, it can never be overcome all at once. Time is needed to erase the overpowering images of the parents.

In each session the patient comes in with some further impulse on his mind that makes him feel guilty. This is the optimal combination of guilt and fantasy spoken of before. The therapist does not disapprove of the impulse; hence, the superego is weakened to that extent during that hour. But the old superego reasserts itself, once the session is over, for it is a psychological fact of life that no psychic phenomenon disappears without a struggle. The next session the patient is back with more forbidden impulses. Again the therapist-projected superego is much more benign than had been thought, and again the patient makes some inroads into his guilt. As this is done over and over again, eventually the superego weakens or disappears altogether and is replaced by conscious rational choices.

Outside, the patient will often be unable to get away from the impulse-superego-punishment sequence, if only for a moment. With the help of the therapist, a substitute parent figure, the patient is able to have long quiet periods in which the superego remains quiescent. Then, as the superego's force is diminished, these quiet periods become longer and longer, until in the ideal case, the patient has permanently reduced his level of anxiety.

The situation here is the same as that with separation anxiety. The loss of one person can only be compensated for by some other human being. The harsh superego of the patient can only be broken down by the repeated presence of a benign person (in this case, the analyst).

As a result of this process, temporarily the patient becomes excessively dependent on the therapist. He believes for a while that only the therapist is forgiving, while the outside world still remains the superego projected from his parents. To some extent, he is of course right in this observation but he is wrong in his estimation of his ability to cope with the disapproval of the outside world.

Alerted to this eventuality, the therapist on the one hand offers gratification by allowing the patient to come and talk, and on the other, offers some insight into the way in which other people relieve anxiety. Gradually the patient begins to acquire more confidence in himself as a result of this continuous contact with a different kind of superego figure.

The procedure could be summed up as follows:

The patient produces material that contains forbidden impulses.

True to his past, the patient punishes himself for these impulses.

The therapist-new superego does not give any punishment, merely understands the impulses.

As this continues, the patient feels less and less threatened by his impulses.

Eventually, he can talk about them freely, which gives him the possibility of rational choice; that is, he can now choose those impulses that can be given reality gratification and discard those that cannot. In either case, he makes his own choice on a conscious, rational basis, whereas before he was driven compulsively to act in certain ways that were too often self-destructive.

After this preliminary, we can return to the outline of the ideal learning procedure.

1) Definition of the Problem

Unlike other learning procedures, the patient in psychotherapy has only a foggy notion of what his problems are. True, he feels certain things bothering him; these are the ego-dystonic symptoms. But quite often, even with the most severe problems, the patient will deny that he has anything bothering him.

This becomes one of the characteristic features of psychotherapy, which differentiates it from other learning procedures. In fact, the patient first has to be told, or first has to clarify what he wishes to learn. A goodly part of psychotherapy then is made up of the consistent effort, based on the material that the patient has produced, to show him that he has certain problems that it is worth his while to look into more carefully. In the beginning, this is the heart of the matter, but it goes on all through the therapy.

Human beings find it difficult to be observant of themselves; rather, they tend to be judgmental. There is a joke about self-analysis: the reason it breaks down is the countertransference. Self-observation is a continuation of the parental judging process. When something "bad" is noted, either the person will see it as correctible, in which case he feels hope, or as unchangeable, in which case he feels despair.

Outside of therapy, people find it hard to make these judgments. They tend rather to think that if something is bad, it will never change (the cliché, after all, is that human nature doesn't change). Thus it arouses anxiety, and then in turn a variety of defense mechanisms.

The presence of the therapist changes this picture. Now that the problems are crystallized out, there is hope that it will change with therapy, even if the process of change is only dimly perceived. Hence, the patient in therapy becomes more willing to talk about his problems.

There are two things that interfere with this willingness. One is the fact that even though therapy strongly underscores the possibility of change, it offers no guarantee. Second, no sooner does the therapeutic process start than transferences and resistances of all kinds come up. Instead of focusing objectively on the inner conflicts, the patient enters into a transference relationship with the therapist. These transferences then have to be resolved before the objective problems are tackled, although in practice the two procedures continue side by side.

It is up to the therapist to help the patient formulate whatever problems he wishes to work on. The therapist provides encouragement; the patient formulates it in his own language. This, however, is an individual matter. If the patient is unable to verbalize freely, the therapist will come to his aid, but if he can verbalize quite freely it is best to leave him alone. This is closer to tutorial learning than to classroom teaching.

Preferably, problems should be formulated in terms of the analytic ideal; that is, at an early stage it is desirable to make clear to the patient that his feelings of unhappiness are intimately linked with his failure to reach some aspect of the ideal. Which aspect this will be depends on a lot of factors, including external circumstances. Here, the tact and ingenuity of the therapist have to be brought into play. If a problem is picked up that is of little consequence, the patient may feel temporarily more comfortable, but the therapeutic outcome will not be as great.

The problem as formulated is always of a relatively simple nature; the simpler the formulation the more impressive it is to the patient.

> Tom came into therapy at his wife's insistence because he suffered from premature ejaculation. In itself, this did not bother him, but he wished to placate her. After the usual exploratory period, the therapist at one point said that Tom seemed to be insecure in all the major undertakings of his life. This made an immediate impression and was picked up by Tom as a deeper motive for seeking therapy.

From one point of view, it does not really matter too much how the problem or problems are formulated by the patient; what counts is that he should be able to formulate it in his own words. For the main goal at this stage of therapy is to increase the motivation of the patient. Every patient comes in with certain resistances to the idea of treatment. *Until it is clear that the patient is adequately motivated in his own terms, everything else is of subordinate importance.*

Thus, the initial stage of finding the problem includes the initial phase of strengthening the motivation, which brings us back to the earlier formulations of the analytic honeymoon and the first treatment crisis. All these stages are necessary to convince the patient that he has a problem that it is worth his while to face.

As an example, take the illustrative case presented in Chapter 2. First of all, the patient refused therapy for a long time, even though he had had a nervous breakdown in the Army. When he did come, it was on the secondary issue of vocational guidance. When he finally accepted therapy, it was only on a trial basis, for two months; he would "look around and see." When he did get under way, the problem he focused on was the sense of aimlessness in his life. This made more sense to him than any comments on his breakdown or his homosexuality or his retreat from women. This is the sort of thing that remains unpredictable in therapy; *a priori* one might guess that he might refuse therapy again, or focus on his sexual conflicts more directly.

At one point, he himself commented that in the early sessions he was filled with a tremendous resentment, which on previous occasions he would have handled by walking out on the situation. Instead, he restrained himself, which provided an opportunity to look at the great resentment that he felt. From this he went on to connect the aimlessness with the bitter feelings about his mother. That was not very far from the realization that he had been living negatively, to get away from her, rather than with some positive goal in mind.

In the meantime, various transference manifestations were investigated, such as the need to say "Thank you" at the end of every session. Through it all, there is a series of steps which are determined by the constellation of psychic forces in the patient's unconscious. Because of this, the therapist is many times forced into a passive position. He has to wait for what the patient produces, has to be alert to what the patient grants or does not grant, in order to make meaningful interpretations. In one sense, it could be said that every patient has every problem; that is why the diagnostic systems fail. But in another sense, this is irrelevant, because what counts is what he sees, not what he is unconsciously suffering from. This vision of his must be carefully nurtured and allowed to grow by the therapist; therein lies the art of therapy.

The patients who experience the greatest difficulty are those who are unable to formulate some aspect of themselves that they wish to change. Such strong denial is found in the most severely disturbed patients. At times, the preliminary period with them may take as long as several years before they can finally put something that they wish to change into words.

2) Roots of the Problem in the Present

From the vantage point of the therapist, the whole process of learning in psychotherapy can be divided into four stages: confrontation, clarification, interpretation, and working-through. The definition of the problem proceeds by a series of confrontations; usually one confrontation is not sufficient for the purpose.

One reason why interpretations are less essential to the process than the beginner ordinarily thinks is that they must always be preceded by a sufficient amount of confrontation and clarification. Thus, all confrontations are based on material that the patient himself produces. Each confrontation is accompanied by a varying amount of anxiety, and for that reason takes time to digest. Analytic tact must be developed, which consists of knowing how to keep anxiety within certain limits. If too much anxiety is aroused, the patient responds with excessive defensiveness; if too little is aroused, a situation of useless reassurance is established.

Although the goal of psychoanalysis can be expressed as expanding the id, strengthening the ego, and dissolving or weakening the superego, the expansion of the libido is still basic to the entire process. The total defensive structure of the patient is built up because his parents refused to permit him certain gratifications in childhood.

Accordingly, confrontations should be guided primarily by the principle of *expanding the libido*. That is, whenever some partially concealed wish appears in the patient's material, the analyst should take advantage of the opportunity to point it out to him. In this way, the analyst presents himself as a different kind of superego figure who is more permissive of the patient's instinctual drives, an idea which gradually seeps through.

What the patient is confronted with depends on the kind of material that he has brought out. Sometimes it may be a simple confrontation with a wish described in a dream. At other times, it may be advisable to point out some repetitive pattern in the patient's life that indicates some concealed wishes. Or, again, the confrontation may rest on some Freudian slip—although this latter is so well understood by now that it generally serves an entirely minor purpose in the course of analysis.

To help in the expansion of the libido it is best for the analyst to speak as bluntly as possible. Four-letter words, such as "fuck," "shit," "prick," "cunt," should be used freely. More abstract scientific language is, first of all, incomprehensible to a good many patients and, second, begins to make therapy sound like a clinical paper rather than a human interaction. Furthermore, since one of the major goals of therapy is to break down the superego, the analyst must behave like a non-superego figure who is not afraid of the four-letter words that are proscribed by common usage in our culture.

> A confrontation that was quite useful with Jerry, a homosexual young man, was the clarification of a period in his life about a year before the analysis began, when he lived in California, with his lover, who was supporting him. It turned out that in this period Jerry hardly ever went out on the streets, and felt extremely depressed. He was confronted with the fact that for all practical purposes he had had a breakdown. Although he rebelled against this confrontation, eventually he accepted it. A second confrontation was that he was bisexual, rather than homosexual.
>
> With these two confrontations—of the bisexuality rather than homosexuality, and the breakdown earlier in California, Jerry's analysis was put on a dynamic footing. Then came the task of exploring these confrontations further, elaborating them, and fitting them into the total life pattern.

It is virtually impossible to predict what confrontation will arouse a responsive reaction with any patient. Sometimes one works, sometimes another. The alert analyst will grope here and there and be guided by how the patient reacts, not by whether his confrontation is "correct" or not. A major criterion is whether the confrontation furthers the flow of material or whether it leads into a useless argument.

The second step in the process is *clarification.* Once the problem has been formulated in the patient's words, it is still necessary to have a good deal of elaboration. Sometimes this will take place in the present, sometimes in the past. The division is for convenience, not because it invariably follows this pattern. However, it is important to realize that the elaboration in the present is just as important, often more so, than its origins in the past.

This is also why one of the most frequently used phrases of the therapists is "Tell me more about it" or "What else comes to mind?" By being noncommittal the therapist makes sure that the patient will continue with his own train of thought rather than follow suggestions of the therapist. For the elaboration, all the material of psychotherapy is brought to bear on the problem. This serves a number of different purposes. First of all, the more material there is, the more is known about the problem, and the more full-blooded it becomes; second, the abundance of material bolsters the inner conviction of the patient that this problem is pretty important in his life; and third, both therapist and patient can then fill in many details of the problem and its relationship to the person's life. It is well to remember that this is an ideal, and that in practice the ideal does not always apply. The amount of material that different patients produce is variable. When there is an abundance of fantasy, it is easy to work with a patient, but this should not be taken to mean that when there is not too much fantasy, the patient is untreatable. Therapy is an individual learning process, and the therapist must be prepared to tailor his techniques to suit the needs of each patient.

Again, coming back to the illustrative case, after it had been established that he was moving through life aimlessly, the patient supplied many details from his previous life and from the present situation. When he came home from work, he had nothing to do. He had no female companionship, no special hobbies that he pursued, or any particular zeal. In short, he was a drifter. He formulated this in terms of patterns that he had had in the past, such as gambling and homosexuality, which had been abandoned.

One reason for getting the patient to tell as much about his life as he can is that the material is often unknown to the therapist and trivial to the patient. After all, as has been stressed, the patient is not a theoretician; he just wants to get well. It is only gradually that the value of all these dreams, fantasies, and memories that the therapist shows such an avid interest in begins to dawn on the patient as well.

This brings up another important point, which is all too often overlooked. Psychotherapy involves a radical shift in the psychological approach to living. In our culture, the usual psychological approach is one of trait psychology: a person is either good or bad, selfish or unselfish, ambitious or lazy, and the like. The patient who comes into psychotherapy uses this psychological framework. The diagnostic system is easier for him to grasp than the dynamics because it fits in with the structure of trait psychology.

It is wise for the therapist to realize that he is gradually teaching the patient a different kind of psychology. Some people take easily to dynamic propositions. Others react to them with much resistance, and find the greatest difficulty in comprehending them. When there is such a difficulty, the therapist must take time out, so to speak, to help the patient understand that this is the way in which it is most profitable to think about himself. Thus the question is not whether or not he is lazy, but what dynamic forces prevent him from undertaking the activities that he wishes to. If he comes with complaints about his wife or parents or children or other intimates, it is necessary to point out to him that the analyst is not there to decide who is right and who is wrong in such situations but to help him understand motivations, both his and those of other people. This indoctrination must necessarily occupy much more time in the beginning of therapy than later on, when it becomes second language to the patient as well. It is also this shift in dynamic psychology that makes the world of psychoanalysis so strange to a great many people.

In connection with the general question of clarification and elaboration, both in the present and in the past, the question frequently arises as to whether outside information is of value. Even leaving to one side the fact that this information is frequently biased either for or against the patient, it is clear that unless the patient produces the material himself, it is useless in therapy, for it is not what the therapist knows that leads to a good result, but how the patient fits it into his whole psychic makeup. This is also the reason why methods of information retrieval, like hypnosis and sodium amytal, are of no value in intensive psychotherapy. Therapy is a gradually growing emotional experience for the patient, and this remains the central fact from beginning to end.

Sometimes, it is even necessary to completely refuse any information that comes from the outside. What counts is the relationship between therapist and patient. If the patient gets the impression that the therapist is, so to speak, spying on him, he is apt to break off in anger. The emotional factors in therapy are more important than the intellectual and the basic principles of transference should guide every case. This is particularly applicable where there is a latent or open battle between the patient and someone very close to him on the outside, such as a marital dispute or an adolescent in a bitter battle with his parents. Sometimes, in such cases, especially with adolescents, it is necessary to advise the outside intimates that they should avoid any kind of contact with the therapist.

3) Roots of the Problem in the Past

This, together with the previous heading, make up the process of elaboration or clarification. Naturally. present and past can only be distinguished for theoretical reasons; in most cases there is a varying mixture of the two. As the patient talks about himself, his life begins to make more and more sense. The basic constellation of every person's life is the early family environment, which must be explored in as much detail as possible. No problem arises out of the blue; it has antecedents, parallels, and origins, which the patient slowly gets to see.

Many patients tend to reject the past as irrelevant. This attitude has a number of different dynamic reasons. First of all, to bring up the past is painful. Immediately the patient starts thinking about how he should have handled such-and-such a situation differently, with the usual rash of guilts and regrets. Secondly, there are enormous gaps in every person's memory—either gaps in the material itself or loss of the feeling surrounding the action. When the patient is so preoccupied with his immediate problem, how to handle it, how to resolve it, how to get out of it, he sees the past as a distracting side issue.

> Many years after a successful therapeutic experience, Al was unexpectedly fired from his job. Reluctantly, he returned to therapy because his reaction was so strong. He walked up and down, could not sleep, could not work, and showed other signs of agitation and depression. In therapy, it took quite a while to get back to the relevant childhood material. What he wanted to do was to go over and over the immediate situation and find out why he had been fired, even though he knew the answer fairly well.

What happens in a case like Al's is fairly typical. Troubled by a real life rebuff, he comes into therapy, and wishes to take up most of his time bemoaning his fate. This is the transference reaction; either he wants sympathy from the therapist or he ascribes to the therapist some magical power to undo the grievous rejection that he has suffered.

Freud once laid down the rule that if a patient talks about the present, the analyst should talk about the past, while if he talks about the past, the analyst should talk about the present. While not invariable, this rule is often helpful, for what has happened to the patient is a rupture in the time connections of his life, so that events seem isolated to him, without any real connection. It is the therapist's job to help him restore those connections and break through the sense of disjointedness.

Although he is ordinarily forced into a passive role, there are many situations where the analyst can inject more activity. One of them is the recall of the past. If the patient consistently stays away from the past, the therapist can from time to time inquire in a general way: "Is there anything in the past which is similar to what is going on now?" or "What could this correspond to in your childhood?" As

long as the therapist has the learning procedure firmly in mind, he will
be able to adjust his activity accordingly.

It should not be assumed that the mere recollection of past events
will in itself have curative value. What counts is really healing the
rupture between present and past, so that the patient can come to
have the feeling that his life is all of one piece. Sometimes past material will be relevant, sometimes present, sometimes both. The emphasis should always continue to be put on the way in which the patient's
awareness of himself and his life is growing.

Just as the elaboration of material in the present involves a shift
to a different kind of psychology, from trait to dynamic, the exploration of the past also involves a new kind of psychology. In greater or
lesser degree, the genetic point of view has to be taught to every
patient. Sometimes it has to be injected almost as a didactic exercise;
the patient must be told in so many words: You are this way because
you were brought up in such-and-such a manner, not because you
are inherently bad or because of external events. The growth process
must be formulated in a number of different ways and must be filled
in with as much detail as can be obtained from the material that the
patient produces.

Two formulations which the writer has found helpful are: Growth
proceeds from mother to father, and away from the family, which
helps to explain the various conflicts involved in interpersonal relations, and second, that growth proceeds from masturbation to intercourse. Even in ordinary language, "intercourse" has the double
meaning of social intercourse and sexual intercourse. The emphasis
on this kind of sexual growth focuses on the need to shift from pre-
genital to genital gratification.

In the pursuit of memory, a particular difficulty arises. Two situations must be distinguished here. First there are those who really are
amnesic before a certain age. This must be taken in stride and other
approaches to the problems adopted. Then there are those who do
remember a great deal, but insist at each point that their memories
are of little or no value. These people are dominated by a kind of
movie version of psychoanalysis, which leads them to believe that
they will recover one memory which will resolve the entire neurotic
conflict. There some simple education is necessary.

In terms of what has happened in the past, again, two types of
people can be distinguished, those who have had some dramatic,
traumatic experience or experiences which have left an indelible im-

pression on their minds, and those who have not. In both of these, the reconstitution of the past is of great importance, but in the latter kind of patient it is apt to take longer to make an impression. However, in the first, the danger arises that the traumatic experience will be dwelt on too long. Thus, no hard-and-fast rule can be set up about the recovery of memories; whatever the patient recovers has to be used as grist for the analytic mill.

Here are some typical instances of patients with deep traumatic incidents in childhood which left a powerful impression:

Cecilia, a 24-year-old actress, originally came to treatment because of severe depressions and a loss of direction in life. The first therapy, which was limited to two sessions a week for financial reasons, led to a compromise resolution when she married a man whom she did not love particularly, but who had a strong passion for her. At least that seemed better than drifting on the fringes of the theater. When she married, the therapy stopped.

Some ten years later Cecilia called in severe panic, asking if she could be seen immediately. By this time she had three children, and was a Westchester matron. But she was so full of anxieties that she could no longer function.

Analysis now revealed that some of her earliest traumatic experiences had erupted from repression, for some unknown reason. From the time she was 3 until she was 6 she had cried continuously, especially at night, complaining all the time that she was frightened. Mother, instead of seeking help, used to punish her by locking her in a closet for hours at a time, including part of the night. She also began to tell her, a remark which was repeated many times throughout her life, that in every generation in their family there was a streak of insanity; in mother's generation it was her brother, a bachelor tax collector who lived with them, while in Cecilia's generation it was Cecilia. Mother offered no remedy, of course.

Shortly after her sixth birthday a man moved into the neighborhood who took a warm interest in Cecilia. He would take her on walks, buy her toys, and be kind to her in other ways. This began the subsequent pattern of her life, which was repeated with her breakdown: panic states, conviction of being crazy, rescue by some strong male figure.

After some initial progress Cecilia's disturbance became increasingly acute. It culminated in a bizarre suicide attempt, in which she stuck a knife into her heart in order "to get her husband out of her skin." This led to hospitalization. When last heard from she had not recovered from the psychotic break.

Charles, a 20-year-old college student, came to analysis because of acute anxiety symptoms that had led him from one therapist to another with little response. Two experiences from childhood stood out in his mind, especially: one, when he was 4½, he was suddenly yanked off to a hospital, put in a dark room, and woke up to find that his tonsils had been removed. The second, from about the age of 6, his father had on a number of occasions "playfully" tried to drown him in a swimming pool.

Charles's personality was one of extreme activity. He could not bear to sit still for even a minute. Even during the analytic hour, he found it virtually impossible to lie on the couch for the full fifty-minute period. In his behavior as an adult, he alternated between overpowering fears, which corresponded to the sudden traumatic removal of the tonsils, and a charm which most girls found difficult if not impossible to resist (as a result of which, he had become a successful Don Juan). Fear of damage and a continual seduction of a large number of women dominated his entire waking thoughts. Again, here, this combination took a long time to overcome.

In the more usual cases, where nothing extraordinary has occurred in childhood, it becomes a matter of patiently working out the variety of conflicts that were found in the family. The therapist should always have an open mind about what might have happened when the patient was a child. There is obviously a connective line between childhood and adulthood, but it is not always easy to grasp.

In the case of Paul, an extraordinarily unusual sexual symptom brought him to treatment: he was unable to ejaculate in the waking state. At 29, he had had only a few "paradoxical orgasms." * He had been married for three years, but had never ejaculated with his wife, although they tried to have sexual intercourse.

What was most striking about Paul's case was that nothing unusual had happened in his childhood. He was the younger son of a lower-middle-class Jewish family in Brooklyn, the kind of family which is seen routinely in clinical practice. Ordinarily, the sexual difficulties of boys in such families are obvious, but never reach the extremes seen in Paul. Why it did go to such an extreme with him remained a mystery. In six months of systematic analysis, the problem cleared up entirely, but few clues were found about why it had developed in the first place, other than the general sexual repression of the family in which he was brought up.

* A sudden ejaculation without accompanying sexual fantasies.

Two extremes may be noted in the reactions of patients to a discussion of their past. One kind becomes defensive about his parents and finds it hard to believe that they could be responsible for his difficulties; these patients maintain an extraordinary amount of guilt about their activities. The other kind of patient tends to blame his parents too much for what has happened; with these it is necessary to help them see that, while the parents began the process, it is the patient who continues it.

SUGGESTIONS FOR FURTHER READING

The topics taken up in this chapter have been largely neglected by most theoreticians. Some papers bearing on the general subject are: R. Fine, "Psychoanalysis and Learning Theory," *Psychoanalysis* 5, 1957; Winter, No. 4. E. Hilgard, Ch. 9 in *Theories of Learning,* 3rd Edition (New York: Appleton-Century-Crofts, 1967). See also: M. D. Pressman, "The Cognitive Function of the Ego in Psychoanalysis," *Int. J. Psychoanalysis* 50, 1969, 187–196. R. Gardner *et al., Cognitive Control* (New York: Int. Universities Press, 1959). H. Hartmann, *Essays on Ego Psychology,* and J. Masserman, *Behavior and Neurosis* (New York: Hafner, 1964).

CHAPTER 14

The Learning Process: Insight and Change

Could I but sit among the audience
and watch the play!
But I must mount the stage, take
part and act,
and once I play a part I'm lost,
forgetting who I am.

A. Strindberg: *The Great Highway*

INCREASED AWARENESS OF VARIOUS ASPECTS OF THE PROBLEM

4) Insight

More has been written about insight than about any other aspect of therapy.

To begin with, however, a correction must be made. There is no one insight that will "heal" the neurosis. That image went out the window more than fifty years ago. Rather, there are many insights that the patient acquires, some far-reaching, some trivial, that he has to work into his thinking, and eventually use for change. Nevertheless, the fact remains that change depends on insight, however dimly perceived or strangely worded.

In the preceding sections, what has been stressed is that the learning process for the patient involves a gradual growth of awareness, with many backward and forward motions; often it is a process of two steps forward and one step backward. In this growth of awareness, insights play the most significant role.

A rare instance of a "cure" in one session can be used to highlight the issues involved. Louis, a 38-year-old singer, came to therapy in great anxiety because he had suddenly lost his job. He was a singer in a Broadway show. Although he had been going along well for quite a while, he unexpectedly found himself unable to sing the part that was assigned to him, and had to leave the show.

Investigation of his life situation revealed that he was homosexual, and involved in a most unhappy relationship with a roommate, from whom he was unable to extricate himself. He had performed well in the show until he was given a more important part, where he had to sing at a wedding. At the same time, his mother, with whom he had had a lifelong quarrel, came to town. When all the factors were put together, what came out was that he had been given a promotion that meant that he was more of a man, and that as a man he had to watch other people get married, which brought back all his Oedipal feelings, at that moment exacerbated by the presence of his mother. When this was brought to light, the anxiety diminished to the point where he could return to the show and give an acceptable performance. The deeper aspects of his pathology he would not touch; he would rather let the whole matter of his unhappy life as a homosexual go.

For its brevity, the above case is certainly unusual. Yet it could be said that the patient succeeded in getting valuable insight in just one session. As soon as this insight was applied the problem disappeared. He did not formulate it in words, but he could be said to have thought, "My conflicts about being a man in real life do not have to affect my behavior on the stage." In capsule form, this is what happens in a great many more complicated cases when insights are reached.

Insight involves seeing relationships between thoughts, events, or wishes that have previously been felt to be entirely separate. It is thus a way of bridging the gap, or breaking down the barriers in the patient's mind. Technically, it can also be seen as a way of breaking through the defense mechanisms.

These interrelationships may exist in the present or they may be connections drawn between the present and the past. In both cases, the relationships may be traced between the conscious and the unconscious.

The stress throughout this book is on what the patient is going through, his learning experience. In Louis's case, he was strongly motivated to understand the sudden fear of the stage that had overcome him, but he was not strongly motivated to grapple with the homosexuality that had plagued him all his life. Thus, insight depends as heavily on motivation as on anything else. The emphasis still remains on strengthening the patient's awareness of his problems and his wish to change.

When the therapy is not sidetracked by too much resistance, what the patient goes through is a gradually growing sense of awareness about himself, his life, his relationships, and his conflicts. In this growing awareness, first he sees this, then that; slowly, he pieces things together. Every stage is difficult because of the anxieties connected with the material that is produced, and the patient's inevitable emphasis on transference and resistance material.

In discussions of insight in other areas of psychology (for example, the Gestalt school), there has been considerable debate as to whether the individual acquires the insight all at once (the "Aha!" experience) or gets it gradually. Both of these are possible, depending on a variety of factors. But even when there is an "Aha" experience, it can only come with a backlog of extensive knowledge of the field. Thus, in all areas of learning, insight depends to a considerable degree on background.

In the process of therapy, this holds as well. The patient, by talking and talking about himself, gets to see much more about his life than he had ever seen before. In this growing self-knowledge, some bits of information may come upon him suddenly, others will have to be worked out slowly and painfully.

Many writers have made much of the distinction between the *emotional* and the *intellectual* insight. It has been argued that intellectual insight is easy to come by, but does not have any real curative value. Patients are pointed to who can spout Freud for hours on end, and yet remain with the same old problems. It is only, they claim, when the insight really hits home, really striking some responsive emotional chord, that it is effective. To the writer's way of thinking, this distinction is of dubious value.

What is noticeable in patients who have all kinds of verbal insights, but do not change, is that their insights miss something essential in what they are doing. A more proper distinction could be drawn between insights that are pursued and insights that are dropped. Those who can verbalize freely not infrequently use this capacity to verbalize as a resistance to following up on the knowledge that they have gained.

Furthermore, careful examination of those patients who are claimed to have all kinds of insights reveals over and over again that certain crucial insights are entirely lacking. They focus on certain aspects of their behavior and leave others entirely out of consideration. In other words, a careful investigation of their self-awareness reveals that they have blocked off a good deal, in spite of their capacity to verbalize something that is very important.

A further distinction should be drawn between insights that are ego-syntonic and those that are ego-dystonic. It is primarily the latter that produce changes, whereas the former can become comfortable subjects for conversation, while the compulsive behavior remains unaltered.

While insight is the unit of the learning process, it is still only a part of the whole procedure. What is necessary is to study with the utmost care the patient's way of learning in the therapeutic situation and to react accordingly.

Every patient has his own idiosyncratic way of learning about himself. Therapeutic skill involves adjusting oneself to each person's different procedures. Some people have an insight and drop it; others immediately want to change; still others forget it and look for a new insight. Many other variations could be described. What counts is to react appropriately to the patient's way of learning rather than to apply in some mechanical fashion the same rules to everybody that comes along. For the experienced therapist, no two patients can be approached in precisely the same way.

Because of the learning block, the growth of every analytic case is slow, awkward, and painful. A major characteristic of the experienced analyst is that he can adjust himself to the patient who is stumbling and fumbling without undue discomfiture.

The majority of patients in analysis may be said to be slow learners. Though cooperative, they offer a variety of resistances that impede the learning process. Many of the insights acquired are so ego-dystonic that it takes some time for them to be grasped and assimilated into the personality structure. A sense of conviction about these insights grows only gradually, very often after an initial period of denial for a greater or lesser length of time.

It is more or less inevitable that the learning process for most patients should be a slow one. In part, this is because the material itself offers a considerable amount of difficulty. A person must learn the dynamic approach to psychology, must understand the genetic roots of his personality development, must grasp connections between the present and the past, must gain some inkling of how his symptoms occurred and what they mean to him in the present situation. At the same time, throughout all there is the constant demand for immediate relief, the transference manifestations, and the resistance that arises when the transference wishes are not gratified. As a matter of fact, most analysts are so convinced that the learning process must be a slow one that when it is speeded up too much, they are suspicious of what is going on. The phenomenon of the "flight into health" has already been discussed in an earlier chapter. In later stages of the analysis there are also similar flights into health that are essentially resistances to a deepening of the process.

Quite often, the patient will grasp certain points about his personality but will bog down when it comes to others. Sometimes there is one particularly crucial point that almost has to be battled out. In the beginning of analysis, this point can be sidestepped; in fact, it is a wise idea to sidestep any such direct confrontation in the beginning. But later on, it may be too crucial to be avoided. In that case, it is absolutely essential for the analyst to maintain his position about that aspect of the patient's personality, and to try to get the patient to see what is really going on.

By and large, the activity of the analyst increases as time goes by. The so-called passivity of the early stages, as has been noted, should really be thought of as a form of dynamic inactivity. In this period, a relationship is established, and everything is subordinated to the establishment of that relationship. If the dynamic inactivity does not lead to such a relationship, then it should be replaced by some more forceful approach that does.

But once the relationship is established, the analyst begins to adopt a more and more active role. It is a mistake to believe that the patient will get better of his own accord. The activity of the analyst centers very largely around interpretations that make the patient's unconscious conscious, making him aware of a variety of ego and superego mechanisms that are affecting his feelings and behavior. Few patients are so gifted that they discover all these things on their own.

More vigorous interpretation, which begins after the initial stages of the analysis have been successfully gone through, introduces a new element into the procedure. Resistances now center not only on the analyst's silence but also on his activity, that is, his interpretations.

The topic of interpretations will be considered in more detail in the next two chapters. In this chapter, the emphasis is on the way in which the patient learns.

The interpretation must be grasped by the patient and eventually assimilated into his understanding of himself. This means that ideally he must be able to give it back in his own words rather than in any kind of technical jargon. As a rule, this is a long and difficult process, especially when the interpretations are unflattering or in some way critical. Yet by and large, interpretations are critical of the patient, since without some criticism no patient ever gets better.

It is unusual to see any two patients learn about themselves in the same way. One learns from dreams, another from free associations, a third from behavior, a fourth may learn from friends who give them the same kind of interpretation that the analyst does. Many other variations are found as well. It is an essential part of the art of analysis to be able to adjust oneself to the particular method of learning of the patient. Here are some clinical vignettes:

A special learning problem came up in the analysis of Larry, a homosexual scientist. Larry could see the dynamics of his homosexuality very clearly; he was well-read in psychoanalysis and nothing that the analyst said came as much of a surprise to him. At the same time, after the initial positive phase of analysis, Larry went into a long period of resistance, where he spent much of his time trying to argue with the analyst about the normal character of homosexuality. In this period, he was essentially being defiant.

At the same time, the analyst noted that although he spent much of his time arguing about whether homosexuality was a normal reaction, he would gradually absorb the interpretations given to him by the analyst. Over and over again, the following would occur: The analyst would give him an interpretation that Larry would vigorously deny. Several sessions later, Larry would come in and say: "You know, I've been thinking . . ." and repeat the interpretation that had been given to him, sometimes word for word. In this repetition, he totally ignored the fact that it had been given to him by the analyst.

Since this kind of absorption of interpretation led to a positive result, in spite of Larry's constant attempt to engage the analyst in arguments about the social normality of homosexuality, the analyst did not point out the resistance to Larry. It was more important to note that this was his way of learning, and to go along with it.

Still another pattern came out in the analysis of Evelyn, a 23-year-old secretary who was an extremely dependent girl. Evelyn was the youngest of four children, and had been bullied, babied, and half-seduced by the older ones, who were all boys. The mother seems to have been retarded, and eventually had committed suicide under rather odd conditions. All the others in the family were still alive.

When Evelyn started analysis, she was functioning at an extremely low level. Her sloppiness was so pronounced that she had been fired from a number of jobs, simply because she was unable to present a sufficiently neat appearance. One job she had lost because she came to work one day wearing two slips, one on top of another. She had never been able to have an apartment of her own, always living in dormitories, such as the Y, or sharing an apartment with an older woman, who immediately became a mother substitute for her.

Although the dynamics of Evelyn's personality were obvious almost from the very beginning, she showed an incredible inability to grasp any of the information that was offered to her. She would come, session after session, relating her problems and conflicts, hear interpretations, go away, and come back the next session and repeat the same thing all over again, as though the analyst had not said anything at all.

At one point, the analyst became rather despairing of his ability to help Evelyn, and suggested that she might go to another analyst, perhaps to a group. At this, she went into a real panic, said that she would never do it, and called him up later to say that she was committing suicide. He assured her that he was not going to drop her, and her panic subsided.

It was clear that Evelyn remained extremely attached to the analyst, which meant that she derived her major gratification from merely coming to the analyst, and paid relatively little attention to the material that came out. At the same time, the material that was brought out was extremely rich and varied, allowing a detailed, dynamic picture of her life to be crystallized. There was no indication that Evelyn understood any of this dynamic clarification. At the same time, she slowly but perceptibly improved in her everyday functioning. She held her job, and actually got several promotions. Her dress improved considerably, although it still left much to be desired. Her relationships with men began to move along more constructive lines; where before she would pick up a man and go to bed with him right away and then feel rejected when he did not call her again, now she was mature enough to wait for some relationship to develop before she felt more attached to the man. Improvements along other lines were noted as well.

In spite of these improvements, Evelyn held on tenaciously to certain conceptions of hers which could be called *idées fixées*. For example, she liked to wear skirts and blouses that showed some of her bare skin in the abdominal area. When queried about this, she insisted that men found this sexy. Nothing could dissuade her from this conviction.

In this case, the patient showed a striking inability to learn anything about herself. At the same time, she made consistent progress. The failure to learn could be seen as holding on to dependency gratification, with the fear that if she did verbalize what was going on in her life, she would be discharged from analysis—an eventuality which she dreaded more than anything else.

The alert reader will of course have noticed that the learning disabilities described go hand in hand with deep-seated transferences and their accompanying resistances. Nevertheless, it is not sufficient to rest at the point of transference resistance without going into the specific learning problems more deeply.

One side effect of a strong transference resistance is that it blocks the patient's capacity to learn about himself. The ways in which this block can occur are, however, much more varied than any particular transference would indicate.

As has been indicated, these learning blocks must be studied in as much detail as the transferences themselves. Once the transferences are resolved, the learning will not just automatically resume its normal course without some guidance, encouragement, and often direct instruction from the analyst.

A case in point is presented by Eissler [49] in a paper written for the *Psychoanalytic Study of the Child*. In this paper, Eissler reports on a woman who was in analysis with him for three years. During this period, she fought him bitterly on every point; every interpretation was met with a denial. Every clarification was met with a contradiction. Eissler could not seem to do anything right, as far as this woman was concerned. The analysis was terminated somewhat prematurely, in Eissler's opinion, because the woman was shifted to another city.

Much to his surprise, some eight years later, he received a letter from her, thanking him profusely for everything that he had done. She reported to him that everything that she had wanted to have accomplished in the analysis she had accomplished.

Eissler takes up the theoretical question of whether this analysis could be considered successful, since the woman was unable to verbalize any of the insights offered to her in the course of the analysis. He considers that she was not adequately analyzed. However, from every point of view, she seems to have resolved her major problems, and moved on into a constructive, happy kind of life. It is clear that

Eissler is taking too rigid a position toward the nature of the analytic cure. The learning block demonstrated by this patient is not at all uncommon. It could be hypothesized that these patients are unable to reach a state of verbal agreement with the analyst, because of some unconscious meaning that such a verbal agreement would imply for them. Instead, they gratify some dependency wish, or release the hostility interminably, as with Eissler's patient. But the fact remains that they do continue in analysis and, in spite of all the negativism and apparent lack of cooperativeness, they reach a result that is considerably better than anything they might have reached in life otherwise.

A particularly difficult and important kind of learning block is seen in those patients who have great difficulty talking about themselves. Their hours are filled with complaints and stories about other people, who inevitably loom much larger in their lives than they themselves. While this over-concern with other people is of course a powerful resistance, from the point of view of the present chapter, it should be looked upon as a maneuver that blocks the patient from learning anything about himself. What he is trying to do is unconsciously force the analyst to intervene in his life situation, to change the other person rather than permit the analyst to give interpretations that will lead to a change within himself. Naturally, within this framework again there are all kinds of variations. There are those who virtually never talk about themselves, and those who place the emphasis on a fair amount of material about themselves. The latter are more easily analyzable than the former. This learning block must be analyzed before anything else is taken up.

To a greater or lesser extent, every patient goes through this resistance. He meets up with love relationships in which he feels abandoned or wronged and will go on at great lengths to try to get some sympathy from the analyst for the rejections that he has suffered. Most patients, however, will be able to see through this defensive ploy and recognize that they have contributed in some measure to the rejection that they feel.

An extreme of this kind of resistance was seen in the case of Harry, a 35-year-old accountant who came to analysis at the insistence of his fiancée. Harry and his fiancée had suffered a similar tragedy in life: Harry's wife had committed suicide and his fiancée's husband had committed suicide. The suicide, however, was not enough to induce

Harry to go to treatment; he needed an additional stimulus from his fiancée.

In the first session, Harry related a fair amount of material about himself. Then, he suddenly switched to other people. His daughter, who was then 4 years old, was temporarily being brought up by his sister; much of the time he spent berating his sister for her misguided efforts to bring up the child and for the mistakes she was making in the education of the child. Or he would go on about some of his business contacts, or about his fiancée.

It was striking that in spite of this attitude, Harry was an analytic enthusiast. He would spend a lot of time going around urging other people to go to analysis, to partake of the wonderful benefits that the procedure had given him. To some extent, this was also a defense, since he was urging others to change, rather than himself.

The defense was so strongly entrenched that after the first few sessions, Harry virtually never said anything about himself. After about a year and a half of trying, the analyst advised Harry to seek some other approach. He did later go into a group, but apparently with little effect.

5) Change

Change is the last step in the learning process, and of course the most important. It is essential to note that it is not one change that is sought, but a whole series. Just as the acquisition of insights is a gradually growing awareness, the attainment of change is really a process of a series of small changes.

The crucial theoretical question is: How does insight lead to change? This must be subdivided into two distinct questions, since change can be either in feeling or in action. The principles that operate in one do not operate in the other.

1. *Change of feeling* requires a consistent working through of the various feelings and thought patterns that have been plaguing the individual all his life. Insights must often be repeated, new material produced and digested, reasons for and against worked out, until finally a big change occurs, especially in the attitude toward the world. In a great many cases, the patient, while able to formulate many insights in the course of therapy, tends to forget them and lead a happier life. As mentioned previously, even after successful therapy, the patient may be able to verbalize very little about what has happened. He feels better, which is all that counts to him. If pressed, the patient can put something in words about what was wrong with him,

but if not pressed, he will forget all about it and live his life without undue suffering. This should be considered a desirable outcome for analysis.

2. *Change of behavior* requires more positive action on the patient's part. After working through all the unconscious dynamics of the compulsive action or actions, the patient still has to do something on his own to change; it will not fall into his lap. At times the therapist may make some suggestion that he give up the damaging activity; at other times the patient will do it on his own. But some action by him is necessary.

This distinction is an important one because so many patients and theoreticians confuse the two kinds of change. If the therapist points out certain fears, for example, the patient may go out and do something to demonstrate that he does not have those fears, and then come back and report his success to the therapist. Until the inner dynamics are worked out, such changes are pseudo-changes, essentially forms of acting out. It occurs quite frequently because the content of a behavioral change is familiar to everybody while the idea of an inner change is derived mainly from the writings of the psychotherapists.

Most patients do not succeed in effecting major changes without a good deal of hard work, lasting in many cases over a period of years. Progress is followed by backsliding; the familiar two-steps-forward-one-step-back progression is often observed. Even insights seemingly solidly acquired are forgotten only to be rediscovered later on. As a rule, it is only the laborious repetition of the same interpretations, analyzing the same dynamics over and over again that leads to permanent changes.

When the patient experiences one beneficial change, he is usually stimulated to go on for more. These are the therapeutic encounters that run most smoothly; there is an analytic honeymoon followed after six months by the first treatment crisis. If this is overcome, the patient believes in therapy and a long middle phase ensues. In this middle phase (working-through) the changes are usually of a gradual nature. After some time, for example, the patient can look back to a few years before, and honestly say to himself that he can never do anything like that again. Finally, he gets to a life situation where he wishes to enjoy himself to the fullest, rather than make further changes. That point is a natural termination for the therapy. Of course, this is only an ideal, which is not too often seen. In practice, it is usually necessary to work through innumerable resistances before a happy ending is reached.

In the illustrative case, the patient had to change both feeling and behavior. His dominant feelings at the time he began therapy were anxiety, anger, resentment, and rebelliousness. All these could be traced to his relationship with his mother and to the identification with a beaten-down father.

Many of the changes in this patient came about silently, without anyone being able to pinpoint the precise time when they occurred or exactly what brought them about. This is more the rule than the exception.

SUGGESTIONS FOR FURTHER READING

Considerable literature on the topic of insight exists. A modern re-formulation of the Freudian position is E. Kris, "On Some Vicissitudes of Insight in Psychoanalysis," *Int. J. Psychoanalysis* 37, 1956, 445–455. The more classical views may be found in: H. Nunberg, "The Synthetic Function of the Ego," in *Practise and Theory of Psychoanalysis* (New York: Nervous and Mental Disease Monographs, 1948). J. Strachey, "The Nature of the Therapeutic Action of Psychoanalysis," *Int. J. Psychoanalysis* 15, 1934, 127–159. An eclectic position is R. Schonbar, "Interpretation and Insight in Psychotherapy," in E. Hammer, ed., *Use of Interpretation in Treatment* (New York: Grune and Stratton, 1968).

The best theoretical consideration of insight from all points of view is J. Richfield, "An Analysis of the Concept of Insight," *Psychoanalytic Quarterly* 23, 1954, 390–408.

For a discussion of analytic variations from pure insight therapy see "Symposium—Variations in Classical Psychoanalytic Technique," *Int. J. Psychoanalysis* 39, 1958, 200–242.

CHAPTER 15

Interpretation: The Analytic Dialogue

They do not hear the melodies I'm singing,
The souls to whom my earliest lays I sang;
Dispersed that throng who once to me were clinging;
The echo is died away that one time rang.
Now amidst an unknown crowd my grief is ringing,
Their very praise but gives my heart a pang,
While those who once my song enjoyed
    and flattered,
If still they live, roam through the wide
    world scattered.

Goethe: *Faust*

Although interpretations are offered by the analyst, and represent his main form of activity, their evaluation depends almost entirely on the *patient's response*. It could be said that there are really two major schools of psychotherapy: the dialogue school and the monologue school. It could even be said that a goodly part of the patient's problem in life is that he is conducting a monologue, while the state of mental health consists in numerous dialogues.

The analytic dialogue can be considered along six different dimensions, depending on the patient's response to the analyst's interpretations.

1) Listening

The first dimension is the simplest, that of listening. Before any possible consequence of any interpretation can be considered, it must be determined whether the patient has listened to what has been said.

The question is by no means trivial. Some patients do not listen at all to what the analyst says, others listen partially; still others gather from the interpretation whatever they please or, more precisely, whatever the superego will permit them to hear at that moment. Sullivan's phrase, "selective inattention," is most appropriate here.

At first sight, patients who do not listen at all may be thought of as completely schizophrenic, unable to comprehend anything of what goes on in their surroundings. Yet even here a more careful analysis forces a correction. The schizophrenic selects out of his environment certain trivial data or observations that he reacts to entirely out of proportion to their significance. Thus he is listening, but in a most autistic manner. The whole basis of technique with the schizophrenic is to find out what he is listening to, and what he is shutting out of awareness.

A schizophrenic woman, delusional and hallucinatory, was being seen analytically in daily sessions. There seemed to be some improvement. Then one day she came in terribly frightened. The voices were not hallucinations, she insisted, they were real. Last night there were musicians in the courtyard who were there just to mock her. Army planes flew over and clinked (her word) her. A few days ago the police had really stopped her and called her a "clinker."

I inquired what had happened the past day to frighten her so. Yesterday when she left, she said, there was a silly grin on my face and she knew that she had upset me. If even an analyst could not get along with her, what was the use? (The patient suffered from the delusion that she harmed everybody she came in contact with.)

At this point I realized what she was reacting to. At the end of the session the previous day her pack of cigarettes was finished, and she wanted to take the empty box along. I laughingly suggested that she leave the empty box in my trash basket, to which she reluctantly agreed. But she had noticed my laugh, and the intensification of her hallucinations followed.

Naturally, in the great majority of analytic patients the interpretation offered by the analyst is heard.

But few interpretations are heard by the patient in the way that they are intended by the analyst. They are first sifted through the patient's unconscious resistances. Out of this comes one point or another, usually related to what the analyst has said, but considerably altered. To get the patient to a point where he listens accurately is a goodly part of the battle.

Lillian, obviously in strong transference, would wander around outside the analyst's office for hours after her sessions were finished. During these meanderings she hit upon various insights. In fact, she said, her best insights came outside the analytic situation, and she was beginning to wonder why she had to bother with the analyst at all. First, I inquired what her feelings were about me. She had been referred by another therapist, who had worked with her supportively over a period of many years. Here, too, she had strong affection and admiration, but verbally she maintained that she had no feelings about him. My question about her feelings about me was interpreted by her as a request that she should enter into a relationship with me. It was only after the question had been repeated a number of times that she grasped the idea that she could express any feelings she wanted to about me, and could begin to probe into the transference.

Cecilia, a 24-year-old actress, showed marked passivity in her life. Fearful of making rounds, she would stay home all day, hoping that some part would come along "somehow." There were few dates with men. She was supported by her parents in another state, so that there was no financial problem.

One day the analyst rather carelessly said to her: "You don't know much about men." Shortly thereafter Cecilia's pattern suddenly changed. She began to go out to bars, staying out until five or six in the morning, and having sex with anyone who asked her. Many times she had sex in cars, which she seemed to think was a particular accomplishment.

When the analyst finally inquired into her behavior, asking what it was all about, she said: "You told me to do it." It then appeared that his remark that she did not know much about men was interpreted as a command to let go with all her hitherto inhibited sexual desires. The comment was taken as a command to reduce her superego prohibitions.

Both of the above examples indicate that the careful analysis of the listening process leads directly into a discussion of transference and resistance. This suggests another way of looking at the transference-resistance phenomenon. Instead of listening coolly and objectively, the patient distorts the remarks of the analyst to fit in with her own emotional needs.

2) Acceptance-Rejection

Naively, one would assume that the analyst's main concern about an interpretation offered is whether the patient accepts it or rejects it. If it is accepted, he tends to feel successful; if it is rejected, unsuccessful. This seems like "common sense."

Experience indicates that it is by no means so simple, but often the reverse. Mere acceptance of an interpretation does nothing until the patient incorporates it into his psychic make-up. If this incorporation does not take place, verbal acceptance is quite meaningless.

Paradoxically, one of the most difficult of all patients to treat is the one who assents too quickly. These are the people who say: "Yes doc, you're so right—anything you say, doc," and then go their merry way.

To them the analyst is a powerful superego figure whom they can handle best by verbal agreement, believing that such agreement will magically dispel their problems. Very often this surface compliance covers up an underlying rebelliousness that the patient is fearful of bringing to the surface.

The basic principle is this: The decisive question with regard to interpretation is not whether it is correct or not, but how the patient reacts to it. Most interpretations by trained analysts, even by relative beginners, are reasonably correct; the problem is rather that insufficient attention is paid to the context in which they are given and received by the patient.

> Rose had great difficulty putting her brassiere on, and decided that she could do it only with her son's help. When the incestuous character of this action was brought out, and tied up with various incestuous conflicts in her childhood, she readily agreed, and shortly thereafter informed me that she had stopped. Years later it was accidentally discovered that she had not really stopped at all, but had merely told me that she had; this in turn was a repetition of an infantile pattern with father.

Just as acceptance is no proof that the interpretation will be worked out properly, rejection is no proof that it will not. Many analysts have been so impressed by the negativistic element in every patient's neurosis that they have even set up a rule that an interpretation cannot be considered successful unless the patient disagrees with it. The rationale behind this statement is that if the interpretation is sufficiently important, it will run up against deep-seated anxieties that the patient cannot be expected to bring to the fore; hence, on the surface there is resistance and rejection. Such a position goes too far toward the other extreme; rejection is not a proof of adequacy, but it should not be considered a sign of failure. What is decisive is how the patient handles the total interpretive process, how he incorporates the dynamic ideas into his psyche, how he tries to effect changes, and the ways in which he does actually change. From this larger point of view, acceptance and rejection are but surface manifestations; it is what comes later that really counts.

It is because rejection is by no means an indication of the inadequacy of an interpretation that resistance analysis can be conducted. Sometimes interpretations have to be offered in the face of intense resistance over a long period of time before they become really meaningful to the patient.

3) Production-Repression

A third way in which the patient can respond is by either producing more material or by blocking and repression. Since, as emphasized throughout, it is the production of material that gets the patient better, here too it is the response that leads to the most successful analyses in the long run.

Certain principles must be reemphasized here. First, each patient's mode of production has to be ascertained and respected. If a patient does not dream much, he cannot be expected to start bringing in four or five dreams a night, as other patients do. If a patient remembers little of his childhood, more will eventually come out, but usually not as much as the patient who from the beginning has many clear memories. Analysis increases productivity, but the increase depends on the base from which it starts. Patients often have the idea that they cannot be analyzed unless they dream prolifically or remember their first five years in detail; these patients have to be reassured on these scores. The scope of analysis must be adapted to the capacity of each patient to comply with the basic rules.

Second, while the analyst must respect the patient's capacity to produce, he should not be satisfied with it. Consistent application of analytic principles, in most cases, leads to a considerably increased productivity. Thus, the patient who dreams little at the beginning will learn to dream more, although not as much as some others.

Analyzability in the classical sense can roughly be equated with this kind of productivity. The patient who dreams, has childhood memories, free-associates—all to greater or lesser degree—can succeed in a classical analysis, regardless of the clinical diagnosis. The patient who does not produce material requires some variation in technique, though the basic goals remain the same.

Productiveness goes on all through the analysis; it is not a matter of having told one's story, and then being through. There is a continuing need for material that will, in the long run, lead to that sense of inner conviction that can result in real change.

The patient is not *per se* interested in producing material. His concern primarily is to get some relief from his symptoms, and the fact that the analyst asks for dreams or childhood memories often strikes him as strange, if not absurd. It is this difference in interest which adds to the continuous tug-of-war that characterizes most analyses, blocking in various degrees the kind of dialogue which is therapeutically most effective.

The question arises here: What about the overproductive patient? There are patients who deluge the analyst with dreams. A colleague in an analytic institute used to bring in his dreams which were often four or five typewritten pages long and took half an hour to relate, much less interpret. Some patients can talk endlessly about their childhood without making the necessary connections with the present-day difficulties. With these patients the problem is to organize the material and its meaning for them, or to help them organize it. Sometimes certain types of material are used as a defense against others; e.g., occasionally patients dream excessively in order to cover up embarrassing everyday material. Many times, too, the excess of material is a prelude to superego punishment, manifested in strong resistances.

Dorothy, a 23-year-old housewife, had a most extraordinary fantasy life. Dissatisfied with her husband, she would daydream of many men coming into her at the same time, sometimes as many as forty or fifty. One movie in which the heroine has control over her husband she saw twenty-four times, and relived it in her mind many more.

In her daily life, she was also an impulse-ridden individual. At 13 she had spent a week having sexual relations with a dog, who had licked her genitals. She prided herself on her rich and varied sex life with her husband, though this meant primarily the release of anal and oral impulses, since she did not really experience orgasms. Constant overeating had led to marked obesity. There was a history of three suicide attempts, all with pills.

Even before the first session she gave evidence of marked ambivalence. She dreamed that on her first visit she went up to the apartment one story above the analyst's. This had both a sexual (her favorite position was to be on top of the man) and resistance meaning (not coming to the right apartment).

For the first year, the transference was largely positive. But the reality situation with her husband who, though fifteen years her senior, was an extremely infantile man, was hard for her psyche to handle. She could not find happiness with him yet she could not leave him.

The anticipated resistance then began to make itself manifest. But, like her strong impulses in general, the resistance was quite marked. She would sometimes be silent for three sessions in a row, then blurt out: "I hate you." Another suicide attempt took place, though apparently without serious intention. She began to attack the analyst, asserting that he had no training, no background, and no understanding; at the same time she maintained that he was treating her because he was secretly in love with her.

The negative transference eventually became positive again, and a long working-through process ensued. Unfortunately the analysis had to be broken off because she moved to another city.

Later reports indicated that the outcome was bad. In another suicide attempt, again apparently without any real intention of killing herself, she took an overdose that caused some brain damage.

This case illustrates the point that it is not merely the quantity of production that counts, but also its nature. When a patient is blind to one area of life, special measures have to be taken to help her become aware of it. In some cases, for example, it is necessary to ask patients not to bring in dreams for a while, or to concentrate on other kinds of material. But all this does not alter the main theoretical emphasis on the central significance of productivity.

4) Action-Discussion

A fourth kind of reaction to an interpretation revolves around action. Some patients take interpretation as a command to action, while others find great difficulty in acting and instead engage in endless discussion.

In popular language, these two opposing positions could be described as (1) Go out and do things, then learn from your mistakes. (2) Look before you leap.

It is clear that both of these points of view can be incorporated into analytic theory today, but as heuristic principles rather than as absolute commands. To one type of patient, action is most tempting because he is constantly looking for suggestions about what to do. To him the careful perusal of fantasy material in analysis is highly irksome; he wants immediate action. The contrasting type of patient is the one who delights in excessive discussion; he can go on for years without any resolution. Nowadays many dependent or pedantic personalities present this problem in analysis.

The resolution to the conflict lies in helping the patient acquire a proper sense of *balance*. In one case, action is called for; in another, discussion. The difference is similar to the one drawn in Chapter 20 between change in feeling and change in action. When action is called for, it must be resorted to; no amount of feeling will suffice. Conversely, action as such will not alter any deep inner feeling.

Approaching the problem in this way leads to a useful technical modification. The ultimate goal is change; interpretation is only the tool. Early in the analysis it quickly becomes clear what the predominant pattern of the patient is—action or talk. The job of the analyst then becomes one of redressing the balance. Almost from the very beginning, interpretations can be geared toward this balance; the degree of success depends on the extent to which this balance is reached.

Two contrasting cases of young men illustrate this principle in practice.

One man came to analysis with a history of excessive sexual activity. For years he had been having sex with two or three girls a night; quite often he would then go home and masturbate. There was little satisfaction in his conquests. Actually, the stimulus toward analysis came when a homosexual acquaintance told him that he (the patient) was really a homosexual at heart, which made him panicky. Here the interpretations were geared toward calming the patient down and allowing him to choose one woman, which he eventually did.

The second patient was one who was extremely withdrawn from the world. For a period in his life he had spent his time sitting in his room drinking tea and listening to records. His income came from part-time jobs and unemployment insurance. He had few human contacts. In this case the interpretations helped him to see how afraid he was of contacts with girls and encouraged him to experiment with various contacts, until he was eventually able to achieve some kinds of relationships.

These two examples bring up the interesting question of whether suggestion is not employed more commonly than theory would lead one to believe. Glover represents the most radical position; he argues that every inexact interpretation is a suggestion; and since he has extraordinarily stringent requirements for "exactness," in his opinion most analysts do rely mainly on suggestion.

To answer this question, distinction must be drawn between suggestion and direction. A suggestion is given to a patient without much explanation; it is a command. Direction, however, is achieved after the analyst gets to know his patient fairly well. Direction is an integral part of the analytic process; without it the patient rightly feels lost. At various points there frequently is a consensus between analyst and patient that certain directions will probably bring fruitful consequences, while others will repeat the old neurotic stagnation. Even when the patient is in sharp disagreement, it is advisable that the analyst take a clear stand on major life issues. This does not mean that the analyst dictates the patient's life, but at least he makes his position known. The analyst should always be a strong figure, yet one who is flexible rather than dictatorial.

Looked at in this light, both action and discussion may be productive of good results in the long run, or may be used as resistances. What is decisive is the working-through of the total design of the patient's life.

5) Thought-Feeling

This category is similar to the previous one, but there are important differences. The contrast here is between an intellectual and an emotional reaction to an interpretation. This contrast has long been noted in the difference between obsessional (thought) and hysterical (feeling) patients. Ideally, the analyst wants release of emotion, yet he also wants the patient to have reasonable control. In this respect, analysis attempts to combine the classical and the romantic views of life in the concepts of the ego and the id.

The patient whose response to an interpretation is one of excessive thought is typically someone who frequently has great verbal command over analytic theory. He can talk about the Oedipus complex, narcissism, penis envy, identification, and so forth, with great facility, but the trouble is that this facility goes too far and becomes too one-sided. He goes on and on about childhood, complexes, and the like, but there is an absence of feeling about what he is saying. Knowledge produces no significant change; there is merely interpretation and more interpretation. Often outsiders who fail to understand the real role of interpretation in analysis are antagonized by these people and see them as living proof that "insight doesn't work."

As pointed out in Chapter 14, closer examination of these patients reveals that while they can verbalize a good many insights, certain ones are invariably missing. Basically they do not genuinely appreciate the significance of feeling. In addition, other insights are missing, usually those related to the transference. Most people who come to analysis confuse true analytic understanding with a series of intellectual insights and fail to grasp both the role of feeling and the significance of transference and resistance. Also, certain other insights are generally simply bypassed by the intellectualizer. For example, a homosexual patient who could spout analytic theory with great ease completely failed to grasp the basic analytic theory of homosexuality. At one point he even wrote out an excellent analysis of a self-destructive relationship that he was about to embark upon, and then proceeded to act it out anyhow!

Another patient who could verbalize analytic theory with great fluency, but felt nothing, completed all his communications about himself in one session. After that he either theorized or talked about other people. Much of his energy went into convincing other people that they had problems. Some of his intellectual insights were fairly good but his affect-block made him blind about himself.

The opposite response is shown by the person who emotes all the time. Usually, the previous type is a man and this one a woman. There is hardly any attempt to think about her situation. Interpretations do not interest her, and often she scarcely pays attention. Analysis for her is a chance to release feelings. One patient would come and spend half the hour crying, then dry her eyes, say she had a good cry, and leave. Hardly any interpretations were offered in her therapy. In spite of this, she felt somewhat relieved by the process.

Popular literature on psychoanalysis is misused by this kind of patient. They read that analysis encourages the release of feeling, which is what they are doing all the time. Why don't they get better?

The answer to this requires first a small theoretical detour. A theoretical distinction must be drawn between *manipulative* and *expressive* emotion. A manipulative emotion involves an unconscious effort to manipulate some other person; an expressive emotion is a direct release. Neurosis relies on manipulative emotion, going back to childhood, for to manipulate is the child's only weapon against inadequate parents. Once the manipulative pattern is set, it becomes internalized and the person then goes through life unconsciously using his emotions to manipulate other people. The release, in such cases, brings some temporary relief followed by a resumption of the old pattern. This is because the "immortal" internalized object, which is the real target of the emotion, remains untouched. There is, as a result, a long-standing repetition of one unsatisfactory emotional experience after another.

A common misuse of this idea is seen with anger. Many people look upon analysis as a means through which they need only relieve their anger to get better. Quite often they consciously try to make the analyst into a target for their anger, sure that all they have to do is "bring it out." The anger is brought out, but the patient does not improve. In these patients, anger was a potent weapon the parents used against them in childhood, and now they are taking revenge against the parents by doing this to other people. But the internalized angry parent-figure is not exorcised by this procedure.

This dynamic can be contrasted with the situation in which anger may really be released with positive results. This occurs in patients who are chronically afraid that if they ever yell at anybody, the roof will fall on them. By venting their anger on the analyst, they discover that this fear is groundless—that it is a neurotic distortion that goes back to childhood. In this case, a modification of the super-ego takes place. What is decisive in this, as in the previous instance, is the inner dynamics of the process, not the release as such.

As before, analytic technique here requires the development of a proper sense of balance. The pale cast of thought must be warmed by passion; hysterical release must be calmed by cool reason. As Fenichel comments, the analyst must always steer between the Scylla of intellect and the Charybdis of feeling; too much of either and the patient will be shattered on the rocks.

6) Self-Involvement—Objectivity

Finally, the patient may respond to an interpretation with excessive self-involvement or with objectivity. In theory, the nature of analysis is stated in terms of a pact between the healthy part of the ego and the analyst. When this pact or working alliance takes place, the patient is able to maintain a certain degree of objectivity about himself which makes for the optimal change. All too often, however, the objectivity is lost in a sea of excessive self-involvement.

The most common form this takes is that of self-blame. Instead of listening to an interpretation calmly, the patient seems to say: "That shows what a bad person I am. How can you ever expect such a person to get anywhere in life?" Often this happens with dreams. The patient comes in saying that he has had a "bad" or a "good" dream, depending on the wishes brought about—thus forgetting that a dream is basically a wish, neither good nor bad.

Rachel, a young woman who had been brought up in an atmosphere of constant and intense quarreling between mother and father, showed such a pattern. Her immediate response to any interpretation was to say: "If I have such wishes, how can you ever expect to help a person like me?" At the beginning of the analysis she gave up masturbation (which she had never practiced to excess anyhow), vowing that as long as she was in analysis she would never masturbate again. This was done to placate the analyst-superego, although he had never said anything about it, and when it was brought up had assured the patient that he did not feel at all disapproving of the practice.

Later, when she had children, the self-blame took a somewhat different form. She began to retract all the negative insights about her mother, because she was afraid that she might be doing the same sort of thing.

In patients with such extreme self-blame, there is a harsh superego and very often, in analysis, a negative therapeutic reaction. In these cases analysis of the superego is more important than any libidinal interpretations. The patient has to be reassured, over and over, that she is worthy of happiness in life, no matter what happened with her parents.

On occasion, the opposite may take place as well: an unrealistic self-approval. One such patient felt that he was somehow special in this world and that the analyst *really* appreciated him, unlike other people. This special feeling concealed a good deal of hostility, which came out only when the positive transference did not resolve his real life difficulties. Before then, his characteristic reaction to an interpretation was to use it as confirmation of his unusual role in the world.

SUGGESTIONS FOR FURTHER READING

Two excellent compendia are available which contain many of the important articles on interpretation. One is L. Paul, ed., *Psychoanalytic Clinical Interpretation* (New York: Crowell-Collier, 1963). The other is E. Hammer, ed., *The Use of Interpretation in Treatment* (New York: Grune and Stratton, 1968).

The discussion in Fenichel (*op. cit.*) is particularly good. Other excellent papers are: R. M. Loewenstein, "The Problem of Interpretation," *Psychoanalytic Quarterly* 20, 1951, "Psychoanalytic Therapy," *Psychoanalytic Quarterly* 20, 1951, 15–30. J. Nydes, "Interpretation and the Therapeutic Act," E. Hammer, *op. cit.* E. Hammer, "Interpretation Technique: A Primer," E. Hammer, *op. cit.* R. M. Loewenstein, "Some Thoughts on Interpretation in the Theory and Practice of Psychoanalysis," *Psychoanalytic Study of the Child* 12, 1957, 127–150. R. Ekstein, "The Nature of the Interpretive Process," in *Children of Time and Space, of Action and Impulse* (New York: Appleton-Century-Crofts, 1966).

The specific topic of this chapter is discussed from a somewhat different point of view in M. Balint, *The Basic Fault* (London: Tavistock, 1968).

A partisan plea is made by E. Glover in, "The Therapeutic Effect of Inexact Interpretation: A Contribution to the Theory of Suggestion," in E. Glover, *op. cit,* 353–364.

CHAPTER 16

Interpretation: The Analyst's Activity

This book, with the new contribution to psychology which surprised
the world when it was published [1900], remains essentially unaltered. It
contains, even according to my present-day judgment, the most valuable
of all the discoveries it has been my good fortune to make. Insight such
as this falls to one's lot but once in a lifetime.

> Freud: Preface to 1932 English
> Edition of *The Interpretation
> of Dreams*

Once the analysis is underway, the activity of the analyst is confined
mainly to interpretations. There are, of course, many other things that
he does, including questioning, suggesting, reassuring, and even on
rare occasions direct intervening in the patient's life. But the activity
that is specifically analytic is *interpretation*. It is the free use of interpretation that distinguishes analysis from all other forms of psychotherapy. Furthermore, the analytic elaboration of interpretation provides an extraordinary enrichment of the therapeutic process that
shifts it to an entirely different plane.

It has already been pointed out that as time goes on there is a change
in the need for interpretation. In the beginning, the most glaring mistake of the novice is the excessive use of interpretation, which often
misses the point and chases patients away more frequently than it
does any good. However, as time goes on and the relationship has been
more securely established, there is an increasing need for interpretation. Once the patient has come to trust the analyst and to rely on him
to help make sense of his life, he looks to interpretations for the
material with which he can grasp his life's dilemmas. At this stage, the
analyst must offer interpretations, and must give them profusely. Just
as the cardinal sin of the beginner is to give too many interpretations,
the cardinal sin of the analyst at the later stages is to give too few.
Without interpretation, the patient will be lost. Of course, one can

always point to a few exceptions of patients who virtually analyze themselves. But these are exceptions rather than the rule. The great majority of patients require consistent, careful, and elaborate interpretation to understand their difficulties and to get over them.

Some comments on the structure of the analytic experience and the nature of the learning involved can be useful here. Essentially, in analysis, the patient comes with certain problems that are disturbing him in his life situation. His attention is expanded to include other problems that had previously escaped his consciousness. For any effective work to be done, the trust of the patient in the analyst must be firmly secured. This process of securing trust takes a variable amount of time, coming very quickly with normal-neurotic patients, and sometimes lasting years with those who are extremely disturbed. Once trust is established, it is used by the analyst to teach the patient. In its essentials, this teaching is not different from any other kind of teaching. The major difference lies in the fact that emotional resistances to the material crop up and keep on cropping up all the way through and these emotional resistances in their turn become the subject for analysis.

Interpretations are the building blocks of the learning process. They come to form the mainstay of the analytic learning because it is only through the careful, painstaking, detailed inquiry into the life situation that light is shed upon the problems that confront the patient. Didactic lectures or books or general propositions are worthless. The patient has to come to grips with the fact that such and such a situation has blocked off a wish, or he did not see the connection between his present behavior and his past, or the like. Analysis follows the pattern of close tutorial instruction, in which every detail has to be worked out with the greatest of precision, rather than a broad global lecture in which general principles are laid down which the student must then work out for himself.

Three types of interpretation can be differentiated: uncovering, connective, and integrative.

1) Uncovering Interpretations

The uncovering interpretation is one in which some concealed wish is brought to the consciousness of the patient. Sometimes the wish is so obvious that it is difficult to see how the patient can conceal it from himself, yet he does. Sometimes the wish is expressed in the material that the patient brings, sometimes the wish is inferred from the material. As a rule, the inference cannot go too deep, since it then leaves the patient behind.

Once the relationship is established, uncovering interpretations go on all through the analysis. They form the heart of the analyst's activity. As long as wishes are present that create some conflict in the patient, they are blocked off to some extent by resistances in one form or another, and these resistances have to be tackled by the uncovering interpretation. It should be noted that once the underlying wish is brought to consciousness, the resistance will then virtually take care of itself, but that merely pointing out the resistance will not be sufficient in many cases to bring out the underlying wish. In theory, this means that id analysis is more primary than ego analysis. All too often, pure ego analysis leaves out the id far too much; numerous examples of this have been given throughout this text.

The uncovering interpretation focuses on the material that the patient brings, but it may, and does in many cases, go beyond that. The criterion is not so much whether the patient has brought the material in clear form, but whether the patient will respond to the interpretation in a constructive way. Here the analyst must be careful not to go off the deep end with interpretations that are either way off the mark, or far too anxiety-provoking, or difficult for the patient to comprehend. By and large, the best rule is to stick as close as possible to the central theses of growth and development.

Since the expansion of the id remains the central task throughout the analysis, it is always wise to pick out some impulse or material closely derived from an impulse as material for the analytic discussion. It is, generally speaking, sufficient for the analyst to point to the impulse, and then to see what the patient does with it. Many times the patient may respond: "So what about it? What do I do about it?" —to which the analyst can fruitfully reply, "Talk about it."

A typical clinical vignette occurred in the case of Sylvan, a 26-year-old homosexual, who verbally denies that he has any interest in women. But he states that he does have one girl, whom he sees a good deal of—Lillian. Once, in their relationship, they tried to have sex (she performed fellatio on him), but it did not satisfy him, and the attempt was never repeated.

One day, Sylvan comes in to report that Lillian now has a boy friend by the name of Harry, with whom she spends a great deal of time. He relates this in an annoyed tone of voice. The analyst responds that he is acting jealous; he replies, "You're damned tootin',

I'm jealous." In the discussion of his jealousy, Sylvan still denies that he has any interest in Lillian as a woman, merely that he wants her to himself as a friend. Nevertheless, a dent has been made in his persistent cry that he is never attracted to any woman.

A considerable difference of opinion exists about the depth to which interpretation should go. In general, the principle is followed that the analyst should work from the surface downward; that is, he should not jump too far beyond what the patient presents to him. On the other hand, there are schools of thought, such as the Kleinian, which almost immediately offer interpretations in terms of the earliest infantile experience.

The decisive factor is not so much how deep the analyst goes, but the purpose that the interpretation is going to serve. Whether this purpose is served or not depends on the patient's reaction to the interpretation. In the beginning of treatment, before the relationship is well-established, the analyst will, by and large, tend to move more gingerly. However, there are many exceptions to this rule as well. There are many times when the analyst has to shake the patient out of a complacent series of denials. Here is a typical example, again from a homosexual patient:

> Jerry, a 23-year-old homosexual, as usual denied any interest in women at the beginning of the analysis. One day he came in with a dream that he saw his mother half-naked and had bitten her breasts.
>
> He laughed at this dream, and intimated that it had no meaning. The analyst picked it up and pursued it, to help him to see that with his denial of his interest in women, he was really covering up a hostility to mother and a hostility to women in general. This made quite an impression on the patient, and brought out many useful memories.

Many people cover up their feelings by a variety of general propositions. Outside of analysis, this goes on a good deal of the time. For example, people will argue at great length that Negroes are inherently inferior to whites, or whether it is environment or heredity that creates their problems. Such generalizations are of no use in analysis. It is desirable whenever possible to bring them down to a particular reaction to another human being.

The best approach, when they occur, is to try to tie them up with the patient's feelings about the analyst. For example, if a woman says that she hates all men, the analyst who is a man may reasonably reply: "Do you hate me too?" If the patient replies in the affirmative, some specific further material will come out; if she replies in the negative, at least a dent in the generalization has been made. At that point, the analyst may even interpret that she does not hate all men, but only some and move on to discuss the men whom she really does hate.

Many times, the analyst who knows his patient well can offer an interpretation which goes beyond the immediate and brings forth a lot of material which would otherwise remain concealed. But this can be done only with patients who have been in treatment for a long time and with whom the relationship is quite secure. Here is a typical example:

> Ruth, a 35-year-old woman who has had a very successful analysis, comes back for some help with her new situation as a housewife. She cannot tolerate remaining home with her two boys, but feels a tremendous urge to go out and work, in spite of what this might do to her marriage, and in spite of the fact there is no urgent economic necessity for it. The analyst who knows her intense incestuous background with her own father, suggests that there may be some fear of incestuous wishes for her own sons. This brings forth a whole mass of material, especially preoccupation with the older son's masturbation.

The uncovering interpretation is the most obvious aspect of analysis and the one with which it is most closely identified on the outside. Many people, as a result of their own analysis, or as a result of reading, acquire a fair amount of ability to make this kind of interpretation. However, an important *caveat* must be entered at this point. The ability to make interpretations depends on the familiarity with the person. No matter how well people know one another in social situations, there is always some backlog of material that remains private and concealed from other people. More often than not, this unknown material will change the meaning of any production on the individual's part, thereby calling for a different interpretation.

For various reasons, the indiscriminate use of analytic interpretations outside analysis may lead to a great deal of confusion on the part of the patient. If it is carried on too extensively it may even interfere with analytic progress. In such cases, it is wise to ask the patient not to discuss the analysis with anybody else. This is apt to be particularly necessary with those dependent patients who grasp every interpretation that anybody else offers them without being able to differentiate between those that are worthwhile and those that are not, or those that are offered with a tendentious purpose and those that are offered with the purpose of helping the individual.

There are two kinds of material that the analyst may focus on: 1) *repetitious* and 2) *unusual*. It will be noted in any analysis that there are certain points that are repeated over and over again by the patient while others crop up only once. Each of these can be utilized to get to the underlying id material.

In the average analysis, there are certain themes that recur over and over again. While the relationship is being established, these themes are developed and explored by means of confrontations, clarification, and elaboration in the past and in the present. At that time it is still too early to interpret these themes in any direct way to the patient. But once the analysis is well underway, the encounter between analyst and patient gets to a much more careful discussion of these repetitive themes. Sometimes they are of a fairly simple nature, and lend themselves to a fairly obvious interpretation, but this interpretation will never do the trick, since the repetition indicates that the themes are deeply rooted in the patient's psyche. Accordingly, a long process of working-through will be necessary to clarify what these themes mean in the life of the patient and how they are to be used for greater self-understanding.

Sometimes these themes are recurrent verbal expressions; other times they may be repetitive patterns of behavior that the patient displays in connection with the analysis. While behavior is more difficult to analyze, sooner or later the recurrent patterns have to be brought into the open and subjected to analytic scrutiny.

When a pattern is deeply rooted in the personality and is repeated over and over again, generally there are a number of wishes embodied in it. Which of these wishes the analyst chooses to bring out depends on a number of factors, chief among them being the receptivity of the patient. However, the receptivity of the patient is not the only consideration. Many times it is necessary to continue interpretation in the face of continued resistance, when the material is so clear that it leaves little doubt. Here is a clinical example:

> Nina, a 28-year-old secretary, came to analysis because of general unhappiness with her life and difficulty in establishing a relationship with a man. The repetitive theme began to come out fairly early that

in terms of her body, she felt ugly, her breasts were too small, her behind was too big, her legs were too thick (cf. p. 113).

The analysis of this theme revealed a number of significant wishes that the patient had concealed from herself. First, there was a homosexual wish to be a man who could admire women; this was transformed into a constant comparison of the bodies of other women with her own. Second, there was the wish to exhibit herself, which again was covered over by the strong conviction that everybody was looking at her disparagingly. Third, anal and oral wishes were brought out in connection with this theme of an unattractive body. The oral wish was the desire to be a little girl again, the baby of the family who would be mothered and smothered by older siblings and admiring adults. This babying had only caused her grief consciously when she reached puberty and could not move on to adequate relationships with the opposite sex. Anal material came out in a deep sense of shame connected with her genitals.

What was unusual with Nina was the persistence with which she denied the analytic interpretations. To her it was simply reality that her body was unattractive. All her life she had handled it by manipulating situations, and that was what she was going to continue to do now. E.g., since she felt so ashamed of her naked body, when she went to bed with a man she would make sure never to let him see her entirely naked while the light was on. Sometimes she would even block herself from going to the toilet until she was sure that he could not see her.

The analysis had to proceed in the face of vigorous denials and requests for assistance in manipulation. For a while it even seemed to resemble a debating exercise, in which she would assert one point while the analyst would assert another.

One manipulative device that she used was to check the analyst's interpretations with other people whom she trusted. It was only as these other people confirmed what the analyst said, and as her positive feelings about the analyst became more and more firmly entrenched, that she was able to work through what she was doing and feeling.

The interpretation of unusual material is likewise of some significance. Most patients who are in analysis are so familiar with the concept of Freudian slips that the little mistakes and slips that occur in every analysis are grasped by the patient himself so quickly that the analyst need do nothing about it.

More important from a practical point of view is the use of the *dream*. It is through the dream, which may come only once or twice, that hitherto repressed material is brought to the surface. Dream material has the further advantage that it meets with the least amount of resistance on the part of the patient.

A striking instance of how an unusual dream was woven into the framework of the analytic experience occurred in the case of Joe, a 40-year-old professional who came to analysis because of dissatisfaction with a second marriage. Since Joe had had some previous experience with the same analyst, the relationship could already be considered established. Shortly after his return, Joe had the following dream: "I am giving birth to a baby, but the trouble is that my body is divided up into sharp oblong rectangles, which leave no room for expansion. The baby has no way of getting out because of that. I am afraid that I am going to die. At this point, I wake up."

The dream brought out more cleary than anything else could have done the strong latent homosexuality in Joe, the identification with his wife, the mother of his children. Although no other material came out which could be interpreted as a wish to be a woman, the dream alone was sufficient to further the analysis a great deal with the various associations it aroused.

Very often, the analysis of repetitive patterns and unusual material is carried out in reference to the past as well as to the present. In fact, in the earlier stages of analysis, it is usually more common to work with the past than with the present, since the present invariably leads to stronger resistances.

In the illustrative case of Jim, the use of the repetitive patterns to bring out his repressed id has been noted in a variety of different ways. A good deal of the material struck the patient himself as rather odd when he looked at it more closely; for instance, the incident where he went to the bank two or three times a day, withdrawing trivial amounts of money, which eventually led the bank to ask him to shift his account to another office, impressed him particularly with his need to make the bank into a mother figure.

Many times other significant behavior or fantasy from the past, which is revealed early in the analysis, can be kept in mind for future reference. While it is not appropriate to interpret at that point, the analyst will store it away. Accordingly, when the opportunity presents itself, the analyst himself may bring up this material and ask the patient to re-evaluate it. This process of the re-evaluation of the life history is a basic one that goes on throughout the analysis. Here is a typical instance.

May, a 25-year-old girl, revealed at an early stage that she had had some sex play with an uncle when she was about 13. He would come down to her apartment, and fondle her breasts from time to time, when there was nobody else home. Naturally she insisted that she derived no pleasure from this action, but she was afraid to deny him.

At an appropriate point, the analyst brought up this material again. He inquired into more details of how the uncle would be let into the apartment. She then revealed that she had become so familiar with his footsteps that she could recognize them when he was still on the staircase. This clearly indicated that she would be sitting around waiting for him to come. He would ring the bell and she would open the door. It was pointed out that she was, after all, under no compulsion to open the door; she was already 13. She knew what was going to happen, and could have prevented it in a number of different ways. It was clear that she enjoyed the feeling of having him play with her breasts. It was also clear that this semiincestuous act had been one of the factors that fixated her sexually and led to a problem of frigidity. Her denial of her own sexual wishes could no longer be maintained.

2) The Connective Interpretation

In this interpretation, the present is tied up with the past. A connection is drawn between childhood and the present-day environment. The essential of the connective interpretation is that it breaks down the barriers between the present and the past.

Note that it is the barrier between the past and the present that has to be broken down. Merely recalling something from the past, or even tying it up with the present is just a first step. The past, after all, is significant only because it is still operative. What leads toward change is the increasing realization of the degree and the manner in which the past is still operating.

With connective interpretations necessarily comes a radical re-evaluation of the life history. This kind of re-evaluation is crucial to every analysis. Every person builds up a personal myth which has been compared to the historical myths that make up what each person knows of the history of his country. Certainly, there is some truth in what the person remembers, just as there is some truth in the events that are stressed in the presentation of a country's history. But these truths are taken out of perspective, while other, more significant truths are concealed. This process of re-evaluation of the life history requires long, persistent, hard work.

At this point again, the question of depth of interpretation can be raised. Connections can be drawn between the present and various periods in the past, but how far back one should go depends on the material available and on the reaction of the patient. Ever since Freud's paper in 1914 on recall, repetition, and work-through, the principle has prevailed that reconstruction is as good as direct recall. However, while this is theoretically true, in practice it still holds that direct recall is subjectively more convincing than a reconstruction. Hence, connective interpretations should try to tie up specific events; reconstructions can then augment the total picture.

As a rule, the amount of information that is collected about the patient's childhood is by no means copious. Hanns Sachs once observed, "Even the deepest analysis does no more than scratch the surface of a dark continent."

In the transference of Jim (cf. Chapter 2) there were numerous ways in which he expressed the wish to be rescued by the all-powerful analyst-mother. The connective interpretations offered helped him to reconstruct his life and to see that at 38 he was really behaving no differently than he had at 3. The same forces that kept him isolated and angry as a child were operative now. It was only when he saw that and realized that he was no longer a little boy of 3 that he could effect some change in his situation.

Usually the connective interpretation is met with a resistance to the effect that the analyst is placing too much stress on the past. What has been done is done, and no longer affects what is going on now. Such an attitude reflects a wish for immediate relief rather than one of trying to understand what has happened in the person's life. Sometimes, the opposite resistance is encountered, where the person pays too much attention to the past, loses himself in recitals of what went on in his childhood, and then does not face up to the fact that these childhood experiences are still operative and still connected with the difficulties that he is now experiencing.

Here is a clinical example:

Herman, a 45-year-old civil service worker, came to analysis because of premature ejaculation and general dissatisfaction with his life. Shortly after he started, it appeared that he was extraordinarily henpecked. In 17 years of married life, he had never gone out alone once in the evening, because of his wife's strenuous objections. At first, Herman accepted this philosophically, feeling that this was simply the way women were and the way marriage was.

As the analysis went on, Herman began to see more and more of his life. But then he began to over-stress the past. He remembered how his whole childhood had been dominated by the cry, "You must not. You must not do this; you must not do that." He never knew what he was permitted to do; he only knew what he was not permitted to do. While it was clear that this kind of childhood experience and his present experience with his wife were similar, Herman stayed away from the connection. As far as he was concerned, the idea was to complain enough about his childhood, so that he could eventually feel free. The emphasis had to be put on the connection between what he had experienced with his mother and what he was now experiencing with his wife. As this connection was pressed more and more, through a variety of interpretations, Herman regained satisfactory potency and began to have some more meaningful life with his wife.

Al, a 40-year-old college professor, was thoroughly dissatisfied with himself because he did not produce enough work. In an atmosphere of "publish or perish" he had already been fired from three different universities and was afraid that he would now be fired from a fourth if he did not publish. It was quite obvious from the material that he produced that Al was strongly attached to his mother. He admitted quite openly that his wife looked like his mother, and said that he had never loved any woman as much as he loved his mother, and so on. At the same time, the connection between this over-attachment to the mother and his difficulty in getting work out remained obscure to him. As far as he was concerned, the inability to work was just a kind of a fluke, for which he could find no explanation. The analyst's insistence on his fixation on his mother he saw as a professional bias.

Material about the attachment to mother became more profuse as the analysis went on. He consciously remembered a number of incestuous fantasies about her and about his sisters. In spite of the overabundance of obvious material, Al continued to deny any connection between the past and the present. Accordingly the analyst's emphasis was on stressing these connections. Eventually, the mother had a stroke and Al had to take over the management of her affairs. When this happened, the anxiety connected with it mounted to such an extent that it forced him to a reconsideration of his feelings about her. In this reconsideration, the connections which had been stressed by the analyst all along finally became worked into his picture of his life.

3) Integrative Interpretation

The integrative interpretation is a much more complex affair. It involves pulling together material from a variety of different sources, to help the patient make sense of his life. As the name suggests, it integrates a whole host of material. It offers a perspective and the consistent framework from which to try to effect further change.

It is obvious that integrative interpretations can come only after the patient has been in analysis for some time. They depend on the availability of a large mass of material which has to be organized. As time goes on, these integrative interpretations play a more and more significant role in the analysis.

It is usually found that the patient, even after a long analysis, has only an isolated, fragmentary image of what has happened to him. After all, most of the time the patient has been involved in a quest for immediate relief. The demand that he understand himself is always met with a certain amount of reluctance. This is why the objectivity of the analyst remains so important. One way in which this objectivity is shown is in terms of integrative interpretations that place the patient's problems and life situation in a more adequate perspective. These integrative interpretations have to be repeated a number of times until the patient is able to formulate a perspective in his own terms.

As time goes on, the emphasis on goals also becomes more and more clear to the patient. Throughout, the analyst is guided by his understanding of the goals of analysis, but the patient is not aware of the nature of this guidance. With the integrative interpretation, the analyst over and over again brings these goals to the attention of the patient and compares his present achievements with what he might achieve if he got over his problems. It is a mistake to believe that the patient will recover satisfactorily without some understanding of what makes for a happy life. It is equally a mistake for the analyst to leave these considerations out of his interpretation.

A good example of effective integrative interpretations came up in the case of Frank, a 35-year-old businessman who came to analysis because of a long history of crippling anxieties. One of his anxieties at the beginning was a fear of the barking of dogs, which had led him to move to a house which was so far distant from any neighbors that no dogs could be heard. Other symptoms were fear of other noises, and a general pervading sense of anxiety. (Cf. pp. 45–63 and 72.)

Frank was the only son of two lower-class Polish parents who had virtually retreated from life in the wake of the depression of 1929. Mother was a strong figure, but father had been, as so often, essentially a nonentity.

The first part of the analysis was a real analytic honeymoon, which lasted for a number of years. Then came the highly negative period, in which no interpretations seemed to hit the mark, and in which all that he could ever reply was that his anxiety remained no matter what the analyst said.

It was at this point that the analyst began to offer integrative interpretations. He would review Frank's life, show him the difficulties that he had experienced, the problems that he had resolved, and the problems that he was still trying to resolve. One of the crucial difficulties was that Frank, inspired by his father's failure with a large company, was determined to leave his firm, one of the largest in the country, and make it in his own business. This preoccupied him to such an extent that he neglected both his work in the large firm and his private businesses. The integrative interpretations helped him to see that he was really carrying out a useless fight against his father which was also translated into a useless fight against the analyst. As this was worked out, he became more satisfied with his very real achievements in life, and reached a considerable degree of happiness.

CONTENT, TIMING, AND MANNER

For theoretical purposes, the content produced by the patient can be subdivided into ego, superego, and id material. But there are several other kinds of material that are important, particularly the life history and anxiety.

While repetition lies at the heart of the entire therapeutic process, it is ordinarily kept within certain limits. When the patient begins to hammer away at certain kinds of material, leaving out of consideration a good deal about his life, the analyst can suspect that some unnamed resistance is operating, and can begin to search for what it might be. If there are clues offered, these can be used. If there are no obvious clues, the analyst can even say to the patient: This is something we have discussed many times before; what are you resisting? Is there something that you have not been able to bring up for one reason or another? Ordinarily, concentration on this kind of question and various subsidiary questions connected with it will highlight the resistances that had hitherto been kept in the background.

For the further analysis of content, while no hard-and-fast rules can be set up for the order in which the material that the patient produces can be handled, for learning purposes it is useful to bear in mind the following order: id, the life history reconstruction, anxiety, superego, and ego-reality. That is, other things being equal, it would be best to interpret id material before anything else, next life history, third anxiety, and so on. But even though this is valid as a general guide, the course of the analysis is always dictated first and foremost by the patient's needs.

The question of timing belongs to the general question of tact in the analytic situation. If an interpretation is not given at the appropriate moment, it may fall flat and completely lose its effectiveness. Nevertheless, it is not easy to determine just what the right time is. Theoretically, the proper time is that at which the patient is most ready for it; this must be gauged from the general knowledge of the patient acquired during the therapy. Once the analyst gets to know the patient, he can estimate to some extent when an interpretation will meet with an adequate reception and when it will not.

However, total precision in this area is entirely out of the question. Some writers, operating on the theory that there is a preconscious derivative that determines free association, try to urge the analyst to find out what the preconscious derivative is and to bring it to the patient's attention. This is an extreme demand which fails far more often than it succeeds. Besides, it is based on a now outmoded view of the mental apparatus. There is so much to be worked out in analysis that the significance of the preconscious derivative is considerably diminished.

Since the main requirement really is to have the patient work out the interpretation rather than to have the interpretation "hit home," timing in that sense is not of such crucial importance. The main consideration is that the interpretation should be given at a time when it arouses a minimum of resistance. That it may arouse some resistance at any time is a factor that must always be given due consideration.

One way of knowing when the patient is ready for some interpretation is by having it come fairly directly out of the material that he presents. The principle is that if his ego will permit certain feelings to come to the surface, then the anxiety is manageable, and the therapist can interpret along those lines.

Timing within the hour is another consideration. Technically, it is a wise idea to let the patient begin every session. No matter how striking some material may be to the therapist, the patient has something else on his mind, and that takes priority.

The manner in which an interpretation is given is likewise of considerable moment. It should be offered in the simplest possible language with due regard for the patient's place in therapy. As a rule it is best to put the interpretation in a direct, forthright manner. However, if a patient is negativistic, it may be wise to phrase interpretations in a cautious way, such as "Don't you think that . . ." or "It seems to me that . . ."

The therapist's language should be clear and free of jargon. Beyond that, it should be as close to ordinary speech as possible. It is important for the analyst to remember that if he tries to present any abstract ideas to the patient, they may be misinterpreted.

A surprising number of analysts, especially women, have difficulty using "dirty language" with the patients. This is a countertransference problem that should be worked out in their own analyses, in much the same way that women in general have to work out their attitudes toward such language in everyday life.

Hammer [50] has called attention to the use of imagery in interpretation. Since interpretation generally has to be given a number of times, it is wise to vary the language.

SUGGESTIONS FOR FURTHER READING

See references to Chapter 15.

One of the few papers dealing directly with the material in this chapter is G. Devereux, "Some Criteria for the Timing of Confrontations and Interpretations," *Int. J. Psychoanalysis* 32, 1951, 19–24.

CHAPTER 17

Working-Through: The Therapeutic Impasse

A conscience darkened
Either with its own or with another's shame
Will find thy speaking to be very harsh.
Nevertheless, all falsehood put aside and
Make thy vision wholly manifest.
And let them scratch indeed then where they
itch.
For if the words thou sayest shall be
unpleasant
At the first taste, life-giving nourishment
They shall become when they have been digested.

Dante: *Paradiso XVII*

As has been noted before, since 1914 the basic concept of all intensive analysis has been *working-through*. By working-through is meant the persistent investigation of conflicts until they are resolved. The emphasis is on time on the one hand and on thoroughness on the other.

Actually it would be more correct idiomatic English to speak of "working out" the problems than working them through. But the literal translation of the German term (*durcharbeiten*) is so well entrenched that no effort will be made to dislodge it.

Working-through is the opposite of the naive image that one or two interpretations are going to "explode the neurosis." The notion of a sudden miraculous change in the personality structure, without long, hard work attached to it, is a holdover of magical beliefs. It is part of the age-old wish that God will take care of all trouble.

While there are occasionally seemingly magical changes that occur with startling rapidity, on closer investigation these turn out to be not a total reconstruction of the personality but an alteration of some

225

attitude that still has to be worked out more carefully. An example of a "miracle" cure in one session was given before, the case of Louis, a singer with stage-fright who recovered after putting together the dynamics in one hour (cf. p. 187). This, however, is a symptomatic recovery, and in the case of the singer the more deep-seated homosexual conflicts and the lifelong misery to which he had exposed himself, remained untouched. It is essential that the analyst give up all hold-overs of magical thinking in his approach to the patient.

While working-through is always of relevance to the whole process, the first important recognition of the need for it comes with the *therapeutic impasse*. The therapeutic impasse is a situation where, in spite of all the efforts of both the patient and the analyst, no progress seems to be made for a long time. Both the patient and the analyst tend to get discouraged by what they conceive of as the lack of progress.

Historically, the existence of the therapeutic impasse has led to the expansion of psychoanalytic insight and technique in many different directions. Every technical procedure, from catharsis on, has led to some successes and some failures. Freud and his successors, by analyz-ing the failures systematically, came to the position that they were due either to resistances on the part of the patient or to counterransferences on the part of the analyst. Accordingly the mainstream of psychoana-lytic thought has concentrated on these two phenomena: resistance in the patient and countertransference in the analyst. At every point in the history of psychotherapy the field has been divided between those who have pursued the mainstream of psychoanalytic thought, with the belief that when difficulties occur they could and should be handled by further analysis, and those who cried that analysis does not work and should be replaced by some other technique. These techniques essen-tially involve reassurance, advice, manipulation, or physiological ap-proaches.

As pointed out in the first chapter, the prepsychological history of psychotherapy is a long one. Advice, suggestion, manipulation, phys-iological assaults (though with different chemical substances) have existed from time immemorial. The analytic criticism leveled at them is essentially the same that has prevailed throughout the ages: first, they have an unsound theoretical basis, in that they ignore the deep-seated and ramified nature of psychological conflicts, and second, in practice they simply do not work. Much of the time these un-analytic tech-niques are buttressed by reports of analyses in which a series of inter-pretations simply has not had the desired effect. What is difficult for both expert and layman to grasp is the idea that working-through becomes the heart of the whole therapeutic process.

The *therapeutic impasse* is the rule rather than the exception in long-term analysis. Resistances mount, the patient feels that he has made no progress for a long time, whether true or untrue, and more and more urgently expresses a wish to quit or to try some other approach.

Sometimes the patient acts out his impasse and despair by consulting another analyst or by trying some other approach or by simply breaking off treatment. Sometimes the analyst himself, especially when he is poorly trained or is up against a problem that he himself has not resolved, dismisses the patient as incurable or as having reached a point that can no longer be passed. Sometimes the patient runs away or uses some external circumstance as an excuse for running away, such as moving to another city, marriage, sickness, change in family circumstances or on the job, and so on. Most of the time, however, the patient sticks it out, and under the influence of the analyst eventually works out his difficulties.

Theoretically, the impasse occurs because a temporary equilibrium has been reached between the forces of fixation and the forces of growth. When, as in the situation being discussed here, a fair amount of therapeutic benefit has already accrued as a result of the analysis, the patient is willing to allow the analyst to help him break through this unstable equilibrium. Essentially relying on the benefits of the past, and on the analyst's conviction, the patient is willing to see it through, even though the immediate gains are entirely unclear.

The underlying forces of *fixation* are represented by the same old neurotic, defensive personality structures that have been encountered all along the line. The only novel element here is that in a sense they are making a more determined stand than ever before, because the imminence of a real change is so great. Since they are essentially the same forces that have been encountered all through the analysis to a greater or lesser extent, the patient has some idea of what is holding him back. This awareness, dim though it may be in many cases, can be used to therapeutic advantage.

The underlying forces of *growth* are represented by the image of the analytic ideal, which is beginning to become more and more clear to the patient. Beyond the neurotic misery that he has suffered from all his life lies the hope, now faintly seen, of a new kind of life in which love, work, pleasure, and the other aspects of the analytic ideal can bring him a kind of happiness that he has never known before. Sometimes all of this can be verbalized by the patient; many times it cannot be verbalized in toto but only to a limited extent.

The old argument about whether analysis should be succeeded by synthesis is generally revived at this point. Synthesis in terms of the conscious direction offered by the analyst to the patient in terms of direct advice or suggestion is certainly undesirable, unless it fits in with the goals of the patient. But synthesis in terms of working out an adequate way of living in which anxieties can be kept to a minimum and handled with the least amount of friction is an essential part of the whole analytic process. It is a mistake to believe that the patient will without further clarification or discussion find his way in the adult world merely because he has worked out certain of the childhood conflicts.

The relevance of synthesis in terms of the analytic ideal is much greater with character analyses that with symptom analyses. In the early days, when symptomatic cases were in the forefront, the analyst could be satisfied if he got the patient over his severely disabling symptoms. Nowadays, when virtually everything that the experienced analyst handles is a character difficulty, it is never sufficient merely to change one disabling symptom. It is almost always desirable to help the person grasp what a different way of life could mean to him.

This emphatically does not mean that the analyst must necessarily impose his own values and convictions on the patient. He may, if he wishes to, offer them to the patient, but it is always up to the patient to choose whatever he finds most desirable. In the long run, the analytic ideal allows for a sufficient amount of variation so that different people can work out their destinies in different ways. As Frederick the Great said, "In my kingdom everybody becomes happy in his own way." The important thing is to help the patient become happy. Less important is the particular way that he chooses.

Clinically, the management of the impasse involves an enormous amount of *repetition* of the most significant points that have been covered before, the life history, integrative interpretations, blockings in the id, mismanagement of reality, and so on.

REPETITION

It is just as well for the analyst to get used to the idea that a great deal of what he has to communicate to the patient has to be repeated over and over again before it becomes really meaningful or really usable. Naturally, the repetition need not be and should not be a literal repetition of the same words, but should involve a tactful reformulation in many different forms of the same or similar ideas.

There are three reasons why so much repetition is unavoidable. First of all, the material of psychoanalytic psychology is difficult to grasp. Now, repetition is a part of every learning process. Thus the first reason is that repetition serves the purpose of reinforcing learning in much the same way that repetition helps in any other teaching situation.

Second, apart from the inherent difficulty of psychoanalytic psychology, there are the special resistances offered to insights into oneself. This is a *special barrier to learning* that does not exist anywhere else. This special barrier to learning is affected by the repetition in several ways. First of all, the barrier involves a denial of whatever the analyst is saying. By insisting on his interpretations, the analyst is battling against this denial. He is thus asserting his authority as a competent professional who is in a position to explain to the patient what is really going on in his life, in spite of the patient's wish to forget it or to deny it, or to repress it in some other way. Second, the impulses that are brought out are generally accompanied by feelings of shame and guilt. If they were discussed in other life situations these feelings would be prominent. By the constant repetition without condemnation, the analyst indicates to the patient that it is all right to talk about such matters with other people. This is another reason why it is so essential for the analyst to be non-judgmental.

Third, the constant repetition serves to give the patient *permission* to think more and more of his instinctual life and of other aspects of his personality that he would otherwise tend to forget or to push into the background. The permission is particularly relevant here, since in the average family id material is forced out of consciousness at a very early age or, more precisely, a good deal of id material is forced out of consciousness, and comes back only in the form of a variety of derivatives, whether as fantasies or as concealed actions of one kind or another.

This point can be tied up with one made earlier, that the most suitable patients for analysis are those with an optimal combination of guilt and fantasy. The fantasy provided by the patient serves to give the analyst material for his repetitions, while the guilt means that he has some anxieties about expressing such impulses, but these anxieties can nevertheless be kept within bounds and eventually overcome. If the fantasy repression is too great, the analyst's repetitions tend to take on a rather tiresome and even boring character, simply because he does not have an adequate amount of material to work with. On the other hand, if there is too little guilt, the repetition has too little effect on the patient. If there is too much guilt, the patient will become too anxious and tend to run away or to resort to some other defense that is destructive to the therapy.

MOVEMENT

While the goal of therapy is change, not all change is desirable. Change itself has to be evaluated in the light of the individual's history, assets, and liabilities.

Two types of patients can be distinguished in analysis: those who present a great deal of movement (that is, those who seem to be changing all the time), and those who present very little movement. Paradoxically, both of these extremes serve as resistances to real analytic progress, though for different reasons.

Excessive movement, where the patient indicates at every session that he is getting better and has given up some old habits or patterns and will never resume them again, is necessarily suspect. In these cases the patient is pushing himself much too hard. He is in effect telling the analyst-parent: "Look, I'm a good boy now, and I'll never do it again." This is the kind of pattern that is seen most often in the acting-out patient with problems of addiction. The defense of denial is still operative. What the patient is denying now are the difficulties that are really involved in changing.

A significant aspect of this denial is the unwillingness to accept any dependency on the analyst. A typical pattern along these lines is seen in, say, the alcoholic. He may come in after a few sessions and say, "Well, I stopped drinking and I've taken a vow that I'll never have another drink, and so the analysis is all over and I don't need you any more. Good-bye, Doctor, and thanks for your efforts." Invariably such vows are broken within a short time, and the patient is back again with the same old problems. While as analysts we cannot speak with authority about the road to Hell, we can certainly say that the road to misery and backsliding is through good intentions.

For any meaningful change to occur, some feeling about the analyst has to be built up in the patient. Another way of putting this is that there has to be some positive transference; purely negative or indifferent transference will lead to minimal changes. Many patients because of their life histories are terribly afraid of warm and dependent feelings about the analyst; these are too reminiscent of what happened with their parents, and re-arouse the conflicts involved in other intimate situations.

On the other hand, too little movement is indicative of an excessive amount of dependency on the analyst. The patient is deriving so much gratification from the relationship *per se* that he sees no great need to effect any changes in his real life. Or it can go even further. If the dependency is strong, real life changes will threaten it and the fear that the relationship with the analyst will be brought to a close becomes greater than the wish to get over the real-life difficulties. Many times, in extremely dependent patients, in fact, the real-life difficulties are minimized because of the satisfaction derived from their dependency. Eventually, in these cases the dependency has to come under analytic scrutiny.

When there is a poor relationship between the analyst and the patient, there may likewise be too little movement. However, these patients will generally leave within a few sessions. What is being discussed here is the lack of movement of patients who have been in analysis for some reasonable length of time. In those patients it is invariably a problem of dependency gratification.

Real movement is necessarily slow and painstaking. It is a mistake to evaluate therapy session by session, as though some miraculous change must occur every time that the patient sees the analyst. The most useful criterion is to look back every six months or year to reflect on how the person is handling his life as compared to the previous checkpoint. It is often useful to evaluate progress during the past year at the onset of a summer vacation.

Evaluating every session is not only ill-advised, it is frequently destructive to progress. Research which concentrates on individual sessions is certainly poorly thought out, since it leaves out of account the real nature of therapeutic movement.

Quite often too much movement generates an over-optimistic feeling in both patient and analyst, which is followed by a letdown. Beginning analysts particularly are apt to be deceived by an excess of movement on the one hand and by a lack of movement on the other. Kris made a profound comment when he spoke of the analyst's first ten years in practice as "the formative decade."

Too little movement generates a feeling of discouragement in both the patient and the analyst. Here it is essential to analyze the feelings on both sides, the resistance in the patient and the countertransference in the analyst. In a considerable number of cases it is found that upon analysis the feeling of too little movement turns out to be deceptive, because the expectations were much too unrealistic. In addition, the kinds of movement that the patient shows may not be too impressive to the outside world or too perceptible to those who do not know the patient intimately.

THE TIME FACTOR IN ANALYSIS

The length of time that the average analysis lasts has become longer and longer over the years. Where in the early history of psychoanalysis three months was considered extraordinarily long, now an average analysis may last anywhere between two and ten years, sometimes even longer. Furthermore, many patients after the conclusion of one analysis and the consolidation of the gains effected there, nowadays often feel the need to go back to the same or to another analyst for more help. This tremendous amount of time has aroused understandable reactions from many quarters, but at the same time it is seriously misunderstood.

Looked at in terms of the medical model, an illness that requires a great deal of time to handle or cure is, generally speaking, a chronic one of considerable severity. While the medical model is not appropriate, at the same time the analogy may be a useful one. Personality difficulties are similar to a chronic disability of varying degrees of severity, which block the person from reaching his true potential in life.

Looked at educationally, the great length of time indicates that there is a great deal to learn and a great deal to digest. As has been stressed throughout this book, the educational model is certainly a much more appropriate one than the medical. From this point of view, the length of time derives from the fact that the undertaking is extraordinarily difficult.

By contrast, therapy that seeks to transform the patient in one weekend (such as nude marathons) or in short three-week cures strikes the professional and the layman as extremely superficial. Comparison can be drawn between a three-week correspondence course in a foreign language, which teaches the individual a few of the everyday phrases needed for travel in the country, and the thorough study of the language that will allow the learner to really read, speak, and write it like a native. A thorough study would necessarily take years, and no substitute for thoroughness in such an adventure has ever been discovered.

Throughout the years there have been innumerable attempts to reduce the time in analysis. Without going into all of these in detail, it can only be said that they have all failed. Freud himself extended the length of time required only because of the difficulties encountered in brief therapy. Originally, in the period of catharsis, he hoped to cure patients in a few sessions. One case that he reports is that of a woman who had recently given birth and who suffered from psychogenic nausea. Hypnosis followed by post-hypnotic suggestion cured her of the symptom in three sessions. But Freud realized that such quick cures left a great deal to be desired. When he moved on to catharsis, he again found that several weeks or a month could help some patients but would not help others.

Around the middle of the nineties, a switch came to psychoanalysis. In his first published analytic case, the case of Dora, the treatment went on daily for three months, at the end of which Dora terminated prematurely. In the case of the Rat Man, whom Freud treated in 1908, the treatment went on for about ten months. Finally, in the case of the Wolf Man, who was in treatment from 1909 to 1914, the therapy lasted five years before the neurotic symptoms were sufficiently dispelled.[51]

In his work after World War I, Freud did engage in analyses of remarkably brief duration. Many of the American physicians who went to Vienna stayed for only three or four months. All of them later expressed a feeling of inspiration combined with a feeling of disappointment.[52] As time has gone on, the length of analysis of the prospective analyst, on which most exact figures are available, has increased steadily. In their review of the published figures of the constituent societies in the American Psychoanalytic Association, Lewin and Ross [53] cite figures to show that the average duration of the training analysis of prospective analysts is anywhere from 150 hours to 1900. Presumably, the psychiatrist (on occasion a Ph.D. psychologist) when he comes into analysis is within culturally normal limits. Yet no matter what realities he starts out with, once he begins to go to psychotherapy, he recognizes in increasing measure the truth of the analytic philosophy.

This is striking evidence that the "normal" in our culture is quite "neurotic." If even the most normal denizens of our culture require so many years in analysis to find lasting happiness it is not surprising that less fortunate mortals have at least as hard a time.

Non-analytic approaches that have attempted to shorten the therapeutic process have been legion, yet none of them have stood the test
of time. Even a naive system like that of Rogers, which began by pro-
claiming that eight weekly sessions of non-directive therapy were
enough to cure virtually anything from mental retardation to schizophrenia, gradually calmed down and became a lengthier procedure
similar to classical analysis. Clinicians, no matter what persuasion
they start out with, once they come to grips with the realities of psychotherapy, are forced to recognize in increasing measure the truth
of the psychoanalytic propositions.

We have already referred to Freud's remark that in the beginning
of his practice he could not get his patients to stay, while at the end
of his practice he could not get them to leave. The paradox is created
by the patients. In the beginning they feel tremendously resentful of
the enormous amount of time involved in analysis. But as they probe
more deeply into themselves and others, that another human being
who is a trained professional will spend such an extraordinary amount
of time with them becomes enormously gratifying.

It is notoriously difficult to present in capsule form the course of a
long-term analysis. Particularly difficult is the presentation of the
working-through. When it is put down in black and white the reader
may say Well, so that is it, what happened? Actually, while it was
going on, there was an enormous amount of ups and downs, backing
and filling, emotions of various kinds, and a whole host of valuable
clinical material. Nevertheless, since it is an impasse, the external impression remains that of an impasse. It is actually only through a careful study of the whole process of the analysis that the impasse and its
resolution can be put in the proper perspective. Here is a clinical
example.

Beatrice, a 26-year-old secretary, came to analysis because of an
unhappy love relationship. After going steady with her for about a
year, her boy friend, a physician, suddenly decided to drop her, under
particularly painful circumstances. She reacted with strong distress
which prompted her to seek out analysis.

Her background was extremely traumatic. Her family left Europe
and went to Mexico during the war years. In Mexico her father left
his wife and two children to marry her mother, who was 15 years his
junior. Father's first family then migrated to Israel, where they still
were at the time of the analysis.

At first the parents' marriage was a true love match, deliriously
happy. Father worked hard and built up an excellent business. But

then, and actually as far back as Beatrice could remember, violent battles began to erupt between mother and father. It was rumored that mother had many lovers. She openly said her father was not a man and he could not satisfy her. Mother would scream and yell at father at the top of her lungs while father would meekly hide his head between his legs. For years mother debated whether to leave father.

During all this fighting both Beatrice and her younger sister, who was born when Beatrice was 6 years old, were seriously neglected. Beatrice remembered how much time she spent alone as a child or with friends and away from her parents. Mother was particularly strong and sometimes actually became involved in physical battles with Beatrice. Father occasionally showed her some love and she became warmly attached to him but with an enormous amount of ambivalence.

When she was 12 years old, mother decided to send her to New York to live with some relatives. There was no special reason for this decision. Evidently it was another facet of mother's dislike of the girl as well as of her wish to maintain lovers without interference from her children. She stayed in New York for a year, then returned home. Finally, when Beatrice was about 18 years old, father and mother were divorced. At first Beatrice sided with father. She went to live with him. One night as she was lying down on the bed, he lay down next to her and put his arms around her. She was horrified, but said nothing.

Father moved to Texas, while mother remarried and moved to Connecticut, leaving Beatrice alone in New York with a number of cousins and other relatives.

The course of the analysis showed, initially, a great deal of progress. She succeeded in liberating herself from the masochistic feelings connected with the rejection by her fiancé. Her sexual reactions improved to the point where she was generally more experienced and more gratified than her partners. Her disorganization was understood in the light of the disorganization of her childhood, and gradually gave way to a more reasonable approach to life. Her feeling about herself was remarkably improved.

Apart from the childhood material, dreams and associations, the analysis concentrated very heavily on her affairs with men. Typically, if the man was potent and could gratify her, she responded well but could not feel any emotional tie to him. However, if the man was impotent or suffered from premature ejaculation she became strongly attached. A long series of affairs ensued, in some of which she would feel cold toward the competent man, and others in which she would feel attracted to the impotent man.

As part of a growing transference in her reaction to the analyst, one day she responded to the approaches of another patient who met her in the waiting room. They spent a weekend together, which made her deliriously happy. Then he suddenly dropped her, without rhyme or reason. She did not understand what he had done but she attributed it to her own inadequacy. This incident brought out a lot of hostility toward the analyst who was accused of mishandling the whole situation so as to block the achievement of her love. It was clear that the analyst had become the bad father who was a strict, puritanical kind of man.

Some time after this incident, she began an affair with another physician, who was the second type of person. Sexually rather shy and not entirely adequate, he was an uncommunicative sort of person who could not make up his mind whether to marry or not.

With remarkable naiveté he spontaneously told her of a childhood incident in which he had slept with his sister, and did not remember whether he had had sexual relationships with her or not. He was obviously overattached to his mother, just like the man whom she had been engaged to and who had dropped her. In the meantime this first fiancé had married someone else, moved to another city, then had begun to call Beatrice. He told her that he was extremely unhappy in his marriage and he wanted to resume the affair with her. She was strong enough to refuse.

The new relationship, after a rather stormy year, did not work out. Without saying so, in so many words, the boy friend simply broke off with her. She had already met his family who were quite enamored of her, but he was clearly too afraid of marriage.

Although she had never been really in love with this second boy friend, his rejection set off an extreme reaction and led to an impasse in the analysis. This impasse went on for more than a year. She did not know where to turn. She became more depressed. A number of bad dreams about her mother appeared, such as one in which she gave birth to a child and her mother took it away, and another in which she was operated on by her mother because there were all kinds of peculiar pipes going through her body which had to be straightened out. She began to fight with her roommate with whom she eventually broke up for neurotic reasons. The difficulties about money which had been resolved for a long time now again came to the fore. There were few men in her life during this period. Her pattern was to reject them as soon as they became interested.

In the meantime she bombarded the analyst with negative feelings, especially about the incident with the other patient for which she blamed him. Sometimes she would not come to the sessions; when the analyst called her up to find out what was going on she said that she might just as well quit, it was all doing her no good.

After about a year of this working-through, she decided to go to school to finish her degree, but in order to do that she had to borrow money from a great many people. She asked for permission to pay half the analytic fee and to defer the remainder until she had graduated. Much to her surprise the analyst assented, commenting that he was willing to be a good father to her in this respect by giving her what she had always longed for from her own father, but had been refused.

The chance to go to school opened up a whole new world for Beatrice. It was the gratification of a long lost dream. She did exceptionally well, and gained scholarships and prizes. One of her professors took an interest in her, fell in love with her, and they were eventually married.

When she left analysis she was somewhat dubious about the relationship because her husband's love was greater than hers and because there were certain difficulties in the way, particularly a previous marriage of her husband's which had left him emotionally and financially drained. But these difficulties were satisfactorily overcome.

It could be said that the resolution of the impasse involved a shift from a masochistic image of love in which she was always deprived, hurt, beaten, damaged, rejected, to a healthy image of love in which she could share her feelings, be loved as well as love, and be treated with decency and respect. Throughout the entire period, however, Beatrice was dubious at every session about whether the analysis would ever get anywhere.

SUGGESTIONS FOR FURTHER READING

In spite of the central importance of working through to the entire psychoanalytic process, the literature on it is meager indeed. Freud's original paper, published in 1914, "Remembering, Repeating and Working-Through" (*S.E.* Vol. XII) is still fundamental.

Some other useful papers are: R. Greenson, "The Problem of Working Through" in M. Schur, ed., *Drives, Affects, Behavior* (New York: Int. Universities Press, 1965), 277–314. W. Stewart, "An Inquiry into the Concept of Working Through," *J. Am. Psychoanalytic Assoc.* 11, 1963, 474–499. S. Novey, "The Principle of Working Through in Psychoanalysis," *J. Am. Psychoanalytic Assoc.* 10, 1962, 658–676. H. Loewald, "On the Therapeutic Action of Psychoanalysis," *Int. J. Psychoanalysis* 41, 1960, 16–33. F. Alexander, "The Problems of Psychoanalytic Technique (1935)," in *The Scope of Psychoanalysis* (New York: Basic Books, 1961), 225–243. H. Schmale, "Working Through," *J. Am. Psychoanalytic Assoc.* 14, 1966, 172–182. P. Greenacre, "Reevaluation of the Process of Working Through," *Int. J. Psychoanalysis* 37, 1956, 439–443.

CHAPTER 18

Working-Through: The Forces of Regression

> We speak a language
> taught we know not how
> And what it is that from us flows
> The listener better than the
> utterer knows.
>
> F. Thompson: "The Hound of Heaven"
> *Poems*

Since the therapeutic impasse rests upon a stalemate between the forces of regression and the forces of growth, the next step is to examine these forces in more detail. The present chapter will discuss regression, the subsequent one growth.

While anything infantile in the character structure may impede the course of an analysis, certain problems occur so frequently that they deserve a fuller discussion. These are particularly: 1) the persistence of childhood patterns; 2) the depth of the regression; 3) the intensity of the transference neurosis; 4) dependency gratification; 5) defiance of the analyst; and 6) external pressures.

1) The Persistence of Childhood Patterns

The persistence of childhood patterns is a psychological fact of life, much as the persistence of physical patterns is a physical fact of life. The human being tends to build up certain patterns and to stick to them, regardless of their consequences in real life. It takes a good deal of training in any area to overcome these patterns.

To take but one example from an allied field, the speech patterns of any individual are determined primarily by the surroundings in which he is brought up. It is rare for anyone above the age of 15 to be able to learn a foreign language with absolute fluency. Experts in linguistics can often spot the birthplace of a speaker within twenty or thirty miles, because of their intimate knowledge of the differences between various localities. If speech can be localized to such degree, surely it can cause no surprise that basic psychological patterns that enter into interpersonal relationships will be hardened as well. The significance of childhood is that no matter what the childhood pattern is it tends to persist. It cannot be said that certain types of childhood experiences are more basic than others; it can only be said that what-ever the person goes through as a child tends to continue in his life. At some point, if he really wishes to change, it has to be worked out in the greatest of detail.

In analysis, these childhood forces must be given a chance to ex-press themselves until they have become sufficiently conscious so that their strength has been spent. There is in fact no real alternative. For if the patient is not given a chance to verbalize the childhood forces, he will act them out.

The amount of time required to bring these childhood patterns to consciousness and talk them out varies with the severity of the trauma. Even if things seem to be going smoothly for the patient at the mo-ment, the phenomenon of the return of the repressed is well known; at some point it will come back to haunt him again. Rather than wait for that point, the analyst prefers to deal with the various derivatives of the repressed material, thus bringing the whole trauma into the light, if he can.

2) The Depth of the Regression

The process of analysis facilitates a varying amount of regression. As will be recalled, the theory of the analytic cure is that a regressive transference neurosis is established, the working out of which leads to a new level of functioning. At the same time, the degree of regres-sion varies from one person to another. It is virtually impossible to predict the depth to which any particular patient will regress.

Frequently when the patient starts to regress, a considerable amount of anxiety is aroused in the analyst. It is well to remember at this point that in general no regression in analysis will go beyond that previously experienced in life.

In regression the patient lets go of a number of ego controls. In such a process he may say and do things that seem entirely foreign to his conscious ego. Some of his actions in turn may frighten him into thinking that he is "much sicker" than was thought to be the case at the beginning of analysis. It is important for the analyst to keep his cool at these points, and to help the patient realize that the regressions will pass by, in much the same way that the childhood patterns spend their force in the course of time.

In the illustrative case of Jim, it might have been anticipated that the patient would go into a much deeper regression than he actually did. For unknown reasons, he did not do so. His sudden love for the woman certainly acted as a defense against a homosexual wish for the analyst. At the same time, it represented a step forward in life, and one that found sanction from many different sources.

The depth of the regression determines how much working-through will have to be done. The deeper it goes, the more working-through is necessary. It is essential to bear in mind in this period that the anxiety experienced by the patient is only temporary. After working out the regression, the patient belongs to those whom William James called the twice-born.

In one type of case the regression starts before analysis, but continues throughout the entire period. A case in which a specific regression to a specific situation occurred during the analysis is the following.

Rebecca, a 22-year-old girl, originally went to therapy because of deep feelings of despair about her life. She could not make friends, and had even contemplated throwing herself off the George Washington Bridge.

Her history can only be presented here in capsule form. She was the older of two children. The family had split its sleeping quarters; Rebecca, as far back as she could remember, had slept with her father, while her sister had slept with her mother. The father was about 20 years older than the mother.

When Rebecca reached puberty, she suddenly became convinced that father was going to rape her. Accordingly she began to sleep in another part of the house. But of course this rape fantasy had devastating effects on her relationships with boys.

In the analysis, Rebecca at first had a positive reaction, and an analytic honeymoon ensued. After about two years, however, she began to regress more and more. She quite consciously set herself the task of changing her body to the form that it had had at the time of puberty. The carrying out of the fantasy meant losing some 50 pounds, reducing from 165 to 115, which she had judged was her weight at the age of 12. The attempt to regain her life situation as of the age of 12 was a deliberate and conscious one and pushed forward with all her effort. Remarkably enough, she even stopped menstruating for a period of about nine months.

The attempt to regain her 12-year-old status stopped when she could not fall below 125 pounds, and endangered her health. The analyst had to insist that she consult a physician when her menses stopped for such a long period. He found nothing wrong with her menstrual cycle but did disclose that her pulse had gone down to about 50 as a result of consistent undernutrition.

The wish to regress was so powerful with Rebecca that when it was frustrated in the analysis, in spite of extensive attempts to work it through, she went to live with a man who was about the same age as her father. Unfortunately at this point the analyst became ill and had to switch her to another therapist. After three more brief therapeutic tries, Rebecca apparently gave up any hope of changing herself and settled down to live with the father figure as long as he would have her.

3) The Intensity of the Transference Neurosis

This third factor in the working-through process is related to the first two, but has a different emphasis. The stress now is on the phenomenological relationship with the analyst. Usually when an intense transference neurosis has to be worked through, it is essentially of a highly positive, often eroticized, nature. It may be accompanied by a persistence of infantile problems or by deep regression, or it may not be. All these factors may vary and do vary with the patient. The only valid generalization is that the more intense the transference neurosis, the more difficult the working-through period will be. At the same time, the working-through will lead to a more radical transformation of the personality.

It may come as a surprise to discover that an intense transference neurosis can occur without a particularly deep regression. Conversely, a deep regression can also occur without a manifestly intense transference neurosis. What is important is to approach the clinical material with an open mind, rather than with theoretical preconceptions.

The following clinical vignette is a good example of an intense transference neurosis that did not involve any profound regression in the girl's actual life.

Ruth, a 22-year-old secretary, came to the present writer after an unfortunate experience with another analyst which had lasted about a year and a half. She had originally gone into treatment for a variety of symptoms including occasional psychogenic fainting spells. With the previous analyst there had been virtually no rapport. He had not given her a chance to ventilate the negative transference. One of his main interpretations was that her head was a vacuum. What he meant was that she was a rather worthless sort of person.

With the new analyst, an entirely different rapport was established from the very beginning. She felt understood and appreciated, and flourished.

She was the younger of two sisters. There had been an extraordinarily intense attachment to the father throughout childhood. He had wanted a boy and had brought her up in many ways to be a boy, giving her a baseball, track equipment, even a football, and introducing her to other sports that ordinarily are limited to boys.

As a result of an accident in a game, Ruth was seriously injured and confined to a hospital for about two years when she was 8 years old. This led to an enormous development of her fantasy life, which was manifested in tales that she spun about her past. She knew that she was making up stories, but could not overcome the compulsion to do so.

When Ruth reached puberty the father, who had never been too successful in business, began going steadily downhill, apparently in reaction to his attraction to his daughter. He began to drink very heavily and could not make a living for about five years. During this period Ruth's mother began to support the family. Violent fights erupted between Ruth and her father when she was about 18. She left home.

A series of love affairs followed, none of which gave her any great amount of happiness. Sexually she felt frustrated, unable to reach any kind of orgasm, either vaginally or clitorally. In her sexual activity she was gratified primarily by the fact that the man wanted her.

Shortly before entering the present analysis she married a man who was about ten years her senior. She did not love him, but felt pleased that he loved her so much. With this man there was a consistent sexual problem because he suffered from premature ejaculation. However, at the time this made no difference to Ruth, since she was unable to reach any kind of sexual pleasure herself.

In the analysis, a considerable liberation occurred. She became freer sexually, improved in her work, felt happy all around, life took on a new flavor.

After about a year and a half of analysis there ensued an intense transference neurosis. She dreamt about the analyst, she consciously wanted him. She had fantasies about lying naked in bed with him, having sex in all kinds of different ways, thought of going off to a different country with him, marrying him, and so on. All of this was communicated to the analyst and the working-through required an understanding of her childhood attachment to father and to an uncle who in some ways was very much like the analyst. At the same time, apart from the attachment to the analyst, there was no regression in her life. Instead, there was a constant progression from one success experience to another.

After about two years of working-through the transference neurosis, Ruth became increasingly dissatisfied with her sexually inept husband who was also just beginning to make his way in the world of work. Where at first Ruth had been pleased by the idea of supporting him through school, now she resented it, since she realized that she was playing out the role of the mother who had supported the family while the father drank himself into a stupor all the time.

One day she met another man, who seemed to offer her much of what she was lacking in her own married life. This other man, who was likewise about ten years older, was a much more sexual person than her husband. He gave her a great deal of warmth, sexuality, and love, as well as a more secure future, since he was already fairly well set in his profession.

At first Ruth though of this other man only in terms of a temporary affair. But gradually the bonds between the two of them became stronger and stronger. In the meantime it appeared that the other man was in many essential respects a substitute for the analyst. She continued to have fantasies about him, and continued to speak of the two men as almost one in her mind.

Finally the other man proposed, and Ruth decided to accept. She left her husband, resolved many of her conflicts, and made a second marriage which was much happier than the first. Although this marriage, too, after a number of years led to some difficulty, on the whole it was a much better resolution for her than her earlier marriage.

It could be argued in this case that Ruth was merely acting out the transference rather than actually resolving her neurosis. This raises the question of whether the transference can ever or should ever really be dissolved or whether on the basis of the transference, the relationship should be entered into. If the transference is compared with the parental situation, then it becomes clear that in the latter the girl who has a good relationship with her father does not break it, but is liberated to move away from it to find a younger man who in most essential respects would be similar to the father. In other words, the positive feelings would be carried over from the father to the husband. Both analytically and sociologically this makes for the most gratifying kind of marriage.

A similar situation occurs in the transference. If the patient has a positive transference, there is nothing wrong with establishing a relationship with another man who is similar to the analyst. The only drawback would be if the other man were chosen because of some accidental criterion such as looks or profession which were similar to the analyst's, while in reality he was pretty unsuitable as a companion or a marriage partner. In the case of Ruth this was not so. The other man, while similar in many respects to the analyst, was still in reality an excellent choice for marriage.

4) Dependency Gratification

Dependency gratification is the most common cause of prolonged analysis. It requires a deep and careful working-through process. Temptations to cut it short or to sidetrack the analysis with some advice or suggestion or manipulation are strongest in this pattern.

Again the dependency is to some extent fostered by the analysis. But to a greater extent it is reinforced by the neurosis and by the real-life situation. Of any ten patients, only some will become extremely dependent, and the amount of dependency will vary from one to the other.

The systematic analysis of dependency is one of the most important contributions of psychoanalytic theory to therapy. In other forms of therapy it is not at all uncommon to decide that the patient is too infantile to benefit from systematic uncovering treatment, and to try to sidetrack him in one form or another. To some extent this holds true in some aspects of medical treatment.

Again, dependency gratification is related to all the factors mentioned before. It can coexist with them in varying degrees, depending on the personality strcture of the individual. But again, when the dependency becomes the major problem to be worked through, the emphasis is on that rather than on anything else.

A number of different types of dependency can be distinguished.

1. The first type of patient is the underlying *fearful, anxious person*. To him, the analyst is a real source of relief and becomes internalized as a constant source of relief. These patients frequently will have some other person or persons on the outside whom they turn to for solace or comfort. If the analyst does not respond to their needs,

it reinforces their search and their attachment to the other person. Many times in these patients the analysis becomes a tug-of-war between the other person who offers them, in addition to the relief, some actual gratification such as sex, and the analyst who offers only words. Often enough these patients become very dependent on the outside source of relief, comfort, or sexuality, and may even rely on them to determine whether they should continue in the analysis.

Since the positive transference as a rule is sidestepped in the beginning, it usually happens that the dependency is reinforced by the analytic process, even though the analyst does not wish to see it happen.

Pamela, a 27-year-old housewife, felt extremely anxious and hesitant about her life situation. She would come in with a million questions about what to do. These would not be answered, but some interpretation would be offered. As soon as it came forth, her anxiety would disappear and she knew exactly what to do. She came to refer to the analyst's interpretations as his "magic wand." After a while she could come in and say, "Wave your magic wand and tell me what to do here." For tactical reasons it was advisable to defer the analysis of this magic-wand image until later on in therapy. But since the analyst had not actually told her what to do, it quickly became clear that the magic wand was something that she had projected to the analyst rather than something that he himself had done.

By contrast, Pamela had a close friend, Charlotte, who was going to a psychiatrist who was treating her in a much more authoritarian manner. Charlotte had a terrible weight problem; she weighed about 300 pounds and was desperately trying to lose to come back to normal. Many of her efforts, including two stints in the Weight Watchers, had failed to make a dent in her problem.

Charlotte's psychiatrist began to run her life in every way. Whenever one of her children was sick she would call him and he would tell her what to do. When her husband did not come home she would call him. When she felt depressed, when she felt beautiful, when she felt timorous, whenever a problem came up, she would call him and he directed her every move.

Under this intensive regime Charlotte became steadily worse. Her weight increased, as might have been anticipated, rather than decreased. Eventually she left to go to another therapist who treated her more analytically.

2. The second type of patient is the one who *projects omnipotence*

to the analyst. Naturally, a certain amount of anxiety goes together with this, but these patients, more characteristically, have a good deal of denial, since they have come through many life crises by finding some powerful figure on whom they could project, or unload their problems. Initially, in the analyses of these patients, it is often necessary to play the role of a powerful figure precisely because the patient is so utterly helpless. But the analyst can then gradually withdraw himself from the situation, leaving more and more of life's intiative up to the patient. When this happens, the patient will protest that too much of a burden is thrown on her, but will gradually learn that she can carry the burden, so that she need not feel so utterly helpless.

In the case of Evelyn (see pp. 113, 191–192) a total state of helplessness was the most outstanding clinical feature. As mentioned, Evelyn had at one time been fired from a job because she could not even dress herself properly. Prior to analysis, Evelyn had never been able to live in an apartment of her own. She had always sought out older girls who would then serve as substitute mothers to take care of her needs. At one point, she deliberately moved into the home of a friend who was married with three children, and the thought that she was the fourth child was not too far from her consciousness. While she was living there, one night she even wet the bed, accentuating the wish to regress to a real infantile stage.

It took several years to establish a relationship with Evelyn. During this period, the analyst had to be a strong figure, advising her about what to do, about where to go, about how to handle herself. For example, Evelyn would constantly be involved in installment plans that got her heavily into debt. Anyone who came along with a likely-looking system for teaching her something or giving her something, costing three or four hundred dollars, which she would have to pay out over a period of time, found a willing customer. The analyst had to point out repeatedly that she did not realize what she was getting herself into, and advised her not to sign any of these contracts without consulting a lawyer. Since she worked in an office with lawyers, and was very friendly with many of them, this was easily arranged.

Once the relationship was established, Evelyn could then be encouraged to move along more independent lines. An unexpected outcome of the analysis was the development of a hidden artistic talent. Evelyn began to paint, and did so well that people bought her paintings. She might eventually have become a professional painter, but the hazards of such an occupation were too great for her.

Later, Evelyn began to go with a fellow who could not make up his mind whether he wanted to marry her or not. In her newly found independence, after about two years of such a relationship, she finally gave him an ultimatum—either marry me or we break up. He still could not make up his mind, whereupon Evelyn, with surprising initiative, rented an apartment away from the boy friend. When she did this, he decided to marry her.

3. The third kind of patient is the one whose dependency derives from an *absence of sexual gratification*. This is most often found in the older woman, with a male analyst, where the man is sometimes the only contact she has with the opposite sex. Paradoxically, but usually, in such cases the woman is not conscious of the sexual attraction, but pursues the analysis ostensibly for other reasons. In these cases it is a mistake to analyze the sexual aspect of the transference too soon, since that would arouse an excessive amount of resistance.

Carole, a 38-year-old, unmarried, handicapped woman, came to analysis because of deep suicidal wishes. She quickly developed a strong erotic transference and deep dependency on the analyst. After the initial hurdles had been passed, during this period, she would talk about the analyst as "that man whom I'm keeping." In spite of her handicap, Carole was able, as a result of the analysis, to establish some relationships with men.

4. The *emotionally isolated person,* particularly those who have, for neurotic reasons, chased everybody away from their lives, except the analyst. These are people with a strong paranoid coloring, who see the whole world as enemies and sooner or later retreat from every intimate relationship that they enter into. As time goes on, the analyst becomes more and more important to them because, no matter what they do, the analyst never deliberately drops them from treatment. Sometimes they leave, only to return when they find how inhospitable the outside world is to them.

At some point here, the isolation must be taken up as an indication of the patient's paranoia, and blocking off of the love feelings. The concept of paranoia is grasped easily enough and can be conveyed to these patients in so many words. Here, as in so many instances, if the analyst honestly tells the patient what is wrong, the patient will be more grateful than resentful.

Rita was a woman who had had an unfortunate psychotherapeutic history. She had been to an Orgone therapist, who had manipulated her body in various ways over a period of 13 years. During this time, she was hospitalized four times.

When she finally left to come to a better trained analyst, she was driven by the paranoid conviction that the Mafia was out to get her. This consciously was based on some vague experience of a man who had once done something illegal which she saw, and she fantasized that he was connected with the Mafia who were going to take revenge on her because of her knowledge of their activities.

In some six months of more systematic therapy, Rita became very attached to her new analyst. The Mafia fantasy began to recede more and more into the background. For some time, the dependency had to be strengthened until Rita was able to make more contacts in the outside world. Once this was done, the dependency could then be analyzed.

5. The fifth type of patient is the one with *little real life potential.* These are people who really, no matter what is done with them, will not get too far in the world. They are dependent in this sense for real reasons, because they do not have the wherewithal to become too independent in the hustle and bustle of modern life. With these patients, it is rarely necessary or even advisable to analyze the dependency in too much detail, until the analysis has gone a great length. Nevertheless, even with these people, analytic understanding through the scrutiny of the usual kind of material is of the utmost importance.

Saul, a 30-year-old carpenter, had gone to the VA for help for seven years after discharge from the service for psychoneurosis. At the end of this period, the VA therapist had kicked him out, telling him that he was too dependent and that he should try to get along as well as he could. After about a year, Saul, in despair, sought out another analyst. This time, he stayed for a number of years, but the therapy was oriented along psychoanalytic lines. While the ideas were difficult for Saul to grasp, he did get the gist of them, and made an adjustment at a much higher level.

6. Finally, there is the dependency of those who are *recovering from a bad therapeutic experience.* It should not be overlooked that in the present-day professional world, a considerable number of therapists are not too well trained. Some of them are so poorly trained or so disturbed that it is undesirable for them to be therapists at all, but the professional societies do not take it upon themselves to become policemen except in extreme instances. Patients who leave such

a therapist after an unfortunate experience and go to a person who is well trained, often become excessively dependent because they regard the well-trained therapist as unique. After all, patients do not know the kind of training that therapists undergo, and assume that if they have a degree they are all alike. In these cases, eventually, it should be pointed out to the patient that he was exposed to a poor technique, not that he was such a poor therapeutic risk.

Ralph, a 35-year-old scientist, was going to a therapist who was interested in "experimentation" and "innovation." One of this therapist's ideas was that the unconscious was a reaction to another person, rather than an expression of one's own innermost desires, as orthodox theory would have it. One day this therapist had a dream that Ralph put his penis in the therapist's rectum. This was interpreted to mean that the therapist had an unconscious awareness of Ralph's homosexuality. This was knocked around for a while by patient and therapist. Several months later, the therapist decided that he did not like Ralph, and dropped him from treatment. Ralph left, terrified that he was really a homeosexual.

When Ralph came to the new analyst, he was quite naturally in a rage. At the same time, inwardly he was terribly frightened that he was not good analytic material and that nobody could really help him. In this case, it had to be pointed out to him from the very beginning that the other analyst was treating him with idiosyncratic theories of his own, and that this had nothing to do with Ralph. In systematic therapy, Ralph made considerable progress.

5) Defiance of the Analyst

A fifth factor that makes for a long and difficult working-through period is a paradoxical one. Many patients, even though they come for help, soon engage in an underground battle with the analyst. After a while, the transference becomes so strong that the major goal of the patient is to defeat the efforts of the analyst. Since the analyst is trying to get him better, one way of defeating him is to stay sick or neurotic. While it is difficult to make the patient aware of the nature of such a resistance, it is still necessary to point it out and try to work it out at some point in the analysis.

In one of his letters to Abraham, Freud comments that several times with patients he had done his utmost to help them only to find himself rewarded with no success. At this point, unconsciously, he gave up the battle against the patient's neurosis. As soon as he did so, the patient began to make progress. It is as though the patient sensed that he had defeated the analyst and now could go on to get better. Other analysts have had similar experiences.

6) External Pressures

The significance of external pressures on the analysis is a highly variable one. At the same time, it should be recognized that in many cases these pressures are of considerable importance in the outcome of the analysis. If they are too great, the working-through problem can be enormous, if not actually impossible. It is essential for the analyst to take these external forces into consideration. If he ignores them he can rightly be accused of sitting in an ivory tower, ignorant of what is going on around him, although this accusation more often applies to the patient than to the analyst.

When the patient feels threatened by reality, a useful question is: What alternatives do you see for yourself? This brings to a head the question of whether the patient is creating problems or whether the problems are such that he simply has to come to grips with the outside world, regardless of his inner conflicts.

SUGGESTIONS FOR FURTHER READING

See references to Chapter 17.

CHAPTER 19

Working-Through:
The Forces of Growth

The love between the sexes is undoubtedly one of the first things in life, and the combination of mental and bodily satisfaction attained in the enjoyment of love is literally one of life's culminations. Apart from a few perverse fanatics, all the world knows this and conducts life accordingly; only science is too refined to confess it.

Freud: *Observations on Transference Love* (*1915*)

It sometimes seems that the forces of regression are so formidable that it is a wonder that the patient ever gets better. Nevertheless, most patients do. This, too, requires clinical investigation and theoretical insight into the forces of growth. It is just as grave a mistake to underestimate the forces of growth as it is to underestimate the forces of regression.

A number of different factors that lead to the growth process can be enumerated. In oversimplified form, it may be said that the therapeutic battle is between the positive and the negative forces in the personality structure. The problem is to allow the positive forces to outweigh the negative, or to facilitate the growth of the positive to the point where they outweigh the negative. For this purpose, it is most essential to understand the positive factors that lie at the analyst's disposal. Seven may be enumerated.

1) The Initial Improvement

From a practical point of view, by far the most important is the experience of an initial improvement. Patients are skeptical people; they have to be shown that this unusual form of therapy has something in store for them. The proof of the pudding for them is in the eating. By and large, the successful patient begins with some initial improvement; that is, he begins by getting better to some extent.

In broad outline, the successful case follows the pattern of an analytic honeymoon, an initial resistance that is overcome—that is, a first treatment crisis—an overcoming of this treatment crisis, a long working-through period, and a satisfactory termination. As has been mentioned (see Chapter 4), the longer the analytic honeymoon lasts, the better the prognosis for the ultimate outcome. But after it has come to an end, and the first treatment crisis has been overcome, the memory of the initial improvement remains with the patient.

Without some initial improvement, prognosis is dubious. In fact, from a practical point of view, if there is no improvement in the first few months, the patient does not stay in treatment. Some patients become impatient after only a few sessions and leave. Absence of improvement makes them dubious of the whole experience.

Usually a patient has gone a certain distance toward the analytic ideal. Initial improvement may involve any or all aspects of this ideal. Then he bogs down in a therapeutic impasse. At this point the working-through process commences. The forces of growth are temporarily equalled by the forces of regression. But the patient has already had some experience of improvement. At this stage, when he begins to question whether the whole experience is worthwhile, it is useful to ask: "Has anything changed since the beginning of analysis?" The patient will then usually reply, "Oh, yes, this and this and this has changed, but I still feel miserable about such and such." The fact that certain things have changed then becomes the strongest of all inducements for him to try to change the remainder.

2) Impulse Release Without Superego Punishment

Of all the aspects of the initial improvement, by far the most important is impulse release without superego punishment. This has already been discussed in the section on the analytic honeymoon, so little more need be said about it here.

As far as the problem of working-through is concerned, particularly in relationship to the ultimate outcome, the impulse release of the early stages is especially significant. It gives the patient an inkling of a different kind of life that ultimately awaits him if he succeeds in working through all his problems. For this reason it is particularly important to stress the positive aspects of the life experience that the individual describes in alaysis.

An instance may be taken from the promiscuous girl, who comes to analysis full of guilt and foreboding that she will be punished for her illicit activity in much the same way that father would have punished her. Generally speaking, these girls derive little pleasure from their sexual activity, which is pursued primarily for the sake of reassuring themselves that they are desirable. The dynamic factor frequently goes back to a crushing mother, from whom they turned to father who was expected to give them some love that they never got from mother. With these patients it is often helpful to say: "You've had so much sex, you must like it." This remark gives the girl the feeling in a way that sex is all right, while it also stamps the analyst as a rather kindly man who is not going to take her to task for her forbidden activities.

It is important to remember that the release of impulse must be handled with the greatest of care by the analyst.

In the case of Jill, a 30-year-old woman who started a love affair with another man because she was dissatisfied with her husband's lack of feeling, the analyst took a superego tack rather than an impulse release tack. He hammered away at the point that Jill was hung up on the other man without adequate expectation that he would leave his wife and marry her. Over and over he pointed out how Jill's thoughts about the other man were obviously fantasy.

While this was true, it was therapeutically entirely beside the point. What was significant was that with the other man Jill for the first time in her life experienced some real sexual pleasure. She experienced the analyst's intensive attempt to wean her away from the other man as an attempt to deprive her of sexual pleasure, that is to restore the old father-superego figure. The analysis came to grief; Jill left treatment after about a year and a half.

3) The Capacity for Love

In dynamic terms the capacity for love is the most important single factor making for analytic success. In oversimplified form, yet still with a large element of truth to it, the struggle in life is a battle between love and hatred. For most people the outcome depends on which of these forces is stronger.

It is hard to say what determines the capacity for love. Certainly, in general, favorable childhood experiences are the most significant. Yet seen as a broad proposition this is apt to be misleading. There are so many families who seem to be fairly normal to the outsider, yet when looked at from the inside have all kinds of neurotic conflicts raging. The child brought up in such an atmosphere is often emotionally no better off than the slum child who is exposed to the most dire economic privations. In evaluating favorable childhood experiences, only those that are emotionally significant should be counted. These, in turn, would be those in which the parents gave the child real love rather than bought them status symbols.

Yet, even when everything is said and done, the capacity for love seems to be to some extent independent of everything else. This is brought out most clearly in the illustrative case of Jim. Certainly no one would have thought that the analysis of such a man would have turned out so well in such a brief time. His background was almost as bad as could be depicted, and he had had a break which was called schizophrenic. He had drifted aimlessly through life before he came to analysis and yet somehow the analyst, who reminded him of the fantasied wealthy Oriental in his adolescence, brought him to life and led him along an entirely new path. In patients like these one is reminded of religious conversions or of what William James called the "twice-born." Balint's concept of the "new beginning" is also appropriate.

Whatever determines the capacity for love, it must be nursed along whenever it appears. But tactically and overtly the analyst should indicate to the patient that this is the way out of his dilemma. At the same time such an indication should not be divorced from the ordinary analytic work. Synthesis and analysis go together.

The main problem that appears clinically and theoretically is to differentiate normal from neurotic love. Many patients come into analysis convinced that they are or have been madly in love and not knowing what has gone wrong. Upon closer examination, their love experiences turn out to be transferences or projections or neurotic holdovers in one form or another.

A goodly part of the analysis must be devoted to helping the patient overcome the neurotic image of love without at the same time discarding the conviction that a real normal love can be found which will make him happy in life. The psychoanalytic theory of love, which runs parallel to the psychoanalytic theory of sexual development, must become part of the ABC of every analyst. It has already been mentioned that love passes through five stages: attachment, admiration, physical enjoyment, total enjoyment, and devotion.* In interpersonal terms they range all the way from being an infant to becom-

* For a fuller discussion see Chapter 1.

ing a parent. Many people have experienced one or another of these aspects of love, but not all are in the desirable combination. The comparison of the ideal developmental scheme with what the patient has gone through provides the framework for the analytic investigation of the patient's love life.

Often it will be found that the patient has been able to experience some aspects of the development of love, but has distorted them in a masochistic manner. Thus there may have been a fair amount of sexual experience and enjoyment, but accompanied by an excessive amount of guilt. Or there may be a devotion to a child, but twisted into a martyr situation. In such cases, it is desirable for the analyst to stress the positive aspects of the patient's adjustment as well as the neurotic. For future relationships the patient must build on these positive achievements, discarding the negative ones.

The most important single criterion for whether love is normal or neurotic is its reality consequences. In normal love the consequences are fulfillment and happiness. In neurotic love sooner or later something will go seriously wrong. There may be some wild enthusiasm for a while, but that soon comes to an end. Many times the neurotic kind of love is a violent protest against the senseless humdrum lives of the patient's parents. But here, too, the result is sooner or later disastrous for the patient.

The capacity for love includes self-love. Love should not be confined merely to a love for another person; to love one's self is in one sense even more basic. If it is left out of the picture the solution offered is one that does not allow the patient an opportunity to develop himself adequately.

Both clinically and theoretically, two kinds of personalities can be distinguished in this respect. The narcissistic individual, in the best sense of the word, is the one who loves himself sufficiently so that he can work independently on his own. Many artists and scientists belong in this category. These people rarely have any loneliness problem, but experience great difficulties in relating to others. The second type is the attached individual, more often than not a woman, who seeks her resolution in making another person happy. These patients get along much better with other people, but suffer terribly from fear and inadequacy when they are forced to spend some time alone.

In both these cases, the love difficulties arise as a result of the excessive pursuit of the personality characteristic; that is, the narcissistic individual becomes too narcissistic and the attached woman becomes over-attached. The task of working-through becomes one of working out the exaggerations of the underlying personality structure, without destroying the positive factors inherent in them.

Probably by far the most common problem that the analyst encounters is that of unrequited or neurotic love. This can be expressed in an unhappy marriage or an unhappy relationship or a crush on some person who does not reciprocate or even know that the crush exists. With this kind of neurotic love there are two possible resolutions: one is to work out the neurotic aspects of the love, leading to an improved relationship with the mate, and the other is to give it up and undertake a new relationship. Which one of these should be adopted depends upon a great many factors. It is necessary in these cases for the analyst at some point to make his position clearly known to the patient, to the effect that the love he is pursuing is impossible or that it is incapable of resolution in the direction in which the patient is looking. In practice, how an analyst proceeds along these lines depends a great deal on his own background, the degree of happiness found in his own marriage, and his own life history.

Some clinical examples can illustrate these principles.

In the case of Ruth cited above (page 241) at first there was a determined effort to adjust herself to her husband, in spite of his sexual difficulties. As so often in such cases, the husband was also in analysis, but unfortunately his analyst pursued a theoretical position that did not permit him to discuss the patient's sex life. As a result there seemed to be no reasonable prospect of ever having a really satisfactory sexual relationship with him. The patient could not know that to some extent this was due to the analyst's bias. All that she did know was that when she tried her husband could not satisfy her. Her solution was to find a different love away from the marriage and to make a second marriage that was much happier than the first.

Meryl, a 40-year-old housewife and schoolteacher, came to analysis because of the difficulties experienced with her older son, who was 17. He had left home after a stormy series of battles with both parents. Meryl was sufficiently sophisticated to realize that there was something she must have done to have created such a situation and sought out analysis.

Meryl's background was a most traumatic one. Her parents had been divorced, and she remained with the mother. The mother remarried, but the second marriage was also an unhappy one. Meryl had not had much to do with her father. At an early age she met her present husband

and married him against the wishes of her family. This was obviously the only way she could get away from the oppression of her home.

In the marriage Meryl seemed to be doing well until a child was born. It was then that the old neurotic complex again came to the fore. She did not understand what was meant by "mother love"; for the first four months of the baby's life she felt nothing whatsoever toward it, then she began to warm up somewhat. When the baby was about a year and a half, Meryl had a "nervous breakdown" which apparently meant that she became extremely anxious, depressed, agitated, and could not function. A local medical doctor advised her to take a rest for her nerves by going away to the country. This she did, but when she returned, she made her adjustment on the basis of having nothing to do with her oldest son, and later with the younger child, who was also a boy.

Investigation revealed that Meryl was openly seductive with her children, walking around without clothing many times, reasoning only that since they were children, they could not be excited or bothered by seeing her in the nude. Increasingly she lost contact with her children, and turned more and more to her professional work and to her relationship with her husband, which remained excellent.

In the analysis Meryl developed a warm, positive transference almost from the very beginning. In the analyst she had found the kind of father whom she had missed all through childhood. Because of the power of transference, it was possible for her to increase her capacity for love considerably. She shared with her son the difficulties that she had experienced in her own life, much to his surprise. As he came to see her more and more as a human being, his initial antagonism toward her diminished. With her husband the main problem in the past had been a kind of coldness which overcame her when she thought of getting closer to him. This too she was able to overcome.

As a result of the positive identification with the analyst she entered into a field that had some therapeutic aspects to it. In both her personal and professional life she found a considerable amount of happiness.

The third case is one that is encountered with great frequency in clinical practice. Leonard, a professional man in his late 20s, had fallen in love with his wife when they were both in their early 20s. The courtship offered no problems and the two were married when they were 21.

After about a year of marriage, more and more difficulties began to come to the surface.

Leonard's wife became more and more depressed. Leonard threw himself into his work, at which he achieved more and more success.

But with her depression and his success the distance between the two of them became successively greater.

When children came, it improved matters for a short while, but not for long. Leonard's wife became a nagging mother who was full of depression and self-pity because of her life as a housewife.

As a result of the various emotional strains that he was suffering under, Leonard developed an ulcer. It was this which led him to analysis originally.

In the analysis, Leonard soon discovered that his early great love which had gone out of the window was based on the sexual frustration of his adolescence. Neither he nor his wife had ever had any appreciable amount of sexual experience before marriage. The love was the classical aim-inhibited form of sexuality. Further he discovered the many ways in which his wife was similar to his mother.

As the analysis went on, Leonard found another girl with whom he again "fell in love." But this time he experienced great sexual difficulties with the other girl. This too he could work out in the analysis as the result of his guilt and fixation on his mother.

After some stormy battles his wife also decided to try analysis. The dynamics in her case were not dissimilar to those in his. With great effort and the determination to resume their happy relationship of adolescence, both Leonard and his wife pursued analysis with considerable vigor. The result was a happy one and the sexual conflicts were overcome. The love feeling was restored, but on a much higher level, and a fairly happy family life ensued.

Naturally, in cases such as Leonard's the outcome of the marriage frequently depends on how the wife will react to her husband's growth. Some will, as here, go into analysis themselves. Many others will take the position that the husband is very sick and that they somehow must coddle him. Still others will withdraw from the whole situation. The way in which the love is finally resolved always depends on the reactions of the other person.

For a happy love to exist there must be some reciprocity on the part of the other person, which is something that cannot be forced.

4) The Positive Transference

This is the fourth factor that builds success in the working-through process. To recapitulate some of the points which have been made before: In any long-term analysis, the positive transference must necessarily outweigh the negative. The negative is worked out only within the framework of an underlying positive transference; if there is no such underlying positive transference, then the patient will simply leave treatment. At the same time, the degree of positive transference will vary from one patient to the other.

Theoretically, positive transference means that the patient has recaptured some of the early good feelings about his parents. For the sake of the parents, the child gives up a variety of infantile pleasures. Similarly, for the sake of the beloved analyst, the patient will give up a variety of neurotic reactions.

5) The Identification With the Analyst

This is related to the previous heading, but focuses on a different aspect of the relationship. Just as the child grows up in a happy family by identifying with the parent of the same sex, the patient grows up by identifying with the analyst. For the most part this identification is unconscious, yet it still plays a fundamental role in the whole process.

When good feelings predominate, the analyst is seen as a benign figure who has all the attributes of a kindly parent from childhood without any of the harsh prohibitions that go along with such a parent. Actually, it is this sense of kindliness, acceptance, affection, warmth, love, or whatever name is given to it, that makes the biggest impression on the patient, together with the opportunity to release his unconscious without punishment. Love and understanding remain the keys to analytic success.

The identification with the analyst can proceed in one or both of two different ways. First and foremost, as a human being, the patient can attempt to be an analyst figure. This might involve on the one hand going around bombarding all his friends and acquaintances with parlor analysis (which is not as bad as it sounds). But on a higher level it involves a deeper sense of compassion for the suffering of other people. Thus, the patient also becomes a kindly parent figure. Many patients are surprised to find out that, as a result of the change in themselves, more and more people come to them for help precisely because they have overcome enough hostility in themselves to be able to offer kindness, affection, and a sympathetic ear to others in trouble.

A second aspect of identification is the professional one. Many patients in analysis, as a result of their own good experiences, wish to become professional analysts. To some extent this may be a temporary hostile identification, but to some extent it may express a real basic change in the personality.

Professionally, it would not at all be a bad idea to admit to the field of therapy only those persons who have previously had a successful therapeutic experience. Certainly the present system, which places the heaviest emphasis on intellectual achievement, when everybody knows that intellectual achievement is the least important part of the analyst's equipment, leaves a great deal to be desired. If all college students, say, at the sophomore year level, could have a personal analysis, or at least if all those planning to go into helping professions had a personal analysis, then a choice could be made on the basis of personality characteristics that are really pertinent to the profession, rather than on the basis of intellectual grades that have little real meaning.

In spite of the difficulties involved, many patients who have had a good therapeutic experience do decide to become analysts. Many of them do not have the professional background, but since they usually have a college degree, they manage to get it without too much difficulty. These people, when they do become analysts, have something to offer to the patient that those who have approached the field in a more orthodox way do not.

6) The Capacity to Resist Regression

Again, it is necessary to see the conflict between the positive and the negative forces in the patient's personality. Many patients, regardless of all efforts put forth by the analyst, go on and on in some negative vein for a long time—sometimes for a period of years, sometimes for a lifetime. If this has gone on too long, the analyst must bring it to the patient's attention, and at some point try to get him to switch from a negative to a positive attitude. Any and all of the factors enumerated in the previous chapter may enter the picture here.

The anxious patient can easily be encouraged to release his anxiety indefinitely, using the analysis as a safe haven. In the therapy of this kind of individual, it is necessary at some point to encourage him to take more steps on his own, by facing the anxiety in the outside world. This is a principle which had already been enumerated by Freud: With a phobic patient it is necessary at some point to tell the patient that he must confront the phobia. The anxious patient is one who has a series of phobias as the central part of his make-up. After enough material has been worked out in the analysis, he must confront his phobic situations, one by one.

With the patient who has *projected omnipotence to the analyst,* two technical devices are particularly useful. One is that the analyst should present himself as a real person, thus breaking down the God-like image that has been created by the patient. This can be done in a variety of ways, such as admitting mistakes or relating something out of the analyst's past to the patient, or telling him in so many words that he is building him up into too God-like a figure. The other technique is to bring the emphasis back to the patient's achievements over and over again. Thus, if the patient is overly grateful to the analyst for any progress that has been made, it is a good idea to say that the analysis is a cooperative effort and that both have contributed to its success.

With an *intense transference neurosis,* again at later stages in the analysis, it is essential to call attention increasingly to the reality factor. The danger with the analysis of the transference neurosis is that there will be an excessive emphasis on the kind of childhood experience that is being repeated over and over again. This is important and absolutely essential for a long time but, if it is continued without enough attention to the reality, there is a danger that the patient will bog down in his childhood experience without being able to see the ways in which the present experience is different. At some point it is useful to ask a patient: What do I really have to offer you, compared with other people? With this question, it is important on the one hand not to play down what the analyst really has to offer—that is, the kind of understanding and warmth that is hard to find anywhere else—but on the other hand, to bring out that many other people do offer reality gratifications that are far different from what the analyst gives. These reality gratifications, after a while, have to be seen as more and more significant in the patient's total readjustment to life.

With an intense transference neurosis, the countertransference tends to become particularly acute. The analyst, flattered by the strong desire of the patient, may find it exceedingly difficult to be objective about what the patient is telling him. Even apart from the obvious exploitation of the transference, such as sexual liaison, or using the patient in some way in the analyst's life (one analyst who had strong countertransference problems in this area had assembled a whole series of assistants, including a lawyer, accountant, secretary, nurse, interior decorator, and so on, all of whom had been former patients of his), there is a more subtle temptation to analyze the patient's new relationships in such a way that they will tend to be broken off in favor of the deep feelings for the analyst. The patient must be helped to realize that reality gratifications play just as much of a part in his finding happiness as do analytic insights and interpretations.

The *dependent patient* will be found to be using his dependency as a defense against aggression and sexuality. As he increases his capacity to be aggressive in the real world and to become aware of his sexual feelings, the dependency will tend to diminish. But from this formulation it becomes clear that the struggle centers around the patient's capacity to express aggression and sexuality. Here, too, the emphasis on reality plays more and more of a role as time goes on.

The *defiant patient* is continuing a useless childhood battle. If his hatred of his parents has been excessive, then this battle may go on for a long time, even indefinitely. Once more, the outcome of the working-through process depends on the degree to which the patient is willing to give up this childhood battle, which can no longer be won, in favor of an adult readjustment, which will lead to some happiness in life. Patients who continue analysis for a long time without much apparent benefit frequently are working out or repeating over and over again a defiance they could not express to their parents, or that they did express in some indirect manner, such as a passive-aggressive resistance.

7) External Pressures

These pressures can mount to a point where the psyche of the individual cannot handle them. It could not be said that the person could not manage this reality situation under any circumstances but, given the combination of emotional difficulties and external pressures, the person comes to grief because these external pressures are temporarily too much for him.

Two types of situations in particular may be singled out that are quite important from a clinical point of view. One is that where other people are needed for a love relationship and they simply refuse to comply. The life of the person is so intertwined with the other that his or her refusal to comply makes for an extraordinarily difficult situation. The other kind of situation is that where economic circumstances create problems that can only be resolved in a way that interferes with the psychological growth.

In general, every attempt is made to help the individual overcome the external pressures in a manner that will further his growth rather than block him. But "no man is an island unto himself" and the outside may simply be too much for the patient. At times it may be necessary for the analyst to step in to try to rearrange some outside situation; at other times, this cannot be done. Here are some clinical examples:

Sybil, an attractive woman in her early 40s, came to analysis after a suicide attempt, which landed her in the hospital. In her despair at ever finding a way out of her dilemmas, she had taken fourteen Seconals.

The situation she was in was one in which her husband, a free-lance artist, refused to take care of the household in an economically responsible way. For a number of years, the family, which then consisted of Sybil, her husband, and one little boy aged 5, had been living on her inheritance from her father. Now the time was approaching when this was running out, and the husband absolutely refused to do anything about it.

Naturally, there were many other neurotic conflicts involved. Sybil was a heavy drinker, and frequently drank herself into a stupor. The sex life of the couple, which had begun brilliantly, had bogged down because of Sybil's drinking and a variety of psychosomatic complaints which afflicted her husband. There were constant disagreements about how to bring up the boy.

Sybil was faced with the choice of trying to work out the relationship with the husband or leaving him. She was already in her early 40s, had had one bad marriage behind her, had a young child, and was faced with a variety of problems. She hoped that the original love between the two could be rekindled.

A further complication ensued when, after some initial benefits from treatment, Sybil suggested that her husband return to his former analyst for more work. At this point the husband flatly said that he had been dismissed by his former analyst as completely cured and that there was absolutely nothing that had to be changed in him. The problems were all in her, and she had to face that unpleasant fact squarely. In reality, her husband had gone to an analyst for about five years, with good results, but had suddenly quit in a fit of temper when the analyst broached the subject of homosexuality to him. Sybil did not know that her husband's statement that the analyst had dismissed him as completely cured was an outright lie, and had no way of handling the situation.

Eventually, Sybil made a good deal of progress with her own problems, but, since her husband refused to try to make any change, the situation there remained quite bad.

Bernie, a 29-year-old unemployed actor, came to analysis because he had lost his voice during a play. After the initial progress, Bernie was faced with the dilemma that, in order to get ahead in the theater, he had to have some financial reserves, which he did not have. In order to keep himself going, he had to work at jobs that interfered with his wish to become an actor. It was often necessary for him to work to pay for the analysis. He could, on the one hand, make analytic progress, working out his life history and his conflicts, while on the other hand, the analytic progress and the necessities of life blocked him from getting back into the theater. Eventually, he reached a compromise in terms of seeking another occupation.

SUGGESTIONS FOR FURTHER READING

See references to Chapter 17.

CHAPTER 20

Termination:
Theory, Practice, and Results

. . . analytical success goes beyond the pathological field altogether. It betokens an understanding . . . of the developmental lines of all the subject's main interests in life . . . so that ultimately one can see his whole life as a gradual unfolding of a relatively few primary sources of interest.

Ernest Jones: *Criteria of Success in Treatment* (*1936*)

In the literature of termination, Freud's last paper, "Analysis Terminable or Interminable," [54] published in 1937, occupies such a fundamental position that it can be used fruitfully as a point of departure for the discussion of the problems involved. Another paper, published in 1963,[55] reviewed the progress made in a quarter of a century since Freud, and offered evaluations of his position by a number of leading analysts.

The question that Freud poses is: Under what circumstances can it be said that an analysis is properly terminated? A subsidiary but important question is: Can the process of analysis be shortened?

The authors of the subsequent article, reviewing Freud's paper 25 years later, subdivide his argument into eight questions: 1) The length of the analysis; 2) termination date; 3) constitutional strength of the drives; 4) activation of latent conflicts; 5) structure of the patient's ego; 6) primary congenital variations of the ego; 7) personality of the analyst; 8) repudiation of femininity.

1) The Length of the Analysis

As time has gone on, the length of the average analysis has increased considerably (cf. remarks on pp. 233–234). In spite of this increase, Freud's remark still holds: That in the traumatic case (what we would call today the symptomatic case), a short, clear-cut result is feasible; where the goal of the analysis is to change the ego-structure, a short, clear-cut result is not feasible.

The main reason for the increase in the length of analysis is that the focus has shifted more and more from the symptoms to the character structure. Even when an immediate symptom is cleared up in short order, the patient has still been made aware of the many difficulties in his character structure that should be worked on. Not infrequently, a symptom clears up without any discussion whatsoever, merely as a result of the development of a positive transference. In these cases, the symptomatic improvement serves as a spur for the deeper, more extensive, analytic work.

> In the course of his analysis, Larry had never mentioned the fact that he had suffered from hay fever since he was a little boy. One day he casually brought out that the hay fever seemed to have disappeared. Its dynamic underpinnings were never systematically investigated, yet it vanished.

The process of ego-restructuring is essentially a learning experience. Like any other learning experience, it can be organized in a more efficient way, but if the material is inherently so difficult, as here, it cannot be appreciably shortened.

The numerous difficulties involved in termination account for the gap between the ideal and the real. Ideally, analysis should continue until a *point of diminishing returns.* As Freud says, it is only when further analysis would effect no appreciable change in the patient's personality that the analysis can really be said to have reached its theoretically desirable solution. Such termination is rarely feasible. In practice, analysis continues until a satisfactory real-life solution is achieved. Such a solution occurs when the patient's anxieties are manageable with the ego-strength acquired. Specifically, this would mean that, as practical goals for the solution of analysis, there should be a satisfactory marital relationship (or a relationship with the opposite sex), work situation, freedom from symptoms, and enough sources of pleasure. When this is accomplished in practice, the analysis comes to an end, even though there may be conflicts visible to both the analyst and the patient.

The illustrative case is a good example.

> At the time of termination, the patient was happily married, had an occupation that he enjoyed and was successful at, was relatively

free of symptoms, and had considerably increased his capacity for pleasure. It could by no means be said that he had worked out all the conflicts about women that had gone on from his childhood, nor could it be guaranteed that he would never again be tempted to indulge in homosexual experiences. Although he liked children, he had made a resolution with a woman who could not bear him any of his own. In spite of all this, the result could be considered to be satisfactory.

The factors that Freud enumerates as most responsible for the length of analysis are the strength of the instincts and the weakness of the ego. To this should be added the gap between a neurotic culture and the analytic ideal. As time has gone on, in fact, this gap between the culture and the ideal looms larger and larger as the main source of the interminable analysis.

2) Termination Date

Setting a date for termination was a device used by Freud in the case of the Wolf Man. This patient, a wealthy Russian who was incapacitated by a variety of obsessional conflicts, had gone on in analysis for some five years without effecting the kind of change Freud considered most desirable. At this point, Freud told him that the analysis would stop in six months whatever he did. The patient was so alarmed by this threat that he produced a number of childhood memories and made further dramatic and significant changes in his personality. This device has since been known as the *end-setting*.

Unfortunately, this device can no longer be widely used because of the availability of analysts. When Freud gave the patient the ultimatum in 1914, there was virtually nobody else available, not even any of Freud's students. Accordingly, the ultimatum meant to the patient: Either get better or get out.

Nowadays, however, when every large city has a considerable number of analysts, the end-setting is interpreted differently by the patient. It means to him that the analyst is no longer sure that the patient's problems will be resolved, and no longer has a desire to work with him. Accordingly, the patient interprets the end-setting as either a suggestion that he go to another analyst or a suggestion that the mode of treatment be altered.

Since this is the way in which the patient is bound to interpret it, it has become more customary to suggest to the patient under these circumstances that if he does not change more within, say, six months or a year, he will then be switched to another person. In some cases, this pressure will produce more changes in the desired direction, but in other cases it will not.

Kubie,[56] in particular, has been the outstanding advocate of switching to another analyst for the termination of a seemingly endless analysis. However, it cannot be said that there is any unanimity of opinion among analysts on this score, and in some cases it seems desirable to continue even though the therapy seems to have bogged down for a long period of time. In other cases, it would seem to be preferable to switch to another person.

3) The Constitutional Strength of the Drives

Freud was always impressed by the power of the id, which he sometimes referred to as the tyranny of the drives. However, while his points are certainly still important, to some extent his theories, as he himself knew, were historically determined.

In practice, the analyst works primarily on the unconscious roots of any impulse, trying to help the patient to see that the compulsive character of his drives is due to some force other than its inherent strength. Certainly, the physiological force behind the drive plays a role, but it is difficult to estimate how much of a role it does play. The drives have to be satisfied up to a certain point, but beyond that point there is considerable leeway in the personality. A great deal of difference also is found between the various drives.

Furthermore, the trend of thinking since Freud has been toward the view that the id itself has its dynamics. If the drive has its dynamics, then the strength displayed in the clinical situation is not due to pure physiology, but also has a large psychological component.

4) The Activation of Latent Conflicts

Many patients are seen who have conflicts that have been pushed into the background. The question is whether these can be brought out and handled or whether they should or must be left alone. In his paper, Freud expressed the conviction that the latent conflicts could not be handled.

However, the thinking on this point has changed considerably with the switch to *character analysis*. Necessarily, every character analysis activities conflicts that were only dormant before. In the chapters on the persistence of anxiety and the working-through of the therapeutic impasse, this point has been made in more detail.

Hence, the question is no longer particularly relevant in the present-day context. What is relevant is whether the analyst can succeed in getting the patient to face his character problems or whether the achievement will have to be confined to purely symptomatic change.

5), 6) Ego Structure

It need scarcely be stressed at this point that ego structure is the dominant theme of modern analysis, together with its genesis, composition, and change.

7) The Personality of the Analyst

As time has gone on, this has proved to be more and more important in the problem of termination. The analyst, as is known, cannot bring the patient further than where he is, yet the analysis of the prospective analyst has proved to be a formidable task. The brief encounters of three or four months duration that Freud tried in the early 1920s would be dismissed as preposterous today. Analysis has become longer and longer, yet the same problems remain.

In his paper Freud remarked that the analysis of the prospective analyst runs up against a special obstacle, inasmuch as he uses analytic theory for defensive purposes. This was true then, and is even more true now. One result is what Glover has called "training transferences" in which one group of analysts approve of themselves and their students, but vehemently disapprove of outside colleagues and their students.

Nevertheless, there seems to be no alternative to the profound soul-searching that modern analysis has become. The growth process is long and formidable, but, like so much else that takes time and effort, it is the most worthwhile in the long run.

8) Repudiation of Femininity

Freud's view that penis envy in women and passivity in men provide a biological bedrock, so to speak, that analysis cannot penetrate further has scarcely stood the test of time. Both are secondary to the crisis of identity that is so characteristic of contemporary man; neither men nor women know what kind of people they really want to be.

Identity crisis and its concomitant alienation lead to a deeper examination of the culture. It is here perhaps that the greatest advances have been made since Freud.

The realization that there are profound dislocations in the culture, which Freud touched only peripherally, has been deepened and expanded in many different directions. A vast amount of material is available documenting the disturbance of contemporary man.

In this area one of the most potent causes of the interminable analysis must be sought. For the individual in analysis learns a way of living that is in many important respects at sharp variance with what is going on around him. It is unfortunately true that ruthless aggression often produces a much better social adjustment than compassionate love. Even overt psychiatric disturbance, as Hitler and Stalin have shown, may be more culture-syntonic than culture-dystonic.

In the long run, successful analysis causes a profound change in the social system. It becomes in that way a method of social reform, concentrating on the change in the individual rather than in the institution.

SOME RECURRENT PROBLEMS

Some problems connected with termination have recurred since the beginning of analysis, and may profitably be discussed here. These are, particularly: 1) the interminable analysis; 2) abrupt premature termination; 3) the shift to another analyst; 4) re-analysis; 5) resolution of the transference; 6) compromise termination; 7) successful and unsuccessful real-life experiences in relation to termination; and 8) alternative or adjunct approaches to analysis.

1) Interminable Analysis

There can be little doubt that this is the most persistent of all problems that the analyst encounters. Freud's experience that in the beginning of his practice he could not get patients to stay, while toward the end he could not get them to leave, has been similar to that of other analysts. A certain number of patients terminate abruptly at an early stage, and cannot be made to stay no matter what the analyst does. Other patients, however, remain indefinitely and seemingly cannot be made to leave, no matter what the analyst does. These "interminable" patients may go on for five or ten years; in some cases they have been known to go on for twenty or thirty years. Both theoretically and clinically, they present great difficulties.

It is assumed, of course, that the experienced analyst will have analyzed the resistances to termination, the nature of the transference, the problems that still persist, and so on. In spite of all this analysis, however, the patient gets up to a certain point and finds himself unable to leave. Sometimes he leaves, only to find his symptoms getting worse, whereupon he rushes right back to analysis. Sometimes, the analyst, in anger or despair, drops him, whereupon he goes to another analyst. It is as though once the desire for analysis gets into his blood he simply will not let go. Put in more theoretical terms, the therapeutic impasse has continued indefinitely. An equilibrium has been reached between the forces of regression and the forces of growth, and it is extraordinarily difficult to break through. Usually such analyses end with whatever seems realistically feasible.

2) Abrupt Premature Termination

This is an undesirable outcome, yet one that happens all too frequently. Sometimes it is a response to a seemingly interminable period where nothing much has happened. Sometimes it occurs because of some unnoticed resistance that has mounted to serious proportions.

This kind of resistance is not inherently different from the resistance encountered early, especially at the time of the first treatment crisis. The difference lies primarily in that the patient has had a much longer period of successful analysis and balks not so much at the analytic process, as such, but at the further change that is specially meaningful to him. Outward events may sometimes release this kind of resistance, and the analyst should be particularly careful in how he handles these, in order to avoid such an eventuality.

3) Shift to Another Analyst

Faced with the choice between an interminable analysis and an abrupt premature termination, many people consider the possibility of a shift to another analyst. On the face of it, this seems quite reasonable since, whatever difficulties lie in the patient, there certainly are some that must be found in the personality of the analyst, and if this were changed, then a satisfactory resolution could ensue. Sometimes the patient decides to shift, sometimes the analyst suggests a shift. In a number of cases the shift is effective not because the new analyst is better, but because the patient begins the same fight all over again. Only this time it may be easier for him to realize that it is a fight that he would carry on against any analyst, so that it becomes all the more important to look into himself more deeply. In other cases the shift may be useful because it opens up areas of the personality that had been neglected in the previous analysis. But then again there are many cases where the shift is ineffectual. Decisions in these cases must always be made on practical grounds.

4) Re-Analysis

So many patients have found it necessary to go back for more analysis that ours has been called the age of re-analysis. Accordingly, a considerable amount of clinical information has accumulated on this point.

Perhaps the most common reason for re-analysis is *an unresolved or mishandled transference situation.* The patient in an analysis of this kind feels thwarted and misunderstood, but quite justifiably. In this frustration, he does not know where to turn. The analyst likewise does not have a good grasp of the problems. Sooner or later, for some extraneous reason, these analyses come to an end. Sometimes the patient goes to another analyst; sometimes he waits for a couple of years. In these cases, one of the first things that has to be done is to straighten out the transference problem created by the previous analyst.

5) Resolution of the Transference

This is one of the most controversial topics in the whole field of psychoanalysis. Some authors argue that the transference should be completely resolved and that not even a trace of gratitude should remain in the patient. He should see that he has overcome his infantile fixations, and should be able to go on his way without remaining in any way dependent upon the analyst. Others argue that the analytical relationship is too powerful an experience to be overcome in this way. Obviously, the theoretical position that the analyst takes toward the transference will determine the manner in which he handles various problems connected with termination. Little can be added here to previous discussions of transference.

6) Compromise Termination

A number of analyses end in a compromise of one form or another. Either the patient is not able to go on for what is euphemistically referred to as external reasons (such as money), or the analyst decides that he has gone about as far as he can go with this patient and therefore suggests that treatment be terminated.

It is certainly safe to say that a fair number of analyses are terminated in this way. They are fully satisfactory neither to the patient nor to the analyst. At the same time a certain amount of progress has been made.

Many times the problem comes up about whether to allow the analysis to terminate in some compromise formation or to pursue it until it has met with a more satisfactory resolution. The answer to this question depends on a variety of factors including practical ones such as time, finances, and the nature of the problem. Theoretically, it is always a wise course to continue the analysis as long as possible but, as Freud had already commented in his first published paper on psychotherapy, the outcome of any psychotherapeutic encounter depends more on practical realities than on anything else.

7) Successful and Unsuccessful Real-Life Experiences in Relationship to Termination

One point at which both patient and analyst often decide to terminate is that where some longed-for success is reached by the patient. Sometimes the patient will attribute this to the analytical work, sometimes not, but in any case it is as though at these stages a natural stopping point has been reached.

Such stopping points are: marriage, the birth of a baby, significant promotion on the job, granting of a degree, and the like. In and of themselves, these achievements do not necessarily, or do not at all, mean that the inner conflicts have been resolved, but most people, including many analysts, will evaluate the resolution of the inner conflicts by means of the amount of success that they lead to in real life.

8) Alternative Approaches and Adjuncts to Analysis

If analysis cannot be satisfactorily terminated, the idea naturally suggests itself that some alternative approach should be adopted. Throughout the years a large number of such approaches have been suggested and tried out by many different analysts. We refer to such theoretical variations as group analysis, Gestalt therapy, rational therapy, behavior therapy, and the like. It is beyond the scope of this book to go into these various techniques in any detail. It can only be said that even though the success of analysis leaves much to be desired, few analysts have been able to have more success with any of the other alternatives. By and large, the analyst prefers to continue with more analysis, either changing his emphasis or sometimes shifting analysts or sometimes with some minor alterations, but all within the analytic framework. Many of these techniques may at times be found useful as adjuncts to analysis, but purely as adjuncts.

RESULTS

Since analytical psychotherapy has been going on for some seventy years, it should certainly be possible to arrive at some reasonable evaluation of the results.

The classical studies in the literature report between fifty and seventy percent of the patients markedly improved. The first such study was published by Fenichel,[57] reviewing the work of the Berlin Psychoanalytic Institute from 1920 to 1930. Next came Jones [58] with a report on the London Psychoanalytic Institute from 1926 to 1936. Alexander [59] reviewed the work of the Chicago Institute for Psychoanalysis from 1932 to 1937. Kessel and Hyman [60] published a survey of patients treated by a variety of analysts up to 1933. More recently, a review of the work of the Southern California Institute [61] has yielded results that are pretty much along the same lines.

These results have been questioned because of the absence of controls, and the possible bias of the investigators, who are determined to make out an adequate case for psychoanalysis. Eysenck has been the most vociferous proponent of the thesis that psychotherapy is totally ineffective, even in certain cases harmful to the patient. Eysenck's work, however, even though it purports to have some scientific rationale, reveals his own biases in favor of behavior therapy and has been adequately refuted by a number of authors.[62, 63, 64]

The problem involved in applying the standard tenets of scientific method to the evaluation of psychotherapy studies are enormous.

It seems abundantly clear, after everything that has gone before, that the only effective method of evaluating the results of psychoanalysis or psychoanalytic therapy is a clinical one. At the present time, no available statistical technique can provide a substitute for clinical judgment. Even the American Psychoanalytic Association,[65] which organized a gigantic fact-finding undertaking in 1952, pursuing a routine statistical course with diagnosis, outcomes, and so on, was faced with the increasing meaninglessness of its results. The committee was so embarrassed by its work that it waited more than ten years to publish even a preliminary report.

A more careful clinical procedure has been developed at the New

York Psychoanalytic Institute.[66] This procedure consists essentially of follow-up interviews with an analyzed patient by a second analyst several years after the termination of analysis. The interviews take place sitting up once a week, and vary in number with different patients from two to seven.

The form of the follow-up interviews is best termed "analytic." Initially structured around the question of results, the interviews remain unstructured around this framework and then the patient takes the lead in introducing and elaborating various themes relating to results. The patient spontaneously communicates in a way that is in the direction of free association and not infrequently with dreams. The follow-up analyst poses occasional clarifying questions that remain in line with the context of the material presented by the patient.

According to Pfeffer, this procedure appears to elicit the necessary information for an adequate evaluation of the results of an analysis. Because of having been analyzed, the patients studied in this way are able freely and meaningly to discuss the symptoms and problems for which they first sought analysis, and the symptoms and problems that emerged in the course of analysis, as well as the current status of all of these. The treating analyst provides the interviewing analyst with information about the patient according to a questionnaire concerning the initial and emerging problems, the course of analysis, the formulation of the patient's central problems, what was achieved analytically and therapeutically by the analysis, and predictions as to what the patient's status in regard to these various problems will be at the time of the follow-up study. This information from the treating analyst is not read by the follow-up analyst until just before the final follow-up interview, thus adding to the opportunity for an unbiased point of view.

Another elaborate research program has been set up by Wallerstein [67] at the Menninger Clinic. Here, too, the number of cases has been quite small, but each one has been studied with the utmost intensity. Although a number of papers on methodology have appeared,[68,69] no final review of the results has as yet been published. Such a review promises to be most rewarding.

While these studies fill in many details in our knowledge, and point to many unanswered questions, it is already clear that psychoanalytic psychotherapy is enormously effective. In spite of the fact that most people come to a therapist only when they have reached a state of desperation, and that both the selection and the training of therapists leaves and has left much to be desired, there is abundant evidence that patients who undergo psychoanalytic therapy move in significant direction towards the analytic ideal. The greatest barrier to further success is undoubtedly the conflicts engendered by a sick culture. If man is offered only the Hobson's choice of an adjustment neurosis or a maladjustment neurosis, how can he be expected to turn out?

Yet at the same time there are cautious grounds for optimism. The understanding of the analytic ideal, with all its implications for a revolution in social and psychological living, is making enormous strides. Therapists are being trained in increasing numbers. An endless flow of people, stimulated by the awareness that a different kind of life is possible for them, streams to the offices of the professionals and even of many amateurs who set themselves up as experts. No one can predict what the future will bring, but this much is already clear: the psychological revolution is here to stay.

SUGGESTIONS FOR FURTHER READING

The literature on termination is surprisingly meager, and much of it is apt to be highly theoretical. Freud's paper is "Analysis Terminable and Interminable," (*S.E.* Vol. XXIII); the reevaluation is A. Z. Pfeffer, "Analysis Terminable and Interminable—Twenty-Five Years After," *J. Am. Psychoanalytic Assoc.* 11, 1963, 131–142.

The best recent paper is R. Ekstein, "Working Through and Termination of Analysis," *J. Am. Psychoanalytic Assoc.* 13, 1965, 57–78. Also useful are: S. Nacht, "Criteria and Technique for the Termination of Analysis," *Int. J. Psychoanalysis* 46, 1965, 107–116. I. Miller, "On the Return of Symptoms in the Terminal Phase of Psychoanalysis," *Int. J. Psychoanalysis* 46, 1965, 487–501. E. Weigert, "Contribution to the Problem of Terminating Analysis," *Psychoanalytic Quarterly* 21, 1952, 465–480. G. Chrzanowski, "Termination in Psychoanalysis," *Am. J. Psychotherapy* 14, 1960, 48–62.

An earlier symposium on the termination of analysis, *Int. J. Psychoanalysis* 31, 1950, still has a number of useful papers. See especially papers by E. Buxbaum (184–190), W. Hoffer (194–195), M. Klein (204), J. Rickman (200–201), and A. Reich (179–183).

On the termination of training analyses see R. Ekstein, "Termination of the Training Analysis within the Framework of Present-Day Institutes," *J. Am. Psychoanalytic Assoc.* 13, 1955, 600–614.

Still interesting is S. Ferenczi, "The Problem of the Termination of the Analysis," in *Final Contributions to the Problems and Methods of Psychoanalysis* (New York: Basic Books, 1955), 77–86.

The results of psychoanalysis and psychotherapy are summarized in R. P. Knight, "Evaluation of the Results of Psychoanalytic Therapy," *Am. J. Psychiatry* 98, 1941 434–446. Also see F. Feldman, "Results of Psychoanalysis in Clinic Case Assignments," *J. Am. Psychoanalytic Assoc.* 16, 1968, 274–300. Critique and discussion are in H. Eysenck, "The Effects of Psychotherapy," *Int. J. Psychiatry* 1, 1965, 97–178. Of the many thoughtful discussions of these topics the best recent one is L. S. Kubie, "Discussion of Eysenck Paper," *Int. J. Psychiatry* 1, 1965, 175–178.

On the general philosophy of results and the concomitant problems, see also R. S. Wallerstein, "The Current State of Psychotherapy: Theory, Practice, Research," *J. Am. Psychoanalytic Assoc.* 14, 1966, 183–225. E. Bibring, "On the Theory of the Results of Psychoanalysis," *Int. J. Psychoanalysis* 18, 1937, 170–189. H. Hartmann, "Psychoanalysis and the Concept of Health," *Essays on Ego Psychology* (New York: Int. Universities Press, 1964). E. Jones, "Love and Morality," *Papers on Psychoanalysis,* 5th edition (London: Bailliere, Tindall and Cox, 1948).

Some miscellaneous works of particular interest are: Joint Comission on Mental Illness and Health, *Action for Mental Health* (New York: Basic Books, 1961). C. Kadushin, *Why People Go to Psychiatrists* (New York: Atherton, 1968). L. Bellak and L. Small, *Emergency Psychotherapy and Brief Psychotherapy* (New York: Grune and Stratton, 1965).

Summaries of large numbers of eclectic studies can be found in: D. R. Stieper and D. N. Wiener, *Dimensions of Psychotherapy* (Chicago: Aldine, 1965). H. H. Strupp and A. E. Bergin, "Some Empirical and Conceptual Bases for Coordinated Research in Psychotherapy," *Int. J. Psychiatry* 7, 1969, 18–90.

Notes

1. H. Brill: "Psychiatric Diagnosis, Nomenclature and Classification," B. Wolman, ed.: *Handbook of Clinical Psychology.*
2. A. Freud: *Normality and Pathology in Childhood,* p. 110.
3. K. Menninger: *A Psychiatrist's World,* p. 672.
4. K. Menninger: *The Vital Balance.*
5. F. Alexander and S. Selesnick: *The History of Psychiatry.*
6. C. Jung: *Psychological Types.*
7. H. Hendin, W. Gaylin and A. Carr: *Psychoanalysis and Social Science Research.*
8. L. Saul and I. Wenar: "Early Influences on Development," *Psychoanalytic Quarterly* 34, 1965, 327–389.
9. M. Klein: *The Psychoanalysis of Children.*
10. A. Freud: *The Psychoanalytical Treatment of Children.*
11. H. S. Sullivan: *Schizophrenia as a Human Process.*
12. J. Rosen: *Direct Analysis.*
13. A. Aichhorn: *Wayward Youth.*
14. M. Jones: *The Therapeutic Community.*
15. F. Alexander and T. French: *Psychoanalytic Therapy.*
16. A. A. Baumeister, ed.: *Mental Retardation.*
17. K. Eissler: *The Psychiatrist and the Dying Patient.*
18. P. Federn: *Ego Psychology and the Psychoses.*
19. H. S. Sullivan: See reference 11.
20. R. Fine: "An Instance of Freudian Analysis," *Case Reports in Clinical Psychology* 3, 1956, 131–138.
21. T. Szasz: "The Concept of Transference," *Int. J. Psychoanalysis* 44, 1963, 432–443.
22. S. Freud: "Observations on Transference Love," *Standard Edition* XII, 158–171.
23. J. McCartney: "Overt Transference," *J. of Sex Research* 2, 1966, 227–235.
24. J. Katz, J. Goldstein, and A. Dershowitz: *Psychoanalysis, Psychiatry and the Law,* p. 722.

25. H. Searles: *Collected Papers on Schizophrenia,* p. 284.
26. R. Fine: "A Note on a Transference Manifestation in Male Homosexuals," *Psychoanalysis and the Psychoanalytic Rev.* 48, 1962, No. 2.
27. I. Bieber et al.: *Homosexuality.*
28. C. Socarides: *The Overt Homosexual.*
29. D. Stieper and D. Wiener: *Dimensions of Psychotherapy,* p. 33.
30. S. Freud: *Standard Edition* XX, p. 160.
31. R. Greenson: *The Technique and Practice of Psychoanalysis,* pp. 85–96.
32. S. Freud: *Standard Edition* X, p. 260.
33. R. M. Lowenstein et al.: "The Silent Patient," *J. Am. Psychoanalytic Assoc.* 9, 1961, 2–90.
34. M. Balint: *The Basic Fault.*
35. J. Frank: *Persuasion and Healing.*
36. O. H. Mowrer: *Learning Theory and Behavior.*
37. J. Frosch: "Severe Regressive States During Analysis: Summary," *J. Am. Psychoanalytic Assoc.* 15, 1967, 606–625.
38. P. F. Cranefield: "Josef Breuer's Evaluation of His Contribution to Psychoanalysis," *Int. J. Psychoanalysis* 39, 1958, 319–322.
39. J. Holzberg *et al.:* "Companionship with the Mentally Ill.," *Psychiatry* 29, 1966, 395–405.
40. L. Merkle and R. B. Little: "Beginning Psychiatry Training Syndrome," *Am. J. Psychiatry* 124, 1967, 193–197.
41. D. Anzieu: *L'Auto-Analyse.*
42. A. Freud: "The Widening Scope of Indications for Psychoanalysis: Discussion," *J. Am. Psychoanalytic Assoc.* 2, 1954, 606–609.
43. E. Glover: *The Technique of Psychoanalysis,* Part II.
44. L. S. Kubie: "Research into the Process of Supervision in Psychoanalysis," *Psychoanalytic Quarterly* 27, 1958, 226–236.
45. M. R. Kramer: "On the Continuation of the Analytic Process After Psychoanalysis," *Int. J. Psychoanalysis* 40, 1959, 17–25.
46. E. Bibring: "Report of Four Countries Conference," *Int. J. Psychoanalysis* 18, 1937, 369.
47. T. Benedek: "Training Analysis—Past, Present and Future," *Int. J. Psychoanalysis* 50, 1969, 437–445.
48. S. Freud: *Standard Edition* XI, 219–227.
49. K. Eissler: "Notes on the Psychoanalytic Concept of Cure," *Psychoanalytic Study of the Child* 18, 1963, 424–463.
50. E. Hammer: *The Use of Interpretation in Treatment.*
51. R. Fine: *Freud: A Critical Reevaluation,* Ch. XII.
52. C. R. Oberndorf: *A History of Psychoanalysis in America.*
53. B. Lewin and H. Ross: *Psychoanalytic Education in the U.S.,* 175.
54. S. Freud: *Standard Edition* XXIII.

55. A. Pfeffer, reporter: "Analysis Terminable and Interminable Twenty-Five Years Later," *J. Am. Psychoanalytic Assoc.* 11, 1963, 131–142.
56. L. S. Kubie: "Unsolved Problems in the Resolution of the Transference," *Psychoanalytic Quarterly* 37, 1968, 331–352.
57. O. Fenichel: *Zehn Jahre Berliner Psychoanalytisches Institut.*
58. E. Jones: *Decennial Report of the London Clinic of Psychoanalysis.*
59. F. Alexander: *Five Year Report of the Chicago Institute.*
60. L. Kessel and H. T. Hyman: "The Value of Psychoanalysis as a Therapeutic Procedure," *JAMA* 101, 1933, 1612–1615.
61. F. Feldman: "Results of Psychoanalysis," *J. Am. Psychoanalytic Assoc.* 16, 1968, 274–300.
62. H. J. Eysenck: "The Effects of Psychotherapy," *Int. J. Psychiatry* 1, 1965, 176–178.
63. L. S. Kubie: "Discussion of Eysenck," see reference 62.
64. E. Zetzel: "Discussion of Eysenck," see reference 62.
65. D. A. Hamburg *et al.:* "Report of Ad Hoc Committee," *J. Am. Psychoanalytic Assoc.* 15, 1967, 841–861.
66. A. Z. Pfeffer: "A Procedure for Evaluating the Results of Psychoanalysis," *J. Am. Psychoanalytic Assoc.* 7, 1959, 418–444.
67. R. S. Wallerstein: "The Problem of the Assessment of Change in Psychotherapy," *Int. J. Psychoanalysis* 44, 1963, 31–41.
68. R. S. Wallerstein: "The Current State of Psychotherapy: Theory, Practice, Research," *J. Am. Psychoanalytic Assoc.* 14, 1966, 183–225.
69. H. H. Strupp, R. Fox, K. Lessler: *Patients View Their Psychotherapy.*

Bibliography

Abt, L., and Reiss, B., eds. *Progress in Clinical Psychology*. Vol. VIII. New York: Grune and Stratton, 1969.

Aichhorn, A. *Wayward Youth*. New York: Viking Press, 1935.

Alexander, F. "The Problems of Psychoanalytic Technique (1935)." *The Scope of Psychoanalysis*. New York: Basic Books, 1961.

―――. "Analysis of the Therapeutic Factors in Psychoanalytic Treatment." *Psychoanalytic Quarterly* 19, 1950, 482–500.

―――, et al. *Psychoanalytic Therapy*. New York: Ronald Press, 1946.

―――. *Fundamentals of Psychoanalysis*. New York: Norton, 1948.

―――. *Five Year Report of the Chicago Institute for Psychoanalysis. 1932–1937*.

―――. *The Scope of Psychoanalysis*. New York: Basic Books, 1961.

―――, Eisenstein, S., and Grotjahn, M. *Psychoanalytic Pioneers*. New York: Basic Books, 1966.

―――, and Selesnick, S. T. *The History of Psychiatry*. New York: Harper and Row, 1966.

Allport, G. *Personality and Social Encounter*. Boston: Beacon Press, 1960.

Altman, L. "Panel Report: Theory of Psychoanalytic Therapy." *J. Am. Psychoanalytic Assoc.* 12, 1964, 620–631.

Anzieu, D. *L'Auto-Analyse*. Paris: Presses Universitaires de France, 1959.

Arieti, S. *American Handbook of Psychiatry*. New York: Basic Books, 1959.

Arlow, J. "Silence and the Theory of Technique." *J. Am. Psychoanalytic Assoc.* 9, 1961, 44–55.

Arlow, J., and Brenner, C. *Psychoanalytic Concepts and the Structural Theory*. New York: International Universities Press, 1964.

Ashby, P. *The History and Future of Religious Thought*. Englewood Cliffs, N. J.: Prentice-Hall, 1963.

Balint, M. *Primary Love and Psychoanalytic Technique*. New York: Liveright, 1953.

―――. "Analytic Training and Training Analysis." *Int. J. Psychoanalysis* 35, 1954, 157–162.

―――. *The Basic Fault*. London: Tavistock, 1968.

Barter, J. Y., and Rerte, M. "Crime and LSD: The Insanity Plea." *Am. J. Psychiatry* 126, 1969, 531–537.

Baumeister, A. A., ed. *Mental Retardation.* Chicago: Aldine, 1967.

Beck, A. T. *Depression.* New York: Harper and Row, 1967.

Bellak, L. "Free Association: Conceptual and Clinical Aspects." *Int. J. Psychoanalysis* 42, 1961, 9–20.

————, and Loeb, L. *The Schizophrenic Syndrome.* New York: Grune and Stratton, 1969.

————, and Small, L. *Emergency Psychotherapy and Brief Psychotherapy.* New York: Grune and Stratton, 1965.

Benedek, T. "A Contribution to the Problem of Termination of Training Analysis." *J. Am. Psychoanalytic Assoc.* 3, 1955, 615–629.

————. "Training Analysis—Past, Present and Future." *Int. J. Psychoanalysis* 50, 1969, 437–445.

Bernfeld, S. "On Psychoanalytic Training." *Psychoanalytic Quarterly* 31, 1962, 453–482.

Bettelheim, B. *The Empty Fortress.* New York: The Free Press, 1967.

Bibring, E. "On the Theory of the Results of Psychoanalysis." *Int. J. Psychoanalysis* 18, 1937, 170–189.

————. "Report of Four Countries Conference." *Int. J. Psychoanalysis* 18, 1937, 369.

Bieber, I., *et al. Homosexuality.* New York: Basic Books, 1962.

Bing, F., McLaughlin, F., and Marburg, R. "The Metapsychology of Narcissism." *Psychoanalytic Study of the Child* 14, 1959, 9–28.

Bird, B. "On Candidate Selection and Its Relation to Analysis." *Int. J. Psychoanalysis* 49, 1968, 513–526.

Blanck, G. *Education for Psychotherapy.* New York: IPTAR, 1962.

Bleuler, M. *The Group of Schizophrenias.* New York: Int. Universities Press, 1950.

Bowlby, J. *Attachment.* New York: Basic Books, 1969.

Boyer, B., and Giovacchini, P. *The Psychoanalytic Treatment of Schizophrenia and Character Disorders.* New York: Science House, 1967.

Brierley, M. "Psychoanalysis and Integrative Living." *Trends in Psychoanalysis.* London: Hogarth Press, 1951. Ch. VI.

Brill, H. "Psychiatric Diagnosis, Nomenclature and Classification," B. Wolman, ed. *Handbook of Clinical Psychology.* New York: McGraw-Hill, 1965. Ch. 24.

Bromberg, W. *The Mind of Man.* New York: Harper and Row, 1959.

Bychowski, G. *The Psychotherapy of Psychosis.* New York: Grune and Stratton, 1952.

Calder, K. T. "How Psychoanalytic Institutes Evaluate Applicants." *Int. J. Psychoanalysis* 49, 1968, 540–547.

The California School of Psychology. San Francisco: Cal. Psychological Assoc., 1969.

Calogeras, R. "Silence as a Technical Parameter in Psychoanalysis." *Int. J. Psychoanalysis* 48, 1967, 536–558.

Caplan, R. *Psychiatry and the Community in Nineteenth-Century America.* New York: Basic Books, 1969.

Chrzanowski, G. "Termination in Psychoanalysis." *Am. J. Psychotherapy* 14, 1960.

Colby, K. "An Experiment on the Effects of an Observer's Presence on the Imago System During Psychoanalytic Free Association." *Behavioral Science, V,* No. 3, July, 1960.

Coltrera, J. "Psychoanalysis and Existentialism." *J. Am. Psychoanalytic Assoc.* 10, 1962, 166–215.

"A Training Program for Psychotherapy." *Council of Psychoanalytic Psychologists.* New York: Council of Psychoanalytic Psychologists, 1968.

Cranefield, P. F. "Josef Breuer's Evaluation of His Contribution to Psychoanalysis." *Int. J. Psychoanalysis* 39, 1958, 319–322.

Cuber, J., and Harroff, P. *The Significant Americans.* New York: Appleton-Century, 1965.

Deutsch, F. "Analysis of Postural Behavior." *Psychoanalytic Quarterly* 16, 1947, 195–213.

————. "Analytic Posturology." *Psychoanalytic Quarterly* 21, 1952, 196–214.

Devereux, G. "Some Criteria for the Timing of Confrontations and Interpretations." *Int. J. Psychoanalysis* 32, 1951, 19–24.

The Diagnostic and Statistical Manual of Mental Disorders. Washington: American Psychiatric Association, 1968.

Eisendorfer, A. "The Selection of Candidates Applying for Psychoanalytic Training." *Psychoanalytic Quarterly* 28, 1959, 374–378.

Eisnitz, A. J. "Narcissistic Object Choice, Self-Representation." *Int. J. Psychoanalysis* 50, 1969, 15–26.

Eissler, K. "The Effect of the Structure of the Ego on Psychoanalytic Technique." *J. Am. Psychoanalytic Assoc.* 1, 1953, 104–143.

————. "Notes upon the Emotionality of a Schizophrenic Patient and Its Relation to Problems of Technique." *Psychoanalytic Study of the Child* 8, 1953, 199–251.

————, ed. *Searchlights on Delinquency.* New York: Int. Universities Press, 1949.

————. *The Psychiatrist and the Dying Patient.* New York: Int. Universities Press, 1955.

————. "Notes on the Psychoanalytic Concept of Cure." *Psychoanalytic Study of the Child* 18, 1963, 424–463.

Ekstein, R. "Trial Analysis in the Therapeutic Process." *Psychoanalytic Quarterly* 19, 1950, 52–63.

————. "Termination of the Training Analysis Within the Framework of Present-Day Institutes." *J. Am. Psychoanalytic Assoc.* 3, 1955, 600–614.

————. "A Historical Survey of the Teaching of Psychoanalytic Technique." *J. Am. Psychoanalytic Assoc.* 8, 1960, 500–516.

————. "Working Through and Termination of Analysis." *J. Am. Psychoanalytic Assoc.* 13, 1965, 57–78.

————. "The Nature of the Interpretive Process." *Children of Time and Space, of Action and Impulse.* New York: Appleton-Century-Crofts, 1966.

————. *Children of Time and Space, of Action and Impulse.* New York: Meredith, 1966.

————, and Wallerstein, R. S. *The Teaching and Learning of Psychotherapy.* New York: Basic Books, 1958.

Erikson, E. *Childhood and Society.* New York: Norton, 1950.

————. *Identity and the Life Cycle.* New York: Int. Universities Press, 1959.

————. *Identity, Youth and Crisis,* New York: Norton, 1968.

Eron, L. *The Classification of Behavior Disorders.* Chicago: Aldine, 1968.

Escalona, S. *The Roots of Individuality.* Chicago: Aldine, 1968.

Eysenck, H. "The Effects of Psychotherapy." *Int. J. Psychiatry* 1, 1965.

Feldman, D. "Psychoanalysis and Crime." Cressey, D., and Ward, D., eds. *Delinquency, Crime and Social Process.* New York: Harper and Row, 1969.

Feldman, F. "Results of Psychoanalysis in Clinic Case Assignments." *J. Am. Psychoanalytic Assoc.* 16, 1968, 274–300.

Fenichel, O. *Zehn Jahre Berliner Psychoanalytisches Institut.* Vienna: Int. Psychoanalytisches Verlag, 1930.

————. "The Problems of Psychoanalytic Technique." *The Psychoanalytic Quarterly* 1941, Albany, N.Y.

————. *The Psychoanalytic Theory of Neurosis.* New York: Norton, 1945.

Ferenczi, S. "The Problem of the Termination of the Analysis." *Final Contributions to the Problems and Methods of Psychoanalysis.* New York: Basic Books, 1955.

Feuer, L. *Psychoanalysis and Ethics.* Springfield, Ill.: C. C. Thomas, 1956.

Fine, R., "An Instance of Freudian Analysis." *Case Reports in Clinical Psychology* 3, 1956, 131–138.

————. "Pre-Doctoral Training in Psychotherapy." *Proc. N.Y. State Psych. Assoc.* New York: N.Y. State Psychological Association, 1960, 16–19.

————. "A Note on a Transference Manifestation in Male Homosexuals." *Psychoanalysis and the Psychoanalytic Review* 59, 1960–61.

————. *Freud: A Critical Reevaluation.* New York: David McKay, 1962.

————. "The Analytic Treatment of a Psychotic." *Psychotherapy* 1, 1964, No. 4, Fall.

————. "The Erotic Transference." *Psychoanalytic Review* 52, 1965.

————. "The Goals of Psychoanalysis." A. Mahrer, ed. *The Goals of Psychotherapy.* New York: Appleton-Century-Crofts, 1968.

Fleming, J. "What Analytic Work Requires of an Analyst: A Job Analysis," *J. Amer. Psychoanalytic Assoc.* 9, 1961, 719–729.

——, and Benedek, T. *Psychoanalytic Supervision.* New York: Grune and Stratton, 1966.

Fliess, R. "Silence and Verbalization: A Supplement to the Theory of the Analytic Rule." *Int. J. Psychoanalysis* 30, 1949, 21–30.

Frank, J. *Persuasion and Healing.* New York: Schocken, 1963.

Frazer, J. *The Golden Bough.* New York: The Macmillan Co., 1949.

French, T. *The Integration of Behavior.* Chicago: U. of Chicago Press, 1958.

Freud, A. *The Ego and the Mechanisms of Defense.* New York: Int. Universities Press, 1946.

——. "Indications and Contraindications for Child Analysis." *Psychoanalytic Study of the Child* 23, 1968, 37–46.

——. "The Widening Scope of Indications for Psychoanalysis: Discussion." *J. Am. Psychoanalytic Assoc.* 2, 1954, 608–609.

——. *Normality and Pathology in Childhood.* New York: Int. Universities Press, 1965.

——. *The Psychoanalytical Treatment of Children.* London: Imago Publishing Co., 1946.

——. "Contribution to Symposium on Acting Out." *Int. J. Psychoanalysis* 49, 1968, 165–170.

Freud, S. *Collected Works* (24 volumes), known as *The Standard Edition.* London: Institute of Psychoanalysis and the Hogarth Press, 1953–1968. Referred to as S.E.

Fromm, E. *Man for Himself.* New York: Rinehart and Co., 1947.

——. *The Sane Society.* New York: Rinehart and Co., 1955.

——, Suzuki, D. T., and De Martini, R. *Zen Buddhism and Psychoanalysis.* New York: Grove Press, 1963.

Fromm-Reichmann, F. *Principles of Intensive Psychotherapy.* Chicago: U. of Chicago Press, 1950.

——. "Psychoanalytic and General Dynamic Conceptions of Theory and of Therapy: Differences and Similarities." *J. Am. Psychoanalytic Assoc.* 2, 1954, 711–721.

Frosch, J. "Severe Regressive States During Analysis; Summary." *J. Am. Psychoanalytic Assoc.* 15, 1967, 606–625.

Geleerd, E., ed. *The Child Analyst at Work.* New York: Int. Universities Press, 1967.

Gitelson, M. "Therapeutic Problems in the Analysis of the 'Normal' Candidate." *Int. J. Psychoanalysis* 35, 1954, 174–183.

Gitelson, M. "On the Identity Crisis in American Psychoanalysis." *J. Am. Psychoanalytic Assoc.* 12, 1964, 451–476.

Glover, E. *Psychoanalysis.* New York: Staples Press, 1939.

————. *The Technique of Psychoanalysis.* New York: Int. Universities Press, 1955.

————. "The Therapeutic Effect of Inexact Interpretation." *Int. J. Psychoanalysis* 12, 1931, 397–411.

Goldstein, M. J., and Palmer, J. D. *The Experience of Anxiety.* New York: Oxford U. Press, 1963.

Greenacre, P. "Re-evaluation of the Process of Working Through." *Int. J. Psychoanalysis* 37, 1956, 439–444.

————. "A Critical Digest of the Literature on Selection of Candidates for Psychoanalytic Training." *Psychoanalytic Quarterly* 20, 1961, 28–55.

————, *et al.* "Symposium on the Evaluation of Therapeutic Results." *Int. J. Psychoanalysis* 29, 1948, 11–32.

Greenson, R. "The Selection of Candidates for Psychoanalytic Training." *J. Am. Psychoanalytic Assoc.* 9, 1961, 135–145.

————. "The Working Alliance and the Transference Neurosis." *Psychoanalytic Quarterly* 34, 1965, 155–181.

————. "That 'Impossible' Profession." *J. Am. Psychoanalytic Assoc.* 14, 1966, 9–27.

————. *The Technique and Practice of Psychoanalysis,* Vol. 1. New York: Int. Universities Press, 1967.

————. "Variations in Classical Psychoanalytic Technique: An Introduction." *Int. J. Psychoanalysis* 39, 1958, 200–201.

————, and Wexler, M. "The Non-Transference Relationship in the Psychoanalytic Situation," *Int. J. Psychoanalysis* 50, 1969, 27–39.

Guerney, B. C., Jr., ed. *Psychotherapeutic Agents.* New York: Holt, Rinehart and Winston, 1969.

Gutheil, E. *A Handbook of Dream Analysis.* New York: Liveright, 1951.

Guttman, S. A. "Panel Report: Criteria for Analyzability." *J. Am. Psychoanalytic Assoc.* 8, 1960, 141–151.

Haak, N. "Comments on the Analytical Situation." *Int. J. Psychoanalysis* 38, 1957, 183–195.

Hamburg, D. A., *et al.* "Report of Ad Hoc Committee on Central Fact-Gathering Data of the American Psychoanalytic Ass'n." *J. Am. Psychoanalytic Assoc.* 15, 1967, 841–861.

Hammer, E., ed. *The Use of Interpretation in Treatment.* New York: Grune and Stratton, 1968.

Hartmann, H. *Ego Psychology and the Problem of Adaptation.* New York: Int. Universities Press, 1958.

————. *Essays on Ego Psychology.* New York: Int. Universities Press, 1964.

————. "Psychoanalysis and the Concept of Health." *Essays on Ego Psychology.* New York: Int. Universities Press, 1964.

————. *Psychoanalysis and Moral Values.* New York: Int. Universities Press, 1960.

————, Kris, E., and Loewenstein, R. M. "Comments on the Formation of Psychic Structure." *Psychoanalytic Study of the Child* 2, 1946, 11–38.

Hendin, H., Gaylin, W., and Carr, A. C. *Psychoanalysis and Social Science Research.* New York: Doubleday, 1965.

Hertzberg, F. *Work and the Nature of Man.* New York: World Publishing Co., 1966.

Hill, L. B. "Anticipation of Arousing Specific Neurotic Feelings in the Psychoanalyst." *Psychiatry* 14, 1951, 1–8.

Hollis, F. *Social Casework.* New York: Random House, 1964.

Holt, R., and Luborsky, L. *Personality Patterns of Psychiatrists.* New York: Basic Books, 1958.

Holzberg, J., *et al.* "Companionship with the Mentally Ill: Effects on the Personalities of College Student Volunteers." *Psychiatry* 29, 1966, 395–405.

Hoppock, R. *Job Satisfaction.* New York: Harper, 1935.

Jackson, D., and Lederer, W. J. *The Mirages of Marriage.* New York: Norton, 1968.

Jackson, S. W., "Aspects of Culture in Psychoanalytic Theory and Practice." *J. Amer. Psychoanalytic Assoc.* 16, 1968, 651–670.

Jacobson, E. "Transference Problems in the Treatment of Severely Depressive Patients." *J. Am. Psychoanalytic Assoc.* 2, 1954, 595–606.

Jersild, A. T., and Lazar, E. A. *The Meaning of Psychotherapy in the Teacher's Life and Work.* New York: Teachers College, 1962.

Joint Commission on Mental Illness and Health. *Action for Mental Health.* New York: Basic Books, 1961.

Jones, E. *Decennial Report of the London Clinic of Psychoanalysis,* 1926–1936.

————. *Papers on Psychoanalysis,* 5th edition. London: Baillere, Tindall and Cox, 1948.

————. "The Concept of a Normal Mind." *Papers on Psychoanalysis,* 5th edition. London: Baillere, Tindall and Cox, 1948.

————. "Love and Morality," Ch. VIII in *Papers on Psychoanalysis,* 5th edition. London: Baillere, Tindall and Cox, 1948.

————. *The Life and Work of Sigmund Freud.* New York: Basic Books, 1953–1957.

————. "Psychiatry Before and After Freud." *Four Centenary Addresses.* New York: Basic Books, 1956.

Jones, M. *The Therapeutic Community.* New York: Basic Books, 1953.

————. *Social Psychiatry in Practice.* Middlesex: Penguin, 1968.

Jung, C. G. *Psychological Types.* London: Routledge and Kegan Paul, 1923.

————. *Modern Man in Search of a Soul.* New York: Harcourt Brace, 1950.

————. *Analytical Psychology.* New York: Pantheon Books, 1968.

Kadushin, C. *Why People Go to Psychiatrists*. New York: Atherton, 1968.

Kairys, D. "The Training Analysis: A Critical Review of the Literature and a Controversial Proposal." *Psychoanalytic Quarterly* 33, 1964, 485–512.

Kanzer, M. "Past and Present in the Transference." *J. Am. Psychoanalytic Assoc.* 1, 1953, 144–154.

Kardiner, A. "Freud—The Man I knew, The Scientist and His Influence." B. Nelson, ed. *Freud and the Twentieth Century*. New York: Meridan Books, 1957.

Katz, J., Goldstein, J., and Dershowitz, A. M. *Psychoanalysis, Psychiatry and the Law*. New York: Free Press, 1967.

Kessel, L., and Hyman, H. T. "The Value of Psychoanalysis as a Therapeutic Procedure." *JAMA* 101, 1933, 1612–1615.

Kety, S. "Biochemical Hypotheses and Studies." In Bellak, L., and Loeb, L., *The Schizophrenic Syndrome*.

Kiev, A. *Magic, Faith and Healing*. Glencoe, Ill.: Free Press, 1964.

Kinsey, A. C., *et al*. *Sexual Behavior in the Human Male*. Philadelphia: W. B. Saunders, 1948.

Klein, H. R. *Psychoanalysts in Training*. New York: Columbia University, 1965.

Klein, M. *The Psychoanalysis of Children*. London: The Hogarth Press, 1932.

———. "On the Criteria for the Termination of a Psychoanalysis." *Int. J. Psychoanalysis* 31, 1950, 78–80.

———. *Envy and Gratitude*. New York: Basic Books, 1957.

———, *et al*. *New Directions in Psychoanalysis*. New York: Basic Books, 1955.

Knapp, P., *et al*. "Suitability for Psychoanalysis: A Review of 100 Supervised Cases." *Psychoanalytic Quarterly* 29, 1960, 459–477.

Knight, R. P. "Evaluation of the Results of Psychoanalytic Therapy." *Am. J. Psychiatry* 98, 1941, 434–446.

———. "Psychotherapy of an Adolescent Catatonic Schizophrenia with Autism." *Psychiatry* 9, 1946, 323–339.

Kohut, H. "Panel Report: Clinical and Theoretical Aspects of Resistance." *J. Am. Psychoanalytic Assoc.* 5, 1957, 548–555.

———. "The Evaluation of Applicants for Psychoanalytic Training." *Int. J. Psychoanalysis* 49, 1968, 548–554.

Komarovsky, M. *Blue-Collar Marriage*. New York: Vintage Books, 1967.

Kovacs, V. "Training and Control Analysis." *Int. J. Psychoanalysis* 17, 1936, 346–354.

Kraepelin, E. *One Hundred Years of Psychiatry*. New York: The Citadel Press, 1962.

Kraft, T. "Psychoanalysis and Behaviorism." *Am. J. Psychotherapy* 23, 1969, 282–287.

Kramer, M. R. "On the Continuation of the Analytic Process After Psychoanalysis." *Int. J. Psychoanalysis* 40, 1959, 17–25.

Kringlen, E. "Schizophrenia in Twins." *Psychiatry* 29, 1966, 172–184.

Kris, E. "Ego Psychology and Interpretation in Psychoanalytic Therapy." *Psychoanalytic Quarterly* 20, 1951, 15–30.

———. "On Some Vicissitudes of Insight in Psychoanalysis." *Int. J. Psychoanalysis* 37, 1956, 445–455.

———. "The Recovery of Childhood Memories in Psychoanalysis." *Psychoanalytic Study of the Child* 11, 1956, 54–88.

Kubie, L. S. "The Concept of Normality and the Neurotic Process." *Practical and Theoretical Aspects of Psychoanalysis*. New York: Int. Universities Press, 1950.

———. "Need for a New Subdiscipline in the Medical Profession." *Archives of Neurology and Psychiatry* 78, 1957, 283–293.

———. "Research into the Process of Supervision in Psychoanalysis." *Psychoanalytic Quarterly* 27, 1958, 226–236.

———. "A School of Psychological Medicine Within the Framework of a Medical School and University." *J. of Medical Education* 39, 1964, No. 5, May.

———. "Discussion of Eysenck Paper." *Int. J. Psychiatry* 1, 1965.

———. "Unsolved Problems in the Resolution of the Transference." *Psychoanalytic Quarterly* 37, 1968, 331–352.

Kut, S. "The Changing Pattern of Transference in the Analysis of an Eleven-Year-Old Girl." *Psychoanalytic Study of the Child* 8, 1953, 355–378.

Lampl-de Groot, J. "On Defense and Development." *Psychoanalytic Study of the Child* 12, 1957, 114–126.

———. "Symptom Formation and Character Formation." *Int. J. Psychoanalysis* 44, 1963, 1–11.

Laughlin, H. P. *The Neuroses*. Washington: Butterworth, 1967.

Leeuw, van der, P. J. "The Psychoanalytic Society." *Int. J. Psychoanalysis* 49, 1968, 160–164.

Leifer, R. *In the Name of Mental Health*. New York: Science House, 1969.

Lesse, S. *An Evaluation of the Results of the Psychotherapies*. Springfield, Ill.: C. C. Thomas, 1968.

Levin, S., and Michaels, J. J. "Incomplete Psychoanalytic Training." *J. Am. Psychoanalytic Assoc.* 13, 1965, 793–818.

Lewin, B. D. "The Analytic Situation: Topographic Considerations." *Psychoanalytic Quarterly* 28, 1959, 455–469.

Lewin, B., and Ross, H. *Psychoanalytic Education in the U.S.* New York: W. W. Norton, 1960.

Lewis, O. *La Vida*. New York: Random House, 1966.

———. *The Children of Sanchez*. New York: Random House, 1961.

Limentani, A. "On Drug Dependence." *Int. J. Psychoanalysis* 49, 1968, 578–590.

Little, M. "Countertransference and the Patient's Response to It." *Int. J. Psychoanalysis* 32, 1951, 32–40.

———. "On Delusional Transference (Transference Psychosis)." *Int. J. Psychoanalysis* 39, 1958, 134–138.

Loewald, H. "On the Therapeutic Action of Psychoanalysis." *Int. J. Psychoanalysis* 41, 1960, 16–33.

Loewenstein, R. "The Problem of Interpretation." *Psychoanalytic Quarterly* 20, 1951, 1–14.

———. "Some Remarks on Defenses, Autonomous Ego and Psychoanalytic Technique." *Int. J. Psychoanalysis* 35, 1954, 188–193.

———. "Some Remarks on the Role of Speech in Psychoanalytic Technique." *Int. J. Psychoanalysis* 37, 1956, 460–468.

———. "Some thoughts on Interpretation in the Theory and Practice of Psychoanalysis." *Psychoanalytic Study of the Child* 12, 1957, 127–150.

———, et al. "The Silent Patient." *J. Am. Psychoanalytic Assoc.* 9, 1961, 2–90.

Lorand, S. *The Technique of Psychoanalytic Therapy.* New York: Int. Universities Press, 1946.

Lorand, S., and Console, W. "Therapeutic Results in Psychoanalytic Treatment Without Fee." *Int. J. Psychoanalysis* 39, 1958, 59–64.

Mahrer, A., ed. *New Approaches to Diagnosis.* New York: Columbia University Press, 1969. In press.

Marcuse, H. *Eros and Civilization.* London: Routledge, and Kegan Paul, 1955.

Masters, W., and Johnson, V. *Human Sexual Response.* Boston: Little, Brown and Co., 1966.

May, R., Angel, E., and Ellenberger, H. F. *Existence.* New York: Basic Books, 1958.

McCartney, J. "Overt Transference." *J. of Sex Research* 2, 1966, 227–236.

Menninger Foundation: *Health-Sickness Rating Scale.* Topeka: Menninger Foundation, 1962.

Menninger, K. *A Psychiatrist's World.* New York: Viking Press, 1959.

———. *The Theory of Psychoanalytic Technique.* New York: Basic Books, 1958.

———. *The Crime of Punishment.* New York: Viking Press, 1969.

———, with Mayman, M., and Pruyser, P. *The Vital Balance.* New York: The Viking Press, 1963.

Merkle, L., and Little, R. B. "Beginning Psychiatry Training Syndrome." *Am. J. of Psychiatry* 124, 1967, 193–197.

Miller, I. "On the Return of Symptoms in the Terminal Phase of Psychoanalysis." *Int. J. Psychoanalysis* 46, 1965, 487–501.

Money-Kyrle, R. "Normal Countertransference and Some of its Deviations." *Int. J. Psychoanalysis* 37, 1956, 360–366.

Mowrer, O. H. *Learning Theory and Behavior*. New York: Wiley, 1960.

Murdock, G. *Social Structure*. Glencoe, Ill.: Free Press, 1949.

Nacht, S. "Criteria and Technique for the Termination of Analysis." *Int. J. Psychoanalysis* 46, 1965, 107–116.

Novey, S. "The Principle of 'Working Through' in Psychoanalysis." *J. Am. Psychoanalytic Assoc.* 10, 1962, 658–676.

Nunberg, H. "The Synthetic Function of the Ego." *Practice and Theory of Psychoanalysis*. New York: Nervous and Mental Disease Monographs, 1948.

Nydes, J. "Interpretation and the Therapeutic Act." In E. Hammer, ed. *The Use of Interpretation in Treatment*.

Oberndorf, C. P. *A. History of Psychoanalysis in America*. New York: Grune and Stratton, 1953.

Odier, C. *Anxiety and Magical Thinking*. New York: Int. Universities, Press, 1956.

Offer, D., and Sabshin, M. *Normality*. New York: Basic Books, 1966.

Olinick, S. L. "Some Considerations of the Use of Questioning as a Psychoanalytic Technique." *J. Am. Psychoanalytic Assoc.* 2, 1954, 57–66.

Opler, M. N., ed. *Culture and Mental Health*. New York: Macmillan, 1959.

Orr, D. W. "Transference and Countertransference: A Historical Survey." *J. Am. Psychoanalytic Assoc.* 2, 1954, 621–670.

Paul, L., ed. *Psychoanalytic Clinical Interpretation*. New York: Crowell-Collier, 1963.

Peplau, H. *Interpersonal Relations in Nursing*. New York: Putman, 1952.

Pfeffer, A. "A Procedure for Evaluating the Results of Psychoanalysis." *J. Am. Psychoanalytic Assoc.* 7, 1959, 418–444.

————. "Analysis Terminable and Interminable—25 Years After." *J. Am. Psychoanalytic Assoc.* 11, 1963, 131–142.

————. "The Meaning of the Analyst After Analysis." *J. Am. Psychoanalytic Assoc.* 11, 1963, 229–244.

Pfister, O. *Christianity and Fear*. London: Allen and Unwin, 1948.

Plog, S. C., and Edgerton, R. B., eds. *Changing Perspectives in Mental Illness*. New York: Holt, Rinehart and Winston, 1969.

Psychoanalysis as Seen by Analyzed Psychologists. Washington: American Psychological Assoc., 1953.

Racker, E. "Notes on the Theory of Transference." *Psychoanalytic Quarterly* 23, 1954, 78–86.

————. "A Study of Some Early Conflicts Through Their Return in the Patient's Relation with the Interpretation." *Int. J. Psychoanalysis* 41, 1960, 47–58.

————. *Transference and Countertransference*. New York: Int. Universities Press, 1968.

Rangell, L. "The Psychology of Poise, with a Special Elaboration on the Psychic Significance of the Snout or Perioral Region." *Int. J. Psychoanalysis* 35, 1954, 313–332.

———. "Some Comments on Psychoanalytic Nosology." In Schur, M., ed. *Drives, Affects, Behavior,* Vol. 2. New York: Int. Universities Press, 1965.

Rank, O. *Will Therapy.* New York: Knopf, 1950.

———, and Ferenczi, S. *The Development of Psychoanalysis.* Washington: Nervous and Mental Disease Publications, 1925.

Rapaport, D. *Emotions and Memory.* Baltimore: Williams and Wilkins, 1942.

———. *The Structure of Psychoanalytic Theory.* New York: Int. Universities Press, 1960.

———. "The Management of an Eroticized Transference." *Psychoanalytic Quarterly* 25, 1956, 515–529.

———, et al. *Diagnostic Psychological Testing.* New York: Int. Universities Press, 1968.

Reich, W. *Character Analysis.* New York: Orgone Institute Press, 1949.

Reider, N. "Transference Psychosis." *J. Hillside Hospital* 6, 1957, 131–149.

Reiff, R., and Riessman, R. *The Indigenous Nonprofessional.* Irvington-on-Hudson, N.Y.: Community Mental Health Journal Monograph No. 1, 1965.

Reik, T. *Listening With the Third Ear.* New York: Farrar, Straus, 1948.

Rennie, T., *et al. Mental Health, in the Metropolis.* New York: McGraw-Hill, 1962.

Richfield, J. "An Analysis of the Concept of Insight." *Psychoanalytic Quarterly* 23, 1954, 390–408.

Rioch, M., *et al.* "NIMH Study in Training Mental Health Counselors." *Am. J. of Orthopsychiatry* 33, 1963, 678–689.

Roazen, P. D. *Freud: Political and Social Thought.* New York: Alfred A. Knopf, 1968.

Robbins, L. N. *Deviant Children Grow Up.* Baltimore: Williams and Wilkins, 1966.

Rogers, C. *Counseling and Psychotherapy.* Cambridge: The Riverside Press, 1942.

Roheim, G. *Magic and Schizophrenia.* New York: Int. Universities Press, 1955.

Roland, A. "The Reality of the Psychoanalytic Relationship and Situation in Handling of Transference Resistance." *Int. J. Psychoanalysis* 41, 1967, 504–510.

Rosen, G. *Madness in Society.* New York: Harper and Row, 1968.

Rosen, J. *Direct Analysis.* New York: Grune and Stratton, 1953.

Rosenfeld, H. "Considerations Regarding the Psychoanalytic Approach to

Acute and Chronic Schizophrenia." *Int. J. Psychoanalysis* 35, 1954, 135–140.

Ross, N. "An Examination of Nosology According to Psychoanalytic Concepts." *J. Am. Psychoanalytic Assoc.* 8, 1960, 335–555.

Rycroft, C. "The Nature and Function of the Analyst's Communication to the Patient." *Int. J. Psychoanalysis* 37, 1956, 469–472.

Sandler, J., and Bolland, J. *The Hampstead Psychoanalytic Index.* New York: Int. Universities Press, 1965.

Sandler, J., and Joffe, W. G. "Towards a Basic Psychoanalytic Model." *Int. J. Psychoanalysis* 50, 1969, 79–90.

Sarbin, T. R. "The Scientific Status of the Mental Illness Metaphor." Plog, S. C., and Edgerton, R. B., eds. *Changing Perspectives in Mental Illness.* New York: Holt, Rinehart and Winston, 1969. Ch. 12.

Saul, L., and Wenar, I. "Early Influences on Development and Disorders of Personality." *Psychoanalytic Quarterly* 34, 1965, 327–389.

Scheibe, K. E., *et al. College Students on Chronic Wards.* New York: Behavioral Publications, 1969.

Schmale, H. "Working Through." *J. Am. Psychoanalytic Assoc.* 14, 1966, 172–182.

Schneer, H. H., ed. *The Asthmatic Child.* New York: Harper and Row, 1963.

Schonbar, R. "Interpretation and Insight in Psychotherapy." In Hammer, ed. *Use of Interpretation in Treatment.* New York: Grune & Stratton, 1968.

Schur, M., ed. *Drives, Affects, Behavior,* Vol. 2. New York: Int. Universities Press, 1965.

Schwab, J. J. "Evaluating Psychiatric Consultation Work." *Psychosomatics* 8, 1967, 309–317.

Scott, W. C. M. "Patients Who Sleep or Look at the Psychoanalyst During Treatment." *Int. J. Psychoanalysis* 33, 1952, 465–469.

Searles, H. *Collected Papers on Schizophrenia and Related Subjects.* New York: Int. Universities Press, 1964.

Sechehaye, M. *Symbolic Realization.* New York: Grune & Stratton, 1956.

Seguin, C. A. *Love and Psychotherapy.* New York: Libra, 1965.

Selye, H. *The Stress of Life.* New York: McGraw-Hill, 1956.

Shakow, D., *et al.* "Recommended Graduate Training Program in Clinical Psychology." *Am. Psychologist* 2, 1947, 539–558.

Shlien, J. M., ed. *Research in Psychotherapy.* Washington: APA, 1968.

Shneidman, E., ed. *Essays in Self-Destruction.* New York: Science House, 1967.

———, and Farberow, N. *Clues to Suicide.* New York: McGraw-Hill, 1957.

Singer, E. *Key Concepts in Psychotherapy.* New York: Random House, 1965.

Socarides, C. *The Overt Homosexual.* New York: Grune & Stratton, 1968.

Sperling, M. "School Phobias." *Psychoanalytic Study of the Child* 22, 1967, 375–401.

――――. "Contribution to Symposium on Psychosomatics." *Int. J. Psychoanalysis* 49, 1968, 250–253.

Spiegel, L. "Acting Out and Defensive Instinctual Gratification." *J. Am. Psychoanalytic Assoc.* 2, 1954, 107–119.

Spitz, R. "Countertransference: Comments on its Varying Role in the Analytic Situation." *J. Am. Psychoanalytic Assoc.* 4, 1956, 256–265.

――――. *The First Year of Life.* New York: Int. Universities Press, 1965.

Stekel, W. *The Technique of Analytical Psychotherapy.* New York: Liveright, 1950.

Sterba, R. "Clinical and Therapeutic Aspects of Character Resistance." *Psychoanalytic Quarterly* 22, 1953, 1–20.

Stewart, W. "An Inquiry into the Concept of Working Through." *J. Am. Psychoanalytic Assoc.* 11, 1963, 474–499.

Stieper, D. R., and Wiener, D. N. *Dimensions of Psychotherapy.* Chicago: Aldine, 1965.

Stone, L. "The Widening Scope of Indications for Psychoanalysis." *J. Am. Psychoanalytic Assoc.* 2, 1954, 567–594.

――――. *The Psychoanalytic Situation.* New York: Int. Universities Press, 1961.

――――. "The Psychoanalytic Situation and Transference." *J. Am. Psychoanalytic Assoc.* 15, 1967, 3–58.

Stotland, E. *The Psychology of Hope.* San Francisco: Jossey-Bass, 1969.

Strachey, J. "The Nature of the Therapeutic Action of Psychoanalysis." *Int. J. Psychoanalysis* 15, 1934, 127–159.

Strupp, H. H. "The Outcome Problem in Psychotherapy Revisited." *Psychotherapy* 1, 1963, 1–13.

――――, and Bergin, A. E. "Some Empirical and Conceptual Bases for Coordinated Research in Psychotherapy." *Int. J. Psychiatry* 7, 1969.

Strupp, H. H., Fox, R. E., and Lessler, K. *Patients View Their Psychotherapy.* Baltimore: The Johns Hopkins Press, 1969.

Sullivan, H. S. *The Interpersonal Theory of Psychiatry.* New York: Norton, 1953.

――――. *Conceptions of Modern Psychiatry.* New York: Norton, 1946.

――――. *Schizophrenia as a Human Process.* New York: W. W. Norton and Co., 1962.

Symonds, P. *From Adolescent to Adult.* New York: Columbia University Press, 1961.

Symposium, "The Termination of Analysis." *Int. J. Psychoanalysis* 31, 1950.

Symposium, "Acting Out." *J. Am. Psychoanalytic Assoc.* 5, 1957, 581–706.

Symposium, "Variations in Classical Psychoanalytic Technique." *Int. J. Psychoanalysis* 39, 1958, 200–242.

Symposium, "The Silent Patient." *J. Am. Psychoanalytic Assoc.* 9, 1961, 2–90.

Symposium, "Acting Out." *Int. J. Psychoanalysis* 49, 1968, 165–230.

Szasz, T. "On the Experiences of the Analyst in the Psychoanalytic Situation." *J. Am. Psychoanalytic Assoc.* 4, 1957, 197–223.

———. "On the Theory of Psychoanalytic Treatment." *Int. J. Psychoanalysis* 38, 1957, 166–182.

———. *The Myth of Mental Illness.* New York: Holber-Harper, 1961.

———. "The Concept of Transference." *Int. J. Psychoanalysis* 44, 1963, 432–443.

Tarachow, S. *An Introduction to Psychotherapy.* New York: Int. Universities Press, 1963.

Tart, C., ed. *Altered States of Consciousness.* New York: Wiley, 1969.

Thompson, C. "Development of Awareness of Transference in a Markedly Detached Personality." *Int. J. Psychoanalysis* 19, 1938, 299–309.

Tolentino, I., and Zapparoli, G. C. "The Psychoanalytic Vocation and the Implications of the Training Analyst's Countertransference on Selection of Candidates." *Int. J. Psychoanalysis* 49, 1968, 555–559.

Waldhorn, H. F. "Assessment of Analyzability: Technical and Theoretical Observations." *Psychoanalytic Quarterly* 29, 1960, 478–506.

Wallerstein, R. S. "The Problem of the Assessment of Change in Psychotherapy." *Int. J. Psychoanalysis* 44, 1963, 31–41.

———. "The Current State of Psychotherapy: Theory, Practice, Research." *J. Am. Psychoanalytic Assoc.* 14, 1966, 183–225.

———. The Psychotherapy Research Project of the Menninger Foundation: A Semifinal View." Shlien, J. M., ed. *Research in Psychotherapy.* Washington: APA, 1968.

———. "Psychoanalysis and Psychotherapy." *Int. J. Psychoanalysis* 50, 1969, 117–126.

Weigert, E. "Contribution to the Problem of Terminating Psychoanalysis." *Psychoanalytic Quarterly* 21, 1952, 465–480.

———. "Countertransference and Self-Analysis of the Psychoanalyst." *Int. J. Psychoanalysis* 35, 1954, 242–246.

———. "The Importance of Flexibility in Psychoanalytic Technique." *J. Am. Psychoanalytic Assoc.* 2, 1954. 702–710.

Wertham, F. *The Show of Violence.* New York: Doubleday, 1949.

Westley, W. A., and Epstein, N. B. *The Silent Majority.* San Francisco: Jossey-Bass, 1969.

Wheelis, A. "The Vocational Hazards of Psychoanalysis." *Int. J. Psychoanalysis* 37, 1956, 171–184.

Winnicott, D. W. "Hate in the Countertransference." *Int. J. Psychoanalysis* 30, 1949, 69–74.

Witkin, H., and Lewis, H., eds. *Experimental Studies of Dreaming.* New York: Random House, 1967.

Wolberg, L. *The Technique of Psychotherapy*. New York: Grune and Stratton, 1967.

Wolman, B., ed. *Handbook of Clinical Psychology*. New York: McGraw-Hill, 1965.

———, ed. *Psychoanalytic Techniques*. New York: Basic Books, 1967.

Wright, E. "Medieval Attitudes Toward Mental Iillness." *Bull. Hist. Med.* 7, 1939.

Zeligs, M. A. "The Psychology of Silence: Its Role in Transference, Countertransference and the Psychoanalytic Process." *J. Am. Psychoanalytic Assoc.* 9, 1957, 7–43.

Zetterberg, H. *The Contraceptive Society*. Bedminster Press, 1969. In press.

Zetzel, E. "Current Concepts of Transference." *Int. J. Psychoanalysis* 37, 1956, 369–376.

———. "Panel Report: The Traditional Psychoanalytic Technique and Its Variations." *J. Am. Psychoanalytic Assoc.* 1, 1953, 526–537.

Zilboorg, G., with Henry, G. W. *A History of Medical Psychology*. New York: Norton, 1941.

Register of Patients

Index